NAZISM,
LIBERALISM,
& CHRISTIANITY

NAZISM, LIBERALISM, & CHRISTIANITY

Protestant Social Thought in Germany & Great Britain 1925-1937

Kenneth C. Barnes

THE UNIVERSITY PRESS OF KENTUCKY

Library of Congress Cataloging-in-Publication Data

Barnes, Kenneth C., 1956-
    Nazism, liberalism, and Christianity : Protestant social thought
in Germany and Great Britain, 1925-1937 / Kenneth C. Barnes.

        p.   cm.
    Includes bibliographical references and index.
    ISBN 0-8131-1729-1 (alk. paper)
    1. Sociology, Christian—Great Britain—History of doctrines—20th
century.   2. Sociology, Christian—Germany—History of
doctrines—20th century.   3. Liberalism—History—20th century.
4. National socialism.   I. Title.
BT738.B2886   1990
261.8'0941'09042—dc20   90-38297

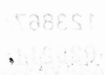

CONTENTS

ACKNOWLEDGMENTS

MY work on this book began at Duke University under the guidance of Charles S. Maier and John Cell. To both I owe great debts, for encouragement when I truly needed it and for insightful criticism that made me think more critically and write more fluently. Joel Colton, Martin Marty, Richard John Neuhaus, William C. Scott, and Richard Soloway also read various versions of the manuscript and offered valuable suggestions.

I am indebted to the many librarians and archivists who greatly aided my research. A.J. van der Bent and the staff of the World Council of Churches Library in Geneva gave me remarkably free use of their very rich archives. In many ways they helped make my time in Geneva more productive and pleasant. The Evangelische Zentralarchiv in Berlin and Lambeth Palace Library in London also graciously granted me access to relevant archival materials. And the librarians at Tübingen University and the University of Chicago gave me invaluable assistance and access to their extensive collections. The Akademisches Auslandsamt in Tübingen helped immensely with housing and adjustment for my family while we were there. I am grateful to Duke University and the German Academic Exchange Service for financial assistance for research in Europe. Concordia University provided financial support and valuable time by awarding me two study leaves to work on the project.

My wife, Debbie, offered support and assistance in many ways. Beside being a patient listener, she has interrupted her own career on several occasions to help relocate a family during research trips abroad.

NAZISM,
LIBERALISM,
& CHRISTIANITY

1. INTRODUCTION

THE Great Depression devastated the economies of Great Britain and Germany and brought social trauma into the daily lives of millions of people. In many ways the two countries were very much alike, both heavily industrialized urban societies with strong, politically active working classes. Both countries experienced the hunger, helplessness, and bewilderment of the depression years with nearly a quarter of the workforce unemployed. Yet the Germans and the British reacted very differently to the economic crisis. The depression further polarized Germany between left-wing and fascist political alternatives. But in Britain, Labour and Tory politicians moved together to form a coalition National Government. The German middle classes brought Hitler to power through their support at the polls and then acquiesced to dictatorship, thereby accepting the radical program of changes Hitler offered. The British, in contrast, muddled through the depression with only piecemeal reform. Despite the charismatic leadership of Sir Oswald Mosley, the British fascist movement never attracted more that a few thousand followers goosestepping through London's East End.

Contrasting mentalities in Great Britain and Germany led to two radically different diagnoses of socioeconomic problems and prescriptions for their cure. These mentalities, of course, are part of macro-divergences rooted in long and different histories. The goal of this study is to examine how these underlying differences were played out in one limited arena, that of the Protestant church leadership, 1925-37. I argue that the social politics of German Protestantism encouraged the radically conservative, authoritarian answers to the problems of the 1920s and 1930s, while Protestant social thought in Great Britain discouraged these answers and pointed followers toward liberalism and gradual reform.

The historical literature concerning Britain and Germany in

the interwar years lacks explicit comparative studies. British historiography generally concentrates on the political squabbles between Labour and the Conservatives or concerns British reactions to what was happening elsewhere in the world. Even the works on British fascism have not asked, in comparative perspective, why there was no radicalization of the middle class, why no pronounced fear of revolution and subsequent turn to the right?[1] German historiography naturally has been preoccupied with the Hitler question, explaining the growth of the Nazi movement by examining its social composition, detailing its progress in meticulous local studies, or searching for the peculiar cultural and intellectual traditions that could have given rise to such a phenomenon. The literature on Germany is indeed rich and varied. However, the comparative literature on the German question generally is confined to comparative studies of fascism, searching for an ideal type among its different national versions. Barrington Moore is one of the few historians to make judgments about the rise of Nazism in Germany based on comparative study of fascist and nonfascist societies.[2]

David Blackbourn and Geoff Eley's recent book *The Peculiarities of German History* has spawned a lively debate on comparisons between German and British history.[3] Despite the seeming dearth of comparative studies, Eley and Blackbourn argue persuasively that the problem with works on the German question is that they are *all* implicitly comparative. Generally, the literature tries to explain why the Germans were not like the British, why they had no successful bourgeois revolution, why they did not make good liberals. Blackbourn and Eley point out forcefully that the idea of German peculiarities, a *Sonderweg,* rests on the assumption that mature capitalism is accompanied by bourgeois liberalism, an assumption that led such scholars as Barrington Moore and Ralf Dahrendorf in their classic and influential studies to posit an orthodox view of an aberrant capitalism with a feudalized, retarded bourgeoisie holding premodern social values. Blackbourn and Eley argue that instead, with the development of mature capitalism in Germany, bourgeois elites simply went another route than liberalism to assure their continuing domination in society.

Labeling the German experience as "peculiar" or "exceptional" has been attractive because it makes the tragedy of German history less threatening. But Eley and Blackbourn's argument against German exceptionality brings our attention back to the similarities of the socioeconomic structures of these two mature capitalistic societies. In fact, given their cultural and ideological differences, their similarities in the 1920s appear all the more striking.

Great Britain and Germany were the two leading industrial countries of Europe in the 1920s. Germany had become Great Britain's equal in industry and trade shortly before World War I. Heavy industry—coal, steel, textiles, and so on—dominated the economies of both countries. Both societies had sharply defined social classes, and the working classes in Britain and Germany were well organized and politically conscious. Union membership in the two countries was the highest in the world on the eve of the war, with some four million in Britain and three million in Germany. The Social Democratic Party in Germany (SPD) and the Labour Party in Great Britain, as well as smaller working-class parties, existed to express politically the interests of working people.

Both countries experienced dramatic political change at the war's end. Historians call the creation of the Weimar Republic in Germany in 1919 a revolution. The revolution did depose one government and establish another. It created a constitution that was parliamentary and truly democratic in a way that the Bismarckian constitution was not. The SPD was now free to use its electoral support for real power. It had been the largest party since 1912. However, Weimar did not usher in state socialism, as many contemporaries had hoped or feared. Britain more quietly experienced profound change after the war with the electoral reform of 1918. The Representation Act of 1918 gave the vote to all men over the age of twenty-one and to women aged thirty and over. Still, some half-million males with the business and university franchises could cast a second vote. But around eight million people voted for the first time in 1918, two million men and six million women. The electorate had doubled. The larger, more proletarian electorate changed conditions for the Labour Party. Like the SPD in Germany, Labour suddenly emerged in the postwar era as a potentially powerful force in national politics.

Therefore, after the postwar changes, the sociopolitical situation was in many ways quite similar in Great Britain and Germany. In both cases socialists participated in executive government—

MacDonald's Labour cabinets, Friedrich Ebert's presidency, and SPD chancellors Gustav Bauer and Hermann Müller—because of their parties' strength in parliament. But in both countries the socialist governments were unable to push through truly socialist reforms because of nonsocialist majorities. Despite socialist participation in government, few of either party's ideals became realities in the 1920s.[4]

Economically, Germany and Britain shared common patterns from the beginning of the 1920s through the depression.[5] Again, the social and economic turmoil of Germany during the five years immediately following the war is well known. Germany was disrupted by civil war, strikes, a coal shortage, hyperinflation, and unemployment following the Ruhr occupation in 1923. But Britain too experienced economic chaos with a coal shortage in 1918-19 and labor strife into the mid-1920s. In early 1919 the Clydeside general strike brought street fighting between police and workers in Glasgow until troops ultimately occupied the entire city. Later that year there were strikes of policemen and railroad workers. And in May, dockworkers refused to load supplies bound for Poland, a country at war with the new Bolshevik regime. Throughout Great Britain there were over three thousand industrial disputes in 1919 and 1920. Compounding these labor difficulties was a phase of inflation in 1919–20 and then high unemployment through the rest of the 1920s. In June 1921 23 percent of the British workforce was out of work, the highest level in British history. There were frequent demonstrations of the unemployed in London; a riot occurred in Liverpool in 1921; and in 1922 several hunger marches converged on London, one from as far away as Glasgow.[6]

Both countries' economic difficulties were brought to a head with traumatizing crises in the mid-1920s. The occupation of the Ruhr and inflation displayed the weaknesses of the German economy: the instability of the mark, the coal problem, the impossibility of making expected reparations payments, and the lack of a coordinated national economic policy. With the General Strike of 1926, Britain's problems were similarly brought to a crisis: the sagging of heavy industry, especially coal, since the war and the industrialists' choice to cut wages rather than to innovate and modernize. The crises were a blow to the labor movement in both countries. Unions that had gained power at the end of the war saw their clout diminished markedly. With the failure of the General

Strike of 1926, the British Trades Unions Congress lost three million members, falling below five million for the first time since 1916. Large numbers of German workers tore up their union cards in 1923. The *Allgemeiner Deutscher Gewerkschaftsbund,* a major German union, dropped from seven to four million members in 1924. After these crises, for both countries the remaining years of the 1920s were relatively more prosperous and stable.

Finally, the depression of the 1930s affected both countries in markedly similar ways. The depression hit home in Europe in May 1931 with the fall of the *Kreditanstalt* bank in Vienna. Afterward, as the flight of capital caused bank failures in Germany, a run on gold in London pulled the British off the gold standard. The result was a spiraling decline in production, especially in the heavy industries, which meant climbing unemployment reaching 20 percent in Britain and one-quarter of the workforce in Germany. Unemployment was unequally distributed by geography and class in both countries, with working-class sections suffering the most. Governments in both countries responded to the financial and social crisis by employing the same orthodox economic remedies: balancing budgets, raising taxes, cutting expenditures and wages. However, at the depth of the depression in 1932-33, the similarities ended. In early 1933 President Hindenburg asked Adolf Hitler, on the basis of his party's strength in the Reichstag, to become chancellor of the Reich. From this point, Germany and Britain moved in opposite directions.[7]

By emphasizing similarities between German and British society I do not intend to gloss over the significant differences in the 1920s: the different effects of the Great War and the Peace Settlement, the more Marxist orientation of the SPD than the Labour Party, the reality of revolutionary violence in Germany 1917-23, and, of course, the dissimilar political traditions in the two countries. However, I want to examine how in Germany and Britain influential groups who helped mold public opinion responded differently to problems that were in themselves quite similar.

The Protestant leadership of the two countries is a particularly significant group for study. It was the Protestant middle classes, after all, who most radically differed in their response to the socioeconomic crises of the depression. As is well known, the Catholic Center Party in Germany, in contrast to the Protestant middle-class parties, the German Democratic Party (DDP), German People's Party (DVP), and German National People's Party (DNVP), did not cave in to Nazi assaults but maintained its electoral support throughout the elections of the early 1930s. The working classes of both countries supported socialist parties that offered similar analyses of the problems and recommended similar solutions. And the working classes, as church historians have demonstrated, were largely outside the church in Protestant Europe by the twentieth century.[8] But the British middle classes generally supported liberal and conservative parties advocating gradual, controlled reform, while the electoral support base for the Nazi movement was the Protestant middle classes. Although the traditional focus has been on a lower-middle-class stratum, Richard Hamilton's study of voting behavior indicates that in urban areas electoral support for the Nazis varied directly according to class, with working classes the least supportive and upper classes the most. In general, recent scholarship alters the traditional view only in suggesting that the Nazi support was more widely middle-class and elite than specifically lower middle class.[9] An examination of the mentality of the Protestant middle classes can therefore aid an understanding of the dynamics of the political decisions made in the early 1930s.

Any historical study of mentalities raises the problems of definition and description. My views on culture and religion owe much to the work of anthropologist Clifford Geertz and sociologist Peter Berger. Anthropologists define culture as learned behavior and ideas. More specifically, I see it as socially sanctioned psychological structures that establish meaning and guide behavior. For the social scientist, religion is a part of culture. It is a set of beliefs, symbols, and practices that serves as a model of a general order of existence and that establishes motivations and directives according to a culturally postulated supernatural entity or force. Therefore, religion is both a model *of* reality and a model *for* action. It explains and interprets what is, as well as what should be. In this view, human beings both individually and collectively strive to make sense of a disorderly world of experience by symbolizing, conceptualizing, and postulating meaning. Religion entails a cognitive ordering of concepts of self, of society, and of the supernatural. The believer constructs a world of culture, which then assumes some objectivity of its own. One externalizes meaning into reality by creating a religious system, but this system is in turn internalized to control moods and actions.

The projected cosmos is seldom static, however. The believer is constantly reflecting on this sacred order. Forces are at work to destroy the solidarity of the system, notably significant change such as death, science, war, and social disruption. The problems of perceived evil and injustice threaten to destroy any confidence that a moral order governs the universe. The religious world view must discern some meaning in pain. The system must constantly be reaffirmed through symbols, rituals, rhetoric, and socialization. When it no longer adequately explains reality or provides acceptable outlines for action, then the model must be changed or discarded.[10]

Because religion is engaged in ordering and giving meaning to objective reality, it is directly related to the political, social, and economic structures of life. I do not imply either a teleological functionalist argument or a Marxist analysis of a dependent structure-superstructure relationship. I see the relationship between structure and ideas as much more complicated. Again, I agree with Geertz, who sees beliefs, symbols, and values as variable not dependently with structural factors but "interdependently."[11] Religion, once created, is not merely a reflection of society. It becomes factual, historical, real, with a structure of its own. Obviously, this anthropological position on culture owes much to a Weberian formulation: human beings in society create ideas that make their changing social situation meaningful. The logic of these ideas then leads to novel social action, creating a new social reality or structure. It is a continuing dialectic.[12] It is one of the purposes of anthropological studies of religion to explore this relation between meaning and structure.

The Life and Work movement is an example of religion making sense of contemporary reality: establishing causation for problems, giving them meaning, and guiding believers toward appropriate actions. Life and Work was an early ecumenical movement organized by leading Protestant churchmen of Europe and America for the purpose of organizing international discussion of social and economic issues. From 1925 to 1937 the movement's conferences, meetings, correspondence, and publications provided a forum within which church leaders from Britain and Germany freely articulated their views on social and economic matters.

The idea that led to the Life and Work movement developed during World War I. Archbishop Nathan Söderblom, primate of

Uppsala, Sweden, lobbied incessantly for an international conference of the churches to lead in peace efforts during the Great
War. Afterward, the World Alliance for Promoting Friendly Relations among the Churches, an ecumenical agency in existence since
1914, gave its support to the idea of a world conference concerning
the church and society. It elected a committee, which made extensive preparations for the conference from 1921 to 1925. Finally, in
August 1925 more than six hundred delegates from thirty-seven
countries attended the Universal Christian Conference for Life and
Work in Stockholm. With Bishop Söderblom as the host, for two
weeks the delegates gave speeches, discussed papers, and attended
worship services at this gathering which marked a milestone in
ecumenical history.

The Stockholm conference inaugurated the Life and Work
movement. Before adjourning, delegates elected a continuation
committee, which met yearly thereafter to perpetuate the work of
the conference. The chief executive elected was the American Henry Atkinson, whose office from 1925 to 1930 was in London. The
conference also established a maze of commissions on youth, labor,
theology, and so on, which met regularly thereafter. In 1926 the
continuation committee created the Social Institute in Geneva, with
its own staff and budget, to be a center of worldwide communica-
tions for the church-social movement. The commissions and the
Social Institute carried out a variety of activities through the late
1920s, such as publishing a newsletter and a quarterly journal, and
planning meetings and study conferences. Its budget and activities
increased until the onset of the depression.

The Great Depression changed the structure and organization
of Life and Work. Reduced income from the churches caused some
retrenchment in Life and Work activities. At the 1930 meeting of
the continuation committee the whole movement was formally
recast into the Universal Christian Council for Life and Work
(UCCLW). The continuation committee became an executive committee, and the Social Institute became the research department of
the UCCLW, with its office remaining in Geneva. Under the new
arrangement Atkinson was succeeded as general secretary by Louis
Henriod, who worked out of the Geneva office and economized by
serving both the UCCLW and the World Alliance as general secretary. The World Alliance was better endowed financially. Andrew
Carnegie, sympathetic to the movement, had created in 1914 a

permanent foundation, the Church Peace Union, which subsidized the World Alliance yearly thereafter. Life and Work was able to weather the financial crisis of the 1930s partly because of its close relationship with the World Alliance.

The 1930s brought many challenges to the Life and Work movement. During the depression years the UCCLW promoted its own studies of the economic crisis and unemployment problem, conducted surveys of the social positions and programs of affiliated churches, and established an annual ecumenical seminar in Geneva to study social questions. Probably most important, the council arranged yearly international conferences on such topics as "The Churches and Unemployment," "The Churches and the World Economic Crisis," and "The Churches and Contemporary Social Systems." By 1933 a new concern had begun to dominate the administration and interest of Life and Work: the rise of the totalitarian state. Hitler's accession to the chancellory and the subsequent *Gleichschaltung* caused a predicament for Life and Work. In 1933 and 1934 Nazi clergymen replaced the former leadership of the German Church Federation, which had originally brought the church into involvement with Life and Work. When a group of German Protestants rejected the Nazi-controlled church later in 1934 and formed their own organization, the Confessing Church, Life and Work was caught in the middle. Each group expected to be received into Life and Work as the official German delegation. For the next three years Life and Work served as a mediator between the two groups, with each participating tenuously.

From 1934 to 1937 the work of UCCLW focused on preparations for the Oxford conference of 1937, the sequel to Stockholm. This time, appropriately, the subject was "Church, Community, and State." Joseph H. Oldham, general secretary of the International Missionary Council, dominated the movement in these years as he coordinated the massive preparations. The conference itself was somewhat anticlimatic: a few weeks before it was to convene, the Gestapo took away the passports of the German delegation members, and they were unable to attend. However, one outcome of the Oxford conference was the recommendation that Life and Work and other ecumenical agencies merge to form the World Council of Churches. Other ecumenical groups moved in the same direction. As a result the UCCLW transferred its functions and responsibilities in 1938 to the Provisional Committee of the World

Council of Churches. Life and Work was no more. But the inter-change between British and German opinion had really ended in June 1937, before the Oxford conference convened.[13]

For the historian, the Life and Work movement displays the strengths and weaknesses of any microcosm. No microcosm truly represents the whole. Life and Work in particular tended to be top-heavy, dominated by two types of participants: high church func-tionaries and intellectuals. Some—William Temple and Joseph Oldham among them—sat in both saddles, being both church administrators and theologians. Missing in such a case study, however, are the reflections of the man or woman in the pew. Unfortunately, few historical sources tap the attitudes of ordinary churchgoers. One can only assume that the ideas of the church leadership were somewhat reflective of the church membership as a whole. This study claims to analyze only the leadership of the churches.

In some ways Life and Work was remarkably representative. It was neither large enough nor sufficiently well organized to exist as an independent entity, as does its descendant, today's World Coun-cil of Churches. Life and Work never aimed to have a voice of its own. Its purpose was to provide an institutional mechanism to pull together social thinkers and church leaders from various countries. Therefore, the records of Life and Work embody all the contradic-tions, ambiguities, and conflicts of opinion that existed already in Protestant social thought in Europe and America. The movement successfully attracted a variety of spokespersons from Germany and Britain. From Britain, Anglicans and Nonconformists, moder-ates and Christian Socialists all attended the conferences. From Germany, the movement attracted social idealists and archconser-vative Lutherans before 1933; after 1933 both the Nazi-controlled state church and the rebel Confessing Christians participated in the movement. No other religious organization, national or interna-tional, drew participation from more diverse ranks.

The stature of the participants in Life and Work makes it especially revealing of the significant religious changes of the 1920s and 1930s. Life and Work attracted the leaders of various social organizations already in existence in the two countries. For exam-ple, the heads of England's Industrial Christian Fellowship and the Christian Social Council worked tirelessly for Life and Work. Similarly, the leaders of Germany's various church-social groups, such as the Inner Mission and the Evangelical Social Congress, were involved from the beginning. Churchmen from the top positions of the national hierarchies were leaders of Life and Work throughout its existence. Guiding the movement in Britain, for example, were Alfred Garvie, the president of the National Council of Free Churches, Anglican Bishops Theodore Woods and George Bell, and William Temple, Archbishop of York. Hermann Kapler, president of the German Church Federation, was a key leader in his country. Life and Work also drew the participation of noted intellectual figures of the interwar years: T.S. Eliot, Arnold Toynbee, R.H. Tawney, Emil Brunner, Karl Barth, Paul Tillich, Reinhold Niebuhr, Paul Althaus. Life and Work was the only international organization through which such outstanding social workers, churchmen, and intellectuals expressed their opinion.

As a microcosm the Life and Work movement therefore has much to offer. The rich sources it generated are very representative of the attitudes of the church leadership of Germany and Great Britain. Such a microcosm allows the advantage of a close exhaustive study of one particular set of evidence instead of the selective use of data drawn from a wide field. I make every attempt to anchor the Life and Work record within the larger context of religious social and economic thought in Britain and Germany. But the case study offers an immediacy, tangibility, and reality unavailable in a more general study.

I hope this work will shed light on the elusive question, how is it that the British middle classes remained confident in gradual reform while the same German classes opted for radical change during the depression? Even larger questions come to mind: how are religious values part of the whole human being, intertwined with the social, economic, and political individual? How do ethical systems explain troublesome situations, prescribe responses, and influence behavior? How do these conceptions of what is right or wrong, possible or impossible, change in response to altered physical realities? I do not expect definitive answers to these questions, merely greater understanding.

2. THE BRITISH AND GERMAN TRADITIONS

THE British churches encountered the social unrest and economic stagnation of the 1920s with an optimistic social gospel that strongly criticized the capitalist system and provided concrete goals for future reforms. German Protestant leaders faced the difficult environment of the 1920s in a much more pessimistic way. They confined their social outreach to charitable endeavors while their criticism was limited to hostile attacks against socialism, the Weimar Republic, and the Versailles Treaty. These striking differences reflect the dissimilar backgrounds of Protestant social thought in the two countries.

In Great Britain, the birthpains of the Industrial Revolution brought a quickening of the Protestant social conscience in the early 1800s. At first, however, the precursors of the British social conscience developed outside the mainstream of the Established Church. The leaders of the Church of England remained for almost a century remarkably immune to the changed social and economic realities brought by industrialization. Before the mid-nineteenth century they were conservative and aristocratic. Overall, Anglican leaders opposed social reform and preached submission to a national order of inequality. Contemporaries were close to reality when they called the Church of England the Tory Party at prayer.[1]

It was not the Anglican hierarchy but parish pastors and laymen and -women who launched the Evangelical movement of the late 1800s, which brought social problems to the attention of the nation. With its nerve center in Clapham, where eminent Evangelicals such as William Wilberforce lived, the movement led campaigns against slavery in the British colonies, denounced squalid conditions in the nation's prisons, and established numerous societies devoted to specific reform causes. The Anglican Evangelicals were joined by Quakers, Methodists, and Baptists in their frantic rush to do good in the early nineteenth century.

Much of the historiography concerning the nineteenth century, from that of J.L. and Barbara Hammond to that of E.P. Thompson, is quick to dismiss the Evangelical movement as a prop for conservative social and political systems. It is true that the Evangelical leaders feared radicalism and revolution. With all their benevolence toward the poor, they wanted no change in the social order; the poor were to stay in their place. The Evangelicals wanted to moralize the working classes so that they would accept their status as a God-ordained fate in life. However, the Evangelical movement with its ubiquitous societies, causes, and immense propaganda did bring the Christian social conscience into the public eye. The movement made clear to the nation that some Protestants saw society as within the domain of Christian morality and direction. It created a group and style of mostly middle-class do-gooders who worked tirelessly and endlessly for moral causes. Indeed many of these societies with their staffs of maids and matrons have carried on to the present day.[2]

This extra-ecclesiastical social reform movement was flourishing while the Church of England in effect hibernated. But apparently neither the Established Church nor the Anglican Evangelicals appealed to the growing industrial proletariat of the nineteenth century. If they were churched at all, the working people of the industrial cities were most likely to attend a Nonconformist chapel. Methodism, for example, grew twice as fast as the population in England between 1800 and 1850. In 1770 only one of fourteen Englishmen was outside the Church of England; by 1851 the religious census showed that nearly half of all churchgoers attended elsewhere. Moreover, over half the nation was unchurched on census Sunday. Attendance was lowest in industrial cities of the north, such as Manchester and Preston, and highest in the agrarian south.[3] Somewhat shocked by the census of 1851, the Anglicans awoke from their slumber and made a vigorous effort throughout the rest of the century to make their message palatable to working people. This meant a new social concern among the Anglican hierarchy.

During the last half of the century the British churches in general threw themselves frantically into charitable work for the poor. It was as if the Evangelical movement had entered the main-stream of the church. The Anglo-Catholic Oxford movement of the 1870s romanticized the Middle Ages and emphasized the historic role the church had played as a charitable institution. New orders of Anglican sisters were organized to work with the poor. The number of charitable institutions continued to climb. In the decade 1850–60 alone, over 140 new societies were organized.[4] The Church of England began a new Working Men's Society in 1876 to train laymen for special work with the poor. The Anglicans and other church groups sponsored adult education programs in all parts of England. So many were giving so much charity to the poor that the Charity Organization Society was organized to coordinate the almsgiving so as not to "pauperize" the poor.[5]

This charitable social work increased in the late 1800s, es-pecially during the economic stagnation of the 1880s and 1890s. The settlement movement epitomized the style of Christian social work in this period. Toynbee Hall in London, for example, brought Oxford undergraduates to the slums for the summers with the idea that contact with the upper classes was necessary for the moral regeneration of the wretched poor. By 1914 there were some forty settlement houses in the major urban centers. Not just Anglicans were involved; the Methodists had their own settlements in Lon-don, Manchester, Liverpool, and elsewhere.[6] In the 1870s Octavia Hill, an idealistic Anglican reformer, introduced a scheme of model houses whereby middle-class landlords would move into tene-ments and teach the impoverished tenants bourgeois and Christian moral values such as piety, thrift, and punctuality. By the late 1870s Hill's seven model housing projects in London were offering pater-nalistic moral training to the poor.

With all this charity and sympathy for the poor, the attitudes of the Anglican and Nonconformist church leaders in the last half of the nineteenth century remained similar to those of the Evan-gelicals in the early part of the century. For most, it was not the economy or the social structure that needed changing; it was the hearts and habits of the poor. The sympathy and concern for the plight of the poor implied reform not of society but of the poor themselves.[7] In the late nineteenth century the Church of England and the Nonconformists were alike in adhering to the principles of contemporary political economy. Despite their philanthropy they wished to preserve the social and economic order. Within their own buildings both Nonconformists and Anglicans retained systems of pew rental that stratified their congregations according to what members could pay. They had no intention of abolishing class. Even the Methodists and Baptists, the most plebeian of denominations in the nineteenth century, were socially and politically conservative.[8]

The few British Protestants who called for reform of society and the economy in the late nineteenth century were outside the mainstream, just as the Evangelicals had been fifty years earlier. But their voices grew increasingly louder and more respectable. Christians who criticized the system itself were lumped together under the label "Christian socialist." The first Christian socialist movement appeared around midcentury as a combination of French utopian socialism and the theology of Frederick Denison Maurice, a professor at King's College, London. Maurice's friend J.M. Ludlow had studied and observed the socialism of Louis Blanc and Charles Fourier in France. He returned to England with the outlines of utopian socialism, which Maurice surrounded with a theology stressing rationalism, pragmatism, and the immanence of God. Greatly influenced by Samuel Taylor Coleridge, Maurice taught that the Kingdom of God was to be a divine order on earth; socialism would be its means. Charles Kingsley became a propagandist for the movement with his novels and tracts which attained a wide readership. The socialism of these men did criticize capitalism's competition, egoism, and inequalities and called for the reform of the economy to make it more cooperative. It did not call for state ownership or intervention.[9]

This Christian socialism was ephemeral, dying out by 1854. But in the 1880s many of the same ideas were revived with a new Christian socialist movement which extended into the twentieth century. The two largest Christian socialist organizations—the Guild of Saint Matthew (1877-1909) and the Christian Social Union (1889-1919)—were both Anglican, but almost all the denominations in England had comparable socialist groups. The Oxford movement of the 1870s ironically aided the Anglican Christian socialist movement by romanticizing the precapitalist medieval economy and social structure. The Anglo-Catholic emphasis on sacraments inspired a theology of sacramental community which the GSM and CSU made a basis for their socialism. This sacramental socialism distinguished the Anglican movement from the Nonconformist ones and also from Maurice's earlier socialism. Otherwise, these two groups shared with the non-Anglican socialist groups a common Maurician rhetoric about the immanence of God in the world, with His kingdom entering all phases of human life, and an optimistic view of man and progress. Their "socialism" was vague and somewhat ambiguous: some members called for Fabian political remedies such as a single tax on land; others recommended voluntary cooperation. But all agreed that the system, the conditions, needed reform not just the character of the poor.[10]

The rise of a Christian critique of social and economic problems corresponded to significant theological changes. The late Victorian years saw in Britain the coalescence of a coherent liberal Protestant theology.[11] The movement in Christian theology away from transcendence and mystery toward reason and man goes as far back as the Enlightenment, and it is not a singularly British movement. Maurice and Coleridge were theological pioneers, but other breakthroughs came in Germany. Theologians there such as Albrecht Ritschl responded to the challenge of science and historical criticism by moving from questions of fact (how was the earth created?) to questions of value (what does the creation mean for man?). Like Maurice in England, Ritschl preferred practical ethical substance in theology to metaphysics. Instead of emphasizing an otherworldly God, liberals looked to God's human form, Jesus: because Jesus Christ is the instrument of man's redemption, Christ is God made meaningful to mankind; the redemption of Jesus Christ is not individual but communal. Finally, Ritschl and other liberals taught that Christians should work toward establishing the Kingdom of God on earth.[12]

In the late nineteenth century, Ritschlian liberalism was more pervasive among Nonconformists than among Anglicans. In the judgment of Thomas Langford, the Church of England felt the impact of Ritschl more in the next century, particularly in the 1910s and 1920s.[13] The Anglo-Catholic movement remained a strong force within the Church of England. In contrast to the Ritschlians, Anglo-Catholics emphasized worship, the sacraments, and the incarnation as the miraculous self-emptying of God into creation. Like Ritschlian liberals, Anglo-Catholics reacted to the challenge of science but in a different way. As the authority of scripture waned, Anglo-Catholics emphasized historic Christianity and the creeds, more than reason, as authoritative.

Despite these differences, Protestants in Great Britain shared many of the same assumptions and emphases. Protestant theology generally had absorbed the prevailing idealistic and evolutionary thought of the day. Its views of an immanent God in human form, Jesus, made Christianity seem more rational and less otherworldly. The liberal view of man as basically good and the confidence in progress and the coming of the Kingdom of God all reflected the optimism of pre–World War I Europe. These ideas fit congenially with the mentality of the comfortable and triumphant middle classes at the turn of the century. Moreover, these optimistic theological premises were a necessary foundation for a social gospel calling for specific reforms and changes to usher in God's kingdom.

Archbishop Michael Ramsay has written that the advent of "modern" theology, as the British call their version of liberalism, came in 1889 with the publication of *Lux Mundi* by a distinguished group of theologians spearheaded by Charles Gore, who went on that year to found the Christian Social Union. At first shocking to an older theological generation, modernism became the dominant stream of Anglican theology until World War II.[14] In the first two decades of the twentieth century the liberal theological outlook and the social gospel of the Christian socialists moved from outside to inside the mainstream of English Protestantism, just as the Evangelical movement had done earlier. The churches moved away from charity and philanthropy—"ambulance" work, as they came to call it—to a thoroughgoing critique of the social and economic order and a call for its reform. As a generation schooled in Christian socialism and theological liberalism moved into the church hierarchies, these ideas became a new orthodoxy.[15]

Statements made by the Lambeth Conferences, the decennial gatherings of Anglican bishops, reflect clearly the change from Victorian philanthropy to social criticism. While the Lambeth Conferences of 1867 and 1878 avoided social and economic questions entirely, in 1888 and 1897 churchmen discussed the matter in great detail. The 1888 conference advocated state action to help the poor with factory-act legislation; the 1897 meeting recommended state aid for the unemployed, sick, and aged.[16] Both conferences spoke out against excessive inequality and poverty, yet the Victorian attitude emphasizing individual guilt and the necessity for personal reform clearly remained. The 1888 report on socialism concluded: "But, after all, the best help is self help." What the poor needed more than an increase in income, it continued, were habits of thrift and self-restraint.[17] The 1897 report agreed that no good could be done for the poor unless they helped themselves: "It is character that they need. It is inspiration."[18] By the 1908 Lambeth meeting this condescending attitude had changed: the reports called again for state intervention to ameliorate conditions but no longer emphasized the moralization of the poor. The 1920 Lambeth Conference stated that the goals of the Labour Party and the Church of England were the same: to secure fullness of life and create a better world. This report went on to condemn unemployment, not the unemployed, as immoral and called for a "living" wage that would allow workers to have noble, honest and complete lives.[19]

William Temple exemplified the new generation of English churchmen. Thomas Langford describes him as an eclectic assimilator of the various threads of social and theological liberalism in English Protestantism.[20] Temple was the son of an Archbishop of Canterbury; his background and education (Rugby and Oxford) were purely aristocratic. But the Christian Social Union and the Student Christian movement inspired him as a youth, and as a young curate he dabbled in various social pursuits. He formed a group called the Collegium, which after 1909 met to discuss ways to relate Christianity to social life. Several of the Collegium members, including Temple, Lucy Gardiner, and Malcolm Spencer, would later be British leaders in the Life and Work movement. The Collegium published works denouncing capitalism; *Competition,* for example, advocated specific policies such as graduated income taxes, death duties, social legislation, and other government remedies.[21] In 1916 Temple even suggested that the state should take over medical services. Two years later he announced to a convocation of churchmen that he had joined the Labour Party.[22] Yet Temple became bishop of Manchester in 1921 and eventually Archbishop of Canterbury, the highest post in the Church of England.

Among the Nonconformists a similar transition from philanthropy to social criticism and political activism took place. Stephen Koss's study of Nonconformity and politics indicates that after years of quiescence the Nonconformists entered the political arena in the early 1900s. Moreover, many Nonconformists moved into the Labour Party in these years.[23] Jeffrey Cox, in his study of the churches in suburban Lambeth, shows that among middle-class Nonconformist churches—Presbyterian, Methodist, Congregationalist—a shift to social and theological liberalism occurred in the first two decades of the century. But the working-class chapels—such as Baptist and Free Methodist—functioned as psychological mutual aid societies, shunning social and political affairs in favor of the personal religious experience.[24]

This optimistic theological liberalism was an analogue to the political liberalism of the period. The culture of liberalism seemed to appeal to many members of the middle and upper classes in the early 1900s. It was not the dour Gladstonian liberalism of a past age but a new liberalism, according to Michael Bentley, an "open and receptive mind, eager for new impressions, brave, poetic, and illogical."[25] But the fate of the liberal religious outlook was not tied to the fortunes of the Liberal Party, as some scholars suggest.[26] On the contrary, the optimism of liberalism surprisingly bloomed again after the war and flourished through the 1920s.[27] The high tide of theological liberalism, according to English church historian Alec Vidler, came in 1929 with the publication of a significant report by the archbishops' commission on theology. Michael Bentley's study of the liberal mind indicates that although the Liberal Party declined in the 1920s, intellectual liberalism did not stabilize itself until after the war.[28] The 1920s were a golden age for the social gospel. After the most destructive war in memory, it is somewhat surprising that the churches managed to cling to their optimism, especially considering the political intrigue abroad and socioeconomic turmoil at home in the 1920s.

In a decade of industrial stagnation, high unemployment, and labor unrest, the churches had ample opportunity to put their social gospel into practice. In the railway strike of 1919, Archbishop Randall Thomas Davidson offered his services as mediator to Lloyd George and the railwaymen's leader, J.H. Thomas; both politely declined his offer.[29] With the General Strike of 1926 several churchmen jumped into the fray. Davidson disapproved of the strike and criticized it as coercive and disruptive in a speech in the House of Lords. But on 7 May he met with a group of Anglican bishops and Nonconformist clergy to prepare a conciliatory appeal by the churches to end the strike. Their message, broadcast on BBC radio and printed in the London *Times,* called for the cancellation of the strike and a renewal of government subsidies to the coal industry.[30] Along with eight other Anglican bishops and eleven Nonconformist leaders, William Temple organized a group called the Standing Conference of the Christian Churches on the Coal Dispute. They tried actual mediation between miners and mine owners with no real success. The intervention of all these churchmen came to nothing and was resented by some conservative parties, including Stanley Baldwin.[31] But it shows that they took their social responsibility quite seriously.

The rhetoric of the social gospel rose to a crescendo in the 1920s. A group of socially minded Anglican bishops brought the social message constantly to the attention of the church hierarchy at every convocation of primates. Charles Gore, Bishop of Winchester until 1924 and mastermind of both *Lux Mundi* and the Christian Social Union, was courted as the grand old man of the Christian social movement in the 1920s. William Temple, Bishop of Manchester after 1922, was clearly the rising star. His Collegium continued to meet and in the early 1920s made plans for the massive Copec conference (Conference on Politics, Economics and Citizenship), the monumental event in the social gospel movement in England in the 1920s. Temple as president of the conference made his name as the unquestioned leader of the Anglican social gospel movement. From 1920 to 1927, he edited *The Pilgrim,* an outlet for expression of opinion on Christian social matters. The respectability of this social gospel within the church was certainly emphasized by his promotion to the Archbishopric of York in 1929.

The scholar of the Christian social movement of the 1920s was Temple's friend from Rugby and Oxford, R.H. Tawney. A professor at the London School of Economics, Tawney was a convinced socialist and member of the Labour Party. He had spent three years at Toynbee Hall and at Oxford had come under the spell of Charles Gore.[32] When Tawney published his *Acquisitive Society* in 1921 it became required reading for socially concerned pastors. Basically, he argued that reorganization of industry along moral lines would make it more efficient and productive. Tawney's new society would be one where moral duties and social obligation, the idea of service, would be the chief motivational principles. In 1926 his

Religion and the Rise of Capitalism chronicled the transition from medieval Catholic communitarianism to modern competitive individualism. Like Weber, he postulated an inadvertent relationship between Protestant ethics and capitalist individualism, but Tawney lamented the modern separation of economics and religion.[33] He thus gave scholarly support to the Anglo-Catholics who romanticized the Middle Ages. Tawney was the economist and historian to whom church leaders looked whenever they needed an expert to support their opinion. In 1918 the archbishops had drafted him as part of a special committee to write a report on Christianity and industrial problems. He also played a large role in the Copec conference.

Tawney and Temple were only part of an extensive network of individuals engaged in the social debate. Some of the old Christian socialist groups had given way to new ones by the 1920s. The Christian Social Union, in which so many of the socially minded bishops had gained their knowledge and experience, dissolved after the war. It had become so respectable, so "establishment," that it had lost its cutting edge. In 1919 it amalgamated with the Navvy Mission Society, a group that maintained missions on construction sites, to form the Industrial Christian Fellowship. The ICF was one of the most vigorous Anglican social organizations in the 1920s, conducting crusades in industrial areas for the working classes and holding meetings full of vague speeches and discussions for its mainly middle-class membership.[34] Many of the CSU people moved right into the ICF—Gore, Temple, even Tawney became members. The ICF dished out the standard social gospel rhetoric: the brotherhood of man, the living wage, a nonpartisan political stance. Like the social gospel in general, its positions were shadowy and ambiguous: it was labeled by various groups both "a cloak for capitalism" and "a camouflage for communism."[35]

Other Christian social groups articulated more concrete remedies for social ills. The newly organized League of the Kingdom of God took a more socialist orientation than the ICF. However, they supported guild socialism rather than state socialism, perpetuating the influence of the Oxford movement in the Church of England. Their guild socialism, a medieval-style syndicalism, recommended a reorganization of the economy into industrial cooperatives. The more conservative guild socialists looked nostalgically to the Middle Ages for guidance and called for voluntary industrial associations. Those to the left called for guild organization to take place after state ownership of industry; this faction was in tune with the guild socialism envisioned by some theorists in the Labour Party.[36] Leaders of the league such as V.A. Demant, Maurice Reckitt, and Ruth Kenyon, were vocal and productive propagandists of their views.[37]

All these various threads of the social gospel movement—individuals, groups, and religious denominations—coalesced in April 1924 with the Conference on Politics, Economics, and Citizenship (Copec) held in Birmingham. Temple and the Collegium initiated the long and extensive preparations for the conference. Temple chaired an ecumenical council that included fourteen Anglican bishops and representatives from the leading church-social agencies such as the ICF. Twelve commissions were organized in 1921 to prepare study reports for the conference; the commissions sent out 200,000 questionnaires to poll public opinion on social questions and the role of the church. The commissions were made up of members from various denominations and walks of life—clergy, professors, writers, businessmen, social workers, civil servants, schoolteachers, Members of Parliament, and others. Yet despite the diversity among the commissions that prepared them, the reports reveal little conflict of opinion in their critique of industrial capitalism. The conflicts emerged over subsidiary questions such as birth control, divorce, temperance, and pacifism.

The actual conference attracted fifteen hundred delegates representing nearly all British denominations and social agencies. The reports and speeches pioneered nothing new; they generally echoed the social criticism of previous decades. The importance of Copec lies in the attention it received. In the view of Edward R. Norman, it provided a whole generation with statements of social teachings. Granted, there were eccentricities in the movement; Norman mentions the feverish sponsorship of every high-minded cause from eugenics to Esperanto and the presence of "too many single women with obsessions" (Lucy Gardiner, the Quaker secretary of Copec, fell out of bed the first night of the conference in a state of estatic delirium).[38] But the conference loudly reaffirmed Christian socialist ideas before the eyes of the nation. Moreover, it made William Temple's reputation as a leading social thinker and an enormously influential figure in the ecumenical circles of the 1920s.

There were a few detractors, notably Hensley Henson, Bishop of Durham, who denounced Copec's almost giddy optimism about the perfectibility of the social order and its meddlesome attitudes in matters of state.[39] But on the whole Copec was received enthusiastically by the churches. A convocation in Canterbury accepted it as expressing the official attitude of the Church of England. The church and secular press reported the conference with approval.[40] Copec was probably the highest moment in the British Christian social movement. After a century of evolution in British Protestant social policy, from neglect to philanthropy to social criticism, the social gospel thus flourished in the 1920s. In Germany by the 1920s, however, Protestant social policy had developed in quite a different way.

The evolution of Protestant social policies in Germany is a much more fragmented story than in Britain, for the social gospel never really entered the mainstream of German religion. Several impediments blocked the growth of an activist social stance in Germany. One was the nature of German theology itself, going back to the Reformation. In many ways, orthodox Lutheran theology was the antithesis of the themes of Protestant liberalism outlined above. Instead of the immanence of God, Luther stressed His otherworldly supernatural character. Instead of the divine-human man, Luther viewed man as a depraved, helpless creature who could do nothing to effect his own salvation. Rather than a synthesis between the world of man and the world of God, Luther posited a dichotomy between the two kingdoms of heaven and earth. This dualism became the ironclad, stereotypical stance of German Lutheranism with the work of conservative dogmatists after Luther and the staid church-state Lutheranism of following centuries.[41]

Although pockets of Calvinism, with its more activist and interventionist stance, were scattered throughout Germany, Lutheran views dominated German social Protestantism. Historical circumstances, such as constant warfare with France in the Calvinist Rhineland and the rise of Lutheran Prussia, had enfeebled German Calvinism by the twentieth century. Also contributing was the forced unification of Lutheran and Calvinist churches in some territories in the early 1800s. In 1817 Friedrich Wilhelm III of Prussia united Lutherans and Calvinists into a state church, the Prussian Union, which comprised half the Protestants in all Germany. In regions where there were sizable Calvinist minorities, such as Württemburg, Nassau, and Baden, princes followed the example of Prussia. When industrialization brought opportunities for more social responsibility in the later nineteenth century, Calvinist social activism had already been diluted by the absorption of the reformed minorities into the united churches. The Lutheran view of social ethics prevailed. Ironically, the great leaders of the German church-social movement in the nineteenth century were Lutheran.

Another hindrance to the development of a social gospel in Germany was the close association there between church and state. Again, the roots of this tradition go back to the Reformation, when the growth of Protestantism took place under the protection of the secular princes. Luther viewed this state control over religion as a temporary expedient, somewhat contrary to his principle of the two kingdoms but necessary to nurture the church through its difficult early years. However, after Luther's death the church remained virtually a department within the civil bureaucracy until the revolution of 1918, when it received autonomy.[42] Three centuries of authoritarian German politics indelibly cast the policies of the German church in a conservative, uncritical, noninterventionist mold.

When a social movement began in response to the growing industrialization of Germany in the nineteenth century, it was, not surprisingly, conservative. Germany experienced a religious revival in the early 1800s. Accompanying it was an awakening of the social conscience, perhaps building upon the pietist tradition of previous centuries. Even though Germans in the past had considered the handling of charity a civil function, not a private affair, the revival brought a strong humanitarian impulse. The sufferings, displacement, and need engendered by the Napoleonic wars also contributed to the growth of private charity. As with the Evangelical movement in Great Britain, charitable organizations were established: orphanages, relief agencies, and prison rehabilitation societies. In the 1830s Theodor Fliedner founded a hospital in Kaiserswerth, which trained Protestant women as nurses. Soon a network of centers was producing the deaconesses, as they were called, who cared for the sick, the poor, orphans, and prisoners. By the 1860s there were deaconess operations in all the large cities of Germany.

A real milestone in the development of a German Protestant social movement was the work of Johann Wichern, which began in the 1830s. A Lutheran layman who had studied under Friedrich Schleiermacher, Wichern was a product of the German religious awakening. In the early 1830s he founded a settlement house for destitute children near Hamburg, the *Rauhe Haus,* which taught residents religious values along with trades and crafts. Wichern's *Rauhe Haus* became a center for the training of missionaries to conduct work among the urban poor. In the 1840s he began his plans for the Inner Mission, which was to be a federation of voluntary charitable organizations throughout Germany, a common agency for social action on the part of the individual territorial churches, the *Landeskirchen.* His opportunity to launch the Inner Mission came with the failed revolution of 1848. In April 1848 an unofficial meeting in Wittenberg of clergy and laymen discussed the church's situation in relation to the revolution. There Wichern unveiled his counterrevolutionary purpose for the Inner Mission: it was to be a stabilizing force for both church and state. The same enemies were attacking both state and church under different guises, he argued; the revolution that shook the state was, on the flip side of the coin, atheism attacking the church. Wichern blamed Communists, not liberals, for the revolution. The manifesto for the Inner Mission, written in 1849, made it clear that the mission's goal was to maintain the state, the royal dynasty, and traditional estates. As an orthodox Lutheran, Wichern argued that any revolt against authority was the work of Satan. A republic would mean godlessness. By ameliorating the social and economic distress of the working classes and by Christianizing them, the Inner Mission would rescue both church and state.[43] As the Inner Mission identified with the counterrevolution, conservatives supported it wholeheartedly.

After 1848 the Inner Mission would dominate the social endeavor of German Protestantism. The mission had no central focus; it simply coordinated the various social and mission activities of existing associations. As one of the few common agencies of the independent *Landeskirchen,* it provided some expression of unity in an ecclesiastically divided land. During the rest of the century the Inner Mission dutifully busied itself with coordinating various charity efforts: Bible and tract distribution; campaigns against drinking, prostitution, and gambling; ministry to prisoners; youth work; rescue missions; street preaching; Sunday schools and various educational tasks. After 1848 voluntary charity thus became institutionalized.

The Inner Mission grew rapidly in the counterrevolutionary 1850s. By 1854 nearly one hundred local charitable associations had affiliated with it. The mission was embraced especially by Prussia, the largest and most important of the German states. Prussia officially incorporated the Inner Mission in 1849, giving it special rights such as franking privileges. Wichern himself became employed by the Prussian government as a penal advisor. By 1861, although three-quarters of its work was in Prussia, 217 paid professional social workers and other staff were working for the Inner Mission throughout Germany.[44] This close relationship with Prussia brought suspicion in homogeneously Lutheran areas such as Hannover and Saxony, where Lutherans feared that the Inner Mission was a guise for the Prussion Union. But when German unification in 1871 did not entail an extension of the union system in the churches, criticism died away, and Lutheran areas joined in the mission's work.

The close relationship between the Inner Mission and the state remained strong. With the growth of the Social Democratic Party (SPD) in the 1860s and 1870s, Wichern and the Inner Mission stayed true to their counterrevolutionary purpose of 1848. Well into the 1870s Wichern continued to portray socialism as an enemy of the church. Atheism was the product of socialism, he said; its success in Europe corresponded to the moral decadence in the land.[45] Wichern maintained that the church dealt with spiritual pauperism, leaving the state to deal with material pauperism. For all its work, the Inner Mission never questioned the validity of the system of government or the social and economic order; in fact, it openly buttressed this order throughout its entire existence. In 1908 a socialist critic noted these characteristics:

> Manifold and numerous as are the undertakings of the Inner Mission . . . they were and remained the services of individuals for individuals, and all bear the marks of charity. . . . This is also shown by the transactions of the congresses of the Inner Mission, where they concern themselves with the numerous ailments of human society, and propose various cures—but solely from the standpoint of Christian charity, the assistance of the socially higher to the socially lower

orders; nothing is heard in these gatherings of an active participation of the masses in their economic, political and spiritual concerns rising to the level of equality.[46]

Although it centralized much charitable work, the Inner Mission was not the only social movement in German Protestantism. The deaconess organization centered in Kaiserswerth continued to supply an army of professionals serving the sick and poor. In 1865 a group of Westphalian Christians opened a home for the epileptic near Bielefeld. Under the leadership of Pastor Friedrich von Bodelschwingh and later his son, Fritz, by the early twentieth century the institution had become a huge community called Bethel, which cared for the epileptic, the mentally retarded, and the sick. Bodelschwingh opened workers' colonies in Bethel and elsewhere to teach unemployed vagrants industrious habits until they were ready to reenter society as contributing members. By the turn of the century Bethel housed four thousand residents and was well known throughout the world as an example of German Christian charity.[47] In method, intent, and style, however, Bethel differed little from the Inner Mission. The German Protestant social movement in the nineteenth century attempted to reform the poor, not society.

The few individuals who called for reforms rather than ambulance work were ostracized from the church establishment. In the 1840s and 1850s, for example, Wilhelm Weitling tried to combine socialism with Christianity to create a "proletarian religion." He was not received even by workers, much less the church. Gustav Werner established model factory communities in Swabia akin to the British industrialist Robert Owen's more famous experiment in New Lanark, Scotland, in the early 1800s. In response, Wichern steadfastly refused to endorse any scheme of Christian socialism. For years he feuded with Victor Huber, an outspoken social critic who founded cooperative societies and housing associations in Berlin in the 1840s.[48]

Only in the late nineteenth century did a social critique coalesce to challenge the social conservatism of German church leaders. The challenge began in the late 1870s with the work of Rudolf Todt and Adolf Stöcker. A country pastor in Barenthin, Todt in 1877 called for state intervention to help exploited members of society. The social theory of the New Testament demanded political action, and Christians should form a political party to implement their ideas, he suggested. In 1878 Todt and Stöcker, the Prussion High Court preacher, founded an association for "Social Reform on Christian and Constitutional Principles." The same year Stöcker formed a political party called the Christian Socialist Workers Party, which advocated national labor associations, higher wages, the eight-hour day, and pensions for widows, orphans, and the aged.

Stöcker was obviously out of tune with the leadership of the church. Quickly, the Inner Mission's central committee divorced itself from him. Kaiser Wilhelm announced that any clergy of a state church holding Stöcker's opinions would lose his freedom of speech. Yet notwithstanding his apparently radical suggestions and the antagonism of church elites, Stöcker's purpose, like Wichern's, was essentially counterrevolutionary. Only his call for Christians to put their ideas into political action was unorthodox. Fearing Communism, Stöcker planned for his Christian Socialist Workers Party to replace the SPD. Todt's book had gloomily predicted a Communist future for Germany, a destiny that Stöcker believed only political action by Christians could prevent.

Bismarck supported Stöcker, recognizing the value of Stöcker's party in dividing the SPD. In 1878 the Iron Chancellor had pushed legislation through the Reichstag outlawing socialism. With the antisocialist laws and Bismarck's support, Stöcker's candidates polled forty thousand votes in Berlin in the 1881 elections to the SPD's mere twenty thousand. Both Bismarck's and Stöcker's ambitions were to steal the thunder from the socialists. Bismarck announced his plans for a social security program in 1881, and the provisions were passed into law later in the 1880s. Meanwhile, however, Stöcker's influence waned. His party's crusade became increasingly anti-Semitic, and his vitriolic propaganda against Jews coincided with violent debates taking place in the Prussian legislature concerning the exclusion of Jews from public schools and universities. When riots, boycotts, and duels resulted from the heated discussion, Stöcker received much of the blame for the controversy. Under pressure from his Jewish banker and adviser Gerson von Bleichröder, Bismarck became increasingly displeased with Stöcker, who in November 1890 lost his post of court preacher.[49]

Before losing his position at court, Stöcker founded the Evangelical Social Congress, which brought him into contact with Protestant liberalism, the other stream of social criticism challenging the quietism of the churches. Since Schleiermacher, theological liberalism with its emphasis on social Christianity had grown primarily in the universities. Albrecht Ritschl, the greatest name in liberal theology, was a professor of theology at Göttingen. After 1887 liberals had their own journal, *Die Christliche Welt,* edited by Martin Rade, which remained a focus of the liberal movement until Hitler suppressed it in 1941.[50] In addition to its university adherents, liberalism appealed to a small number of clergy and educated laity mainly in large-town parishes where the ecclesiastical patronage was the town council. Liberals were unrepresented in the General Synod of the Prussian Church or the *Oberkirchenrat,* the High Church Council.[51]

The weaknesses and difficulties of liberalism were illustrated by Adolf von Harnack's problems in receiving his appointment to the University of Berlin in the late 1880s. Harnack was the greatest Ritschlian, having picked up the mantle from his aging mentor. His reputation as a theologian was already made; he had a wide following especially in Britain and America. When the Berlin faculty offered him a chair, the Prussian High Church Council refused to accept him, invoking a privilege granted it in 1855 to evaluate the doctrinal soundness of any theologian called to the university. Finally, in 1890, the case went before the kaiser for a decision. Young Wilhelm II decided in favor of Harnack, who took the post to become Germany's premier theologian for the next three decades.[52]

The year 1890 was pivotal in the fortunes of Protestant liberalism in Germany. Besides Harnack's victory, the government sent other friendly signals to the liberals. Bismarck resigned that year, and the Reichstag refused to renew the antisocialist laws. The new kaiser's display of idealism and openness to novel ideas gave hope to liberals.[53] Conditions for the working classes should be improved, he announced. On cue, the Prussian High Church Council issued a circular letter calling for pastors to confront the needs of workers and their families, and to persuade them to shed their prejudices against church and kaiser.[54]

Also in 1890 Stöcker's Evangelical Social Congress provided a new outlet for liberalism. Harnack had aided Stöcker in founding the congress, and liberals very quickly took over its leadership. For the next four decades it remained a center of social studies of a rather academic nature. Each year in the 1890s, from eight hundred to a thousand pastors, professors, and laymen assembled to discuss such questions as housing, the ten-hour day, unemployment, and the relationship between Christianity and social democracy. Besides Harnack and Stöcker, active participants included Martin Rade, Friedrich Naumann, Max Weber, Ernst Troeltsch, and the noted theologians Julius Kaftan, Wilhelm Hermann, and Adolf Deissmann. Having taken over the congress's leadership from Stöcker, Friedrich Naumann and Harnack revolted against him. Declaring the gospel to be pro-Semitic, Harnack persuaded the organization to take a stand against Stöcker's anti-Semitism. When liberals asked him to resign his vice-presidency in 1896, Stöcker left the congress with a group of supporters to form a rival group, the Church Social Congress.[55] He also revived his anti-Marxist political party, the Christian Social Party.

Although the early 1890s were the zenith of the popularity and prestige of Protestant liberal fortunes in Germany, the bloom of Kaiser Wilhelm's idealism and receptivity was beginning to fade. Liberals started to criticize the kaiser's "new course" as "in substance the old."[56] A wave of reaction brought liberalism and the Christian social movement into ill repute.[57] Karl Ferdinand von Stumm, a prominent Rhineland industrial magnate, began a propaganda campaign against the entire church-social enterprise. Conservatives and representatives of big business in the Reichstag and the Prussian Landstag attacked Christian activism in loud debates, denouncing the Evangelical Social Congress as a seedbed of socialism. The conservative press recommended that church authorities investigate antiauthoritarian and democratic clergy. Church councils in Prussia, Hesse, and Brunswick called pastors on the carpet for flirting with socialism. Speeches at the Inner Mission's Congress of 1895 sharply distinguished between the spheres of politics and religion. And the Prussian High Church Council, the *Oberkirchenrat*, speaking with authority to half the Reich's Protestants, passed a decree forbidding pastors' involvement in social-political agitation, declaring that such activities distracted from the mission of the church to save souls.[58] After the decree, Kaiser Wilhelm wrote to his tutor in Bielefeld: "Stöcker is finished, just as I have predicted for years. Political pastors are an absurdity. . . . Pastors should be concerned with the souls of their congregations and with nurturing neighborly love, but should leave politics out of the picture, since it does not concern them."[59] Satisfied with his success, the industrialist von Stumm published the Kaiser's telegram in his paper, *Die Post*.

So by the late 1890s a reactionary retrenchment had taken place against liberal social criticism, extending even to the conservative Stöcker and his followers. Once more the church took its cues from the government. When the political climate became more restrictive and conservative, the church restrained social criticism by the clergy, and the budding critique of social and economic conditions was left to wither until the next generation. Many clerics dropped out of the Evangelical Social Congress after the 1895 decree, leaving it an isolated bastion of Ritschlian liberalism. As the years went on, its visibility declined, its speeches becoming more academic. Martin Rade, editor of *Die Christliche Welt*, admitted at the twentieth meeting of the congress in 1909 that the congress had little effect on the churches. And even the character of German liberalism changed somewhat after the ecclesiastical reaction of the mid-1890s: it became more narrowly theological, turning the social question over to party politics.[60]

In the fortunes of Protestant liberalism from 1890 to 1918, Friedrich Naumann was a case in point. Having worked in Wichern's *Rauhe Haus*, Naumann was an Inner Mission pastor in Frankfurt when he came to the realization that the Inner Mission's ambulance work was not enough; the conditions had to be changed as well. As one of the most active leaders of the Evangelical Social Congress, he embraced socialism and proclaimed that the Kingdom of God on earth was the process of accomplishing social justice. Using the congress and *Die Christliche Welt* as his forum, he poured out the same sort of vague Christian socialist rhetoric that was common at the same time in England. With the attacks against Christian activism in the mid-1890s, Naumann found himself repeatedly in trouble with authorities of the church and the Inner Mission. He was also a central target for the propaganda of von Stumm and others.

But when the conservative reaction again placed a barrier between the church and political action, Naumann reevaluated his own ideas and entered a new phase. By the late 1890s even he was saying that Christ had established no Christian-social program. Like the conservatives, he too began to separate religion and politics. His Christian-social activism became national-social. He came to the conclusion that Christians should express their convictions not through Christian activism but through secular politics. To this end he founded a new party, the *Nationalsozialer Verein*, a nonrevolutionary reformist party. Essentially he tried to incorporate moderate socialist ideals under liberal bourgeois leadership. Throughout the World War I years he continued to vent his convictions in the political arena rather than in ecclesiastical circles.[61]

Thus, after its golden days in the early 1890s, Protestant liberalism remained outside the leadership of the German churches well into the twentieth century. In the inhospitable political climate of Germany after 1895, religious liberalism moved into academic isolation. Liberal leadership remained in universities, not in church hierarchies; Harnack, for example, was barred from any position in the Prussian church through the first decades of the twentieth century. Or, like Naumann, liberals moved their activist ethic into secular politics and adopted a dualism similar to that of the conservatives, though they worked for different political ends. Neither form of liberalism was a strong or popular alternative to Lutheran social conservatism, which still held force in the Protestant hierarchies and the Inner Mission.[62]

The end of the war and the revolution of 1918 set a new agenda for the German churches' social, political, and economic concerns. The revolution of 1918 left conservatives in control of church administrations in Germany. While reforming the institutional structure of the church, the revolution left the fortunes of liberals and conservatives unchanged. In religion, unlike other areas of culture, the "outsiders" did not become "insiders" in the Weimar Republic.[63] But churchmen now had to cope with socialists who held real political power. During the early days of the revolution, leaders in the church feared its impact. Socialists generally favored disestablishment of the churches in Germany. Beyond this the SPD had no religious policy, since for years they had called religion a personal matter. Nevertheless, a widespread perception persisted that the SPD was not just indifferent to organized religion but against it.

That view was reinforced by socialist actions in the early revolutionary days. The socialist Adolf Hoffmann had recently written a piece of anti-Christian propaganda, *Die Zehn Gebote und die besitzende Klasse,* denouncing the Ten Commandments as a prop for capitalism. In November 1918 the Independent Socialist Party (USPD) appointed "Ten Commandments Hoffmann," as he was known, as Prussian Minister of Education and Public Worship. Hoffmann promptly announced plans to cut church subsidies, confiscate church property, abolish theological faculties in universities, and change church holidays to nature festivals. When he banned school prayer, compulsory religious instruction, and attendance at worship services by students, the public perceived these laws as the beginning of the removal of all religious education in the schools. A storm of Catholic and Protestant protest forced him to resign in January 1919, and three months later his decrees were rescinded.[64] In early 1919 Protestant leaders organized a propaganda campaign to support the DVP and DNVP, parties favoring Protestant interests, even to the extent of having pastors tell congregations how to vote.[65]

Finally, with support of the Center Party and the liberal Democratic Party (DDP), Protestants staved off complete disestablishment. While declaring that there was no state church, the Weimar constitution did allow the national government to establish by legislation fundamental principles for religious associations. With the new constitution the churches retained their status as public corporations and kept their subsidies from state and local governments. Religious instruction and theological faculties in universities were continued. On a local scale, since the constitution changed the relation of church to state, the individual *Landeskirchen* had to reconstruct their polity. In almost every case, the existing structures of church government were reaffirmed, and leadership remained in the hands of conservatives hostile to the new Weimar regime. Rights formerly held by the princes were merely handed over to consistories and church councils; high ecclesiastical officials, considered civil servants before the revolution, after 1919 became officials of the church. Only in Brunswick, Saxony, and Prussia did liberals and socialists in the legislatures push for more democratic church constitutions or for disestablishment of the church from the state. Nowhere were they successful. What the churches received from the new constitutions of 1919 was essentially what they wanted: greater independence from a state that most Protestants perceived as hostile but retention of the churches' special privileges and state subsidies. The German churches constitutionally arrived at a settlement somewhat like that of the Church of England, established yet autonomous.[66]

Another outcome of the 1918 revolution for the churches was growing centralization. In 1919 the *Kirchentag,* an assembly of representatives of the provincial churches, established a confederation called the *Kirchenbund* to represent their common interests. The *Kirchenausschuß,* a committee of thirty-six individuals representing the *Landeskirchen,* became the executive body for this church federation, and its administrative offices were set up in Berlin. Entailing more ecclesiastical centralization than Germany had possessed since the Reformation, the *Kirchenbund* came to speak for German Protestantism in the 1920s.

Although the churches emerged in the early 1920s unified and less dependent on a state now dominated by the left, on both counts the constitutional changes of the revolutionary days were a conservative victory. Retaining their hold on the *Landeskirchen,* conservatives dominated the new *Kirchenbund* administration. The leaders were clearly antagonistic to the new republic.[67] The *Kirchentage* of 1919 and 1922 became podiums for anti-republican speeches. The new president of the *Kirchenausschuß,* Reinhard Moeller, lamented the loss of the old *Kaiserreich*'s glory and with it "the ruler and dynasty which we loved."[68] The president of the 1922 *Kirchentag,* Baron Wilhelm von Pechmann, declared: "The changes which have befallen public life in Germany in the last three years . . . have not only struck at the very marrow of the German people but represent a serious danger for the Protestant church."[69] Karl Wilhelm Dahm argues that most Protestants regarded the Weimar government as "usurpers, traitors, and atheists, in short as enemies."[70] This antagonism toward the Weimar regime became more concrete with the churches' tangible opposition to socialist parties and their identification with the parties of the right. Though officially "above parties," the church prohibited pastors from joining the Communist Party, and it certainly looked with disfavor on the SPD. The anti-Christian attitudes of some socialists, such as Adolf Hoffmann, were not easily forgotten. Throughout the 1920s socialist publications such as *Vorwarts* and *Lachen Links* repeatedly criticized the church as monarchist and conservative; they attacked state subsidies, religious education in schools, and church festivals. The *Kirchenbund* office in Berlin kept a file of such left-wing criticism. The most influential and widely circulated Protestant periodical in Germany, the *Allgemeine Evangelisch-Lutherische Kirchenzeitung,* printed frequent antisocialist editorials, particularly before elections, and openly endorsed Paul von Hindenburg in the 1925 election. It rejoiced when the conservative elderly general won the election: "After six and a half years of this unblessed revolution, the German people have called a man in his prime who is best able to be a savior of the fatherland. The fog has lifted." [71]

The academic liberals generally identified with the *Deutsche Demokratischepartei* (DDP), which entered the first coalition government with the SPD and Center Party. Friedrich Naumann was the DDP's first president, and Martin Rade, still editor of the liberal *Christliche Welt,* was a member of the party's executive committee. [72] However, most church leaders clearly favored two parties of the right, the DNVP and DVP. In the early years of the Weimar Republic the more right-wing party, the DNVP, had the closest ties to the church leadership. The DNVP was the revamped old German conservative party, which had absorbed several right-wing and even anti-Semitic parties from imperial days. One of these was Stöcker's Christian Social Party, led after Stöcker's death in 1909 by his son-in-law, Reinhold Mumm. In the Weimar years the DNVP was still dominated by Junkers, industrial elites, and higher bourgeoisie, with many army officers, bureaucrats, and conservative intellectuals. The party made no bones about its preference for monarchy over democracy. It stood strongly against Bolshevism and was overtly anti-Semitic. [73] Its stance against Marxism as destructive to both state and religion echoed Wichern's call in 1848 and attracted many Protestants. Daniel Borg estimates that throughout the Weimar years the DNVP received the most votes of active Protestant church members, with the DVP running a poor second. [74] In each of the *Kirchentage* of the 1920s, several delegates were DNVP members of the Reichstag. Protestant clergy were frequent speakers at DNVP party rallies. Therefore, despite the official neutrality of the church, the public easily associated the church with the DNVP. Just as in nineteenth-century Britain the Anglican Church had been called the Tory Party at prayer, in the 1920s in Germany the following jingle summed up the situation: "Die Kirche ist politisch neutral—aber sie wählt deutsch national" (The church is politically neutral, but it votes DNVP). [75]

During the Gustav Stresemann era, 1923-29, some Protestant churchmen moved closer to the DVP. At first Stresemann and the party took a cautious attitude toward the republic. They regretted the loss of the monarch, and with many industrialists in the party, they were opposed to radical economic experiments and Communism. To compete with the DDP for middle-class votes, the party platform was fairly moderate, calling for democratic suffrage and for freedoms of the press, speech, and assembly. The DVP first came to the support of the republic with Stresemann's great coalition of 1923, but its influence quickly waned after Stresemann's death in 1929. The election of Hermann Kapler to the presidency of the *Kirchenausschuß* in January 1925 signaled a similar temporary rapprochement between church and republic in the Stresemann years. Following the chauvinistic speeches of his predecessors Frederick Winckler and Reinhard Moeller, Kapler's pronouncements were more conciliatory in tone. A strong leader but no ideologue, Kapler personally knew and respected Stresemann and closely aligned his politics with the DVP. Under Kapler the church in 1925 joined celebrations for the anniversary of Weimar democracy. In 1927 he denied allegations that the Protestant churches were antirepublican. He proceeded to work for a treaty between the Prussian church and the Reich which would grant the church more independence in exchange for loyalty to the republic. Acceptance of the treaty in 1930 was a victory for Kapler and the moderate conservatives in the church over the right wing, which opposed the treaty.[76] Under Kapler's leadership the German church also participated in the ecumenical movement. This moderation among conservatives was, however, ephemeral. The moderate Kapler would be forced out of office when Hitler became chancellor in 1933.[77]

Besides the church's conservative reaction to the revolution and new republic, it also strongly reacted against the fortunes of Germany at the end of the war. Most Protestant clergy had vigorously supported German aims in the Great War. Even the university theologians, divided as they were between pan-German chauvinists and liberal theologians, were practically united in their support of German war efforts.[78] Like most Germans, the leadership of the Protestant churches accepted the stab-in-the-back view of Versailles. The three *Kirchentage* of 1919, 1921, and 1924 condemned the hunger blockade against Germany during the war, the expropriation of German foreign missions, and the Versailles *Diktat*. The church journals and *Kirchliches Jahrbuch* denounced the war-guilt concept and the forced payment of reparations. As late as 1929, on the tenth anniversary of the Versailles Treaty, the *Kirchenausschuß* issued a new declaration condemning the treaty.[79]

Even liberal criticism had weakened by the 1920s. The former bastion of Protestant liberalism, the Evangelical Social Congress, had moved markedly toward the center. After the war the ESC was at a turningpoint, badly divided between moderate and Christian socialist factions. At the thirty-fourth congress in 1921 the power struggle came to crisis. Following a radical Christian socialist speech, President Otto Baumgarten proposed his resignation and the placing of the leadership in Christian socialist hands. Then Arthur Titius, a moderate professor of theology from Berlin, gave an emotional address against socialism. Christ, he said, might be socialist; but for Germany, socialism meant class warfare, which was destructive to the church. Titius won the day, and thereafter the ESC toed a moderate line.[80] Christian socialist groups, such as Paul Tillich's *Kairos* circle, remained isolated though vocal critics throughout the Weimar years, receiving constant ridicule from the church establishment.[81] The liberal challenge weakened through the 1920s, while the conservative social mentality remained intact.

Protestant social conservatism became thus more entrenched in the 1920s. The past provided a tradition not of social activism but of conservative quietism, state subservience, and ex post facto charity work. The brief challenge to this conservatism by Protestant liberalism was quickly ostracized outside the mainstream of the churches. With the end of the war and revolutionary settlement the churches became freed from control by the new center-left state in the early 1920s. Meanwhile, fears of socialism and resentment against economic chaos and the loss of the war intensified the bitter feelings of German church leaders toward the republic. These patterns show that the German church leadership was indeed keenly interested in the social question. And although they proclaimed themselves "above parties," they could quickly rise to explicit political criticism and even intervention when the traditional status quo was threatened.

Historical traditions help explain the very different social stances in postwar Britain and Germany. Actually until the late nineteenth century British and German Protestant social positions had been quite similar. Both the Church of England and the German Protestant churches largely ignored the plight of the working classes until becoming frightened by midcentury revolution and unrest. For the Germans, the failed revolution of 1848 inspired vigorous new efforts to pacify the working classes by converting them to Christianity and treating the symptoms of socioeconomic distress via Wichern's Inner Mission. The 1848 revolutions in Europe also shocked the English, inspiring Maurice's Christian social movement of 1848-54. A spate of industrial novels that appeared in the late 1840s and 1850s advocated Christian responsibility in the capitalist economy.[82] Even more, the census of 1851 had brought Anglicans to the shocking realization that the working class was largely outside the church. For the rest of the century both Anglicans and Nonconformists, like the Germans of the Inner Mission, rushed headlong into charitable work of many sorts.

By the end of the century, however, patterns in the two countries had diverged. British Protestantism moved from philanthropy to reform, from charity to social criticism. Protestant liberalism and the social gospel grew into the mainstream of the British churches by the 1920s. No such transition took place in Germany. After a brief struggle between 1890 and 1895, conservative orthodoxy retrenched and kept its hegemony over the leadership of the German churches. In the land of Schleiermacher, Ritschl, and Harnack, Protestant liberalism and the social gospel were left to wither on the vine, isolated in the universities; they remained outside the hierarchy and even the social agencies of the German churches. By the 1920s the hero for British social Protestantism was Frederick Maurice, a so-called Christian socialist of the 1850s and precursor of liberal theology. The German hero, however, was Maurice's contemporary Johann Wichern, the avowed anti-Communist counterrevolutionary of 1848.

The actions of the British and German churches in the 1920s illustrate the huge differences between them. British bishops and archbishops tried to mediate in strikes in 1919 and 1926; a former member of the Labour Party became Archbishop of York in 1929. German churchmen, though they claimed no party affiliation, supported conservative political parties and generally opposed the revolution and the republic. The huge Copec conference, probably the most significant church assembly in Britain in the 1920s, demonstrated the state of British social Protestantism with its explicit criticisms and calls for reform. Receiving wide press coverage in Germany in 1924, Copec prompted the 1924 *Kirchentag*'s "Social Message," a comparative work of the assembled German churches.[83] The message said very little, however; it had no concrete sociopolitical analysis or recommendations. Moreover, in the words of Karl Kupisch, the historian of the twentieth-century German church, it was made in a spirit of patriarchalism.[84]

These monumental differences are most clearly reflected in the Life and Work movement.

3. PROTESTANT SOCIAL THOUGHT

1925-1929

WITH such different backgrounds and traditions, both the British and German churches came to be involved in the Life and Work movement. The established churches of both England and Germany were at first reluctant participants in the emerging international ecumenical social movement. As plans for the Stockholm conference progressed in the early 1920s, the Church of England balked at entering into a movement that claimed to be Protestant. Emphasizing their historical and theological links with Roman Catholicism, Anglican leaders were placated only when Eastern Orthodox Christians agreed to join the movement. Once involved, however, Anglicans were among Life and Work's most enthusiastic supporters. The climate of church opinion favored such a movement. With its internationalism, the young ecumenical movement was widely perceived as doing, in church circles, the work of the League of Nations (even better perhaps, for Life and Work involved the Americans).

The British members of the Life and Work committee abridged the Copec reports to become the official British contribution to the Stockholm conference of 1925.[1] Nearly all of the British delegates to the Stockholm conference were veterans of Copec. Archbishop Davidson considered Copec to be the official British preparation for Stockholm.[2] Under the leadership of Theodore Woods, Bishop of Winchester, the British delegation at Stockholm was large and official. About half of the delegates represented the Church of England; the remaining delegates represented Baptist, Methodist, Presbyterian, Unitarian, and other church bodies. The major groups within the British church-social movement, such as the Industrial Christian Fellowship and the League of the Kingdom of God, were all represented at Stockholm. Apart from the United States, Britain sent more delegates than any other country.[3]

The British also took a leading role in Life and Work after Stockholm. British church leaders served in executive positions of the continuation committee. Two key British churchmen, one Anglican, the other Nonconformist, epitomized the British representation to the international movement of the 1920s. Theodore Woods, Bishop of Winchester, was president of the British section of Life and Work and played a large role at Stockholm and the continuation committee thereafter. Having served parishes in industrial cities such as Manchester, Huddersfield, Bradford, and Southwark before becoming Bishop of Peterborough in 1916, he was well known as a spokesman for the liberal social gospel. He initiated discussion programs in Peterborough between workers and employers. At Anglican convocations of the clergy he spoke out for a greater and more active church concern for social and economic matters. He wrote letters to the *Times* and advocated nationalization of mines and railways after the war. He tried to mediate the national railway strike in 1919, and the same year he attended the Trades Unions Congress in Glasgow. As a recognition of his work, Woods was appointed to the historic see of Winchester in 1923.[4]

Besides Woods, Alfred Garvie was probably the most active British representative. His background made him uniquely qualified for ecumenical work. The son of Scottish parents, Garvie was born in 1861 in Russian Poland. He attended a German school in Poland and so as a schoolboy spoke fluent Polish, English, and German. He finished his education in Edinburgh and at the universities of Glasgow and Oxford. He left the Scottish Kirk for Congregationalism and in 1903 became professor of theology at Hackney and New Colleges, Congregationalist institutions associated with the University of London. Eventually he became dean of the Faculty of Theology at the University of London. In 1919 he became president of the Congregational Union of England and Wales, and in 1923 he was elected president of the National Council of Free Churches, a post he held into the 1930s.[5] Garvie was very active in Copec, Stockholm, and the continuation committee, serving as coeditor of the journal *Stockholm* from 1928 to 1931. Because he spoke German, he made a special effort to build bridges between the ecumenical movement and the German delegation. A warm-hearted, affable man, Garvie sat with the Germans at Stockholm conference sessions. This was a conspicuous action; contemporaries noted that Germans sat apart from the rest of the delegates. He was in frequent correspondence with German church authorities and seemed to enjoy their trust and respect. With his language ability, his prominent role in the Free Churches, and his indefatigable personality, Garvie was well suited to represent the views and interests of the non-Anglican community.

Until 1929, British participation in Life and Work was through individuals such as Garvie and Woods. There was no constituent body in Britain for Life and Work. The archbishops continued to appoint the Anglican members of the continuation committee, and the other churches simply chose their own representatives. But in 1927-28 Theodore Woods and some other Life and Work enthusiasts began plans for the formation of the Christian Social Council, an interdenominational English agency that would incorporate the Copec movement and represent Life and Work in England. The council was inaugurated officially in January 1929 with a service at Westminster Abbey. The Church of England and the National Council of Free Churches each appointed half of its sixty members. Half of the Anglican representatives came from the ICF and half from the church's Social and Industrial Committee.[6] Life and Work thus claimed a wide and significant representation of Anglicans and Nonconformists in the movement. In fact, the British—and the Americans—were so enthusiastically involved that the Germans complained throughout the decade of Anglo-Saxon domination.

Given the prevailing political atmosphere in the years immediately following the war, the German churches received no invitation to the first planning meetings for Stockholm. Instead, Archbishop Söderblom invited a few individuals, all known to be moderates or liberals, to represent Germany unofficially. One of these was Friedrich Siegmund-Schultze, a Protestant pastor who ran a settlement house in Berlin. He had corresponded with Söderblom during the war and long supported his calls for a conference.[7] Siegmund-Schultze was active in the World Alliance for Promoting Friendly Relations among the Churches. As editor of its German mouthpiece, *Die Eiche*, he made himself unpopular by his expression of pacifist and antinationalist views. His criticism of German mistreatment of allied prisoners caused German censors to blot out sections of his journal in July 1915.[8] After the war he attended the organizational meetings for the Stockholm conference in 1925 and wrote glowing accounts of the plans in *Die Eiche*.[9]

Other Germans involved in the plans for Stockholm were Adolf Deissmann, theology professor at Berlin and member of the Evangelical Social Congress since the 1890s, and Julius Richter, who had many contacts with the Christian leaders of other lands through his involvement with the international missionary movement. Also on the executive committee for Stockholm was Walter Simons, president of the Evangelical Social Congress after 1925. Having represented Germany at the Versailles conference, Simons was also a functionary of the Weimar government; he served as head of the German Supreme Court from 1922 to 1929, as foreign minister in 1920-21, and as interim president of the republic between Ebert's death and the installation of Hindenburg.[10]

In 1921 the planning committee for Stockholm agreed upon the need for an official German presence and an invitation followed. At the first meeting of the *Kirchenausschuß* of the newly inaugurated German Church Federation in May 1922, the committee voted to participate in the Stockholm conference.[11] Of course, soon afterward German relations with the Allies fell apart with French occupation of the Ruhr. It took careful coaxing by Archbishop Söderblom from 1922 to 1924 to get the German church actually committed to the Stockholm idea.[12] Söderblom, the enormously prestigious Swedish prelate, was the key figure in winning over the conservative Germans to the ecumenical movement. A Lutheran from neutral Sweden, Söderblom had been a professor at Leipzig before World War I. His son was a German officer in the war, and Söderblom had publicly criticized the treatment of Germany by the Allies.[13] If any foreign leader could win the Germans to ecumenism, it was Söderblom.

The Life and Work record shows the reticence of conservative Germans to participate in a movement that was both international and church-social. As the conference approached, the division in German Protestantism became all the more striking. The price paid for official participation of the German churches at Stockholm was the exclusion of liberals from the conference preparations. As the official representative body of the German church, the *Kirchen-*

ausschuß was responsible for the preparations of German studies for Stockholm. The four volumes it produced completely bypassed liberals such as Siegmund-Schultze, Deissmann, and Richter, who had been the strongest German supporters of the conference from the beginning.[14] Bitter about being excluded from the Stockholm preparations, Siegmund-Schultze complained to church authorities in Berlin and severely criticized the preparations in *Die Eiche*.[15] During the spring of 1925 he organized his own preparations for the conference. His summer 1925 issue of *Die Eiche* contained articles titled "Deutsche Beiträge zur Allgemein Konferenz du Kirche Christi für Praktisches Christentum," written by himself and Adolf Harnack, Theodor Kaftan (brother of Julius Kaftan), A.W. Schreiber, and others outside the church hierarchy. Apparently Siegmund-Schultze thought he was providing a liberal counterpart to the official, more conservative preparatory work of the *Kirchenausschuß*. What is ironic and perhaps suggestive of the transition of liberalism in Germany is that none of these *Beiträge* dealt with the social and economic themes of the upcoming conference. Instead, each article concerned ecumenism. The liberals offered no social message.

The feud between liberals and conservatives continued when the delegates to Stockholm were selected. The *Kirchenausschuß* chose forty-five of the German delegates, the individual *Landeskirchen* the remaining eighteen. The *Kirchenausschuß* certainly dominated the German delegation: twenty-eight of its thirty-six members traveled to Stockholm as delegates. President Moeller of the executive committee was adamant that the renegades Siegmund-Schultze and Theodor Kaftan not be included in the German delegation.[16] Siegmund-Schultze attended Stockholm only after receiving a personal invitation from Söderblom. Söderblom also bypassed the German authorities by inviting the aging Adolf Harnack, who declined the invitation for reasons of health.[17] The other extraofficial Germans present at Stockholm—Deissmann, Simons, and Richter—attended because of their long-standing membership on the planning committee for the conference.

One effect of this struggle was the extraordinarily official German participation in Life and Work in the 1920s. Members of the *Kirchenausschuß* wrote many of the reports for Stockholm themselves; otherwise they chose articles by professors, clergy, and leaders of the various Christian-social groups. All reports bore the stamp of approval of the *Kirchenausschuß*. The reports also included a "Social Message of the German Churches" written by the social subcommittee of the *Kirchenausschuß* and presented to the first meeting of the *Kirchentag* in Bethel in 1924. Liberals criticized the report as inadequate.[18] Though short (only four pages) and very general, the Social Message was the first statement on the social question ever to have the endorsement of the assembled Protestant churches of Germany.

Again at the Stockholm conference, the *Kirchenausschuß* was careful to present the official views of the German church government. The fact that nearly the entire committee traveled to Stockholm for the conference underscores this. Hermann Kapler, who had become president of the *Kirchenausschuß* in January 1925 and was thus the head of the German delegation, made sure that the German delegation stood united on national and international issues by convening the *Kirchenausschuß* for a special meeting in the summer to prepare the German position for Stockholm. Kapler asked the German delegates to assemble in Berlin for an evening of instructional meetings before traveling as a group to Sweden.[19] The German delegation was disciplined to speak for a conservative church and a national government that had drifted markedly to the right in recent years. The German Foreign Office subsidized the travel cost for German delegates, explaining that it was willing to further this religious endeavor "so far as this work in a foreign land lies in the general German interest." Kapler assured the government of conservative President Hindenburg and Chancellor Hans Luther's center coalition that the church delegation would be in line with official policy on political questions.[20] Several observers at the conference and afterward remarked how closely the German delegates represented the characteristic positions of their church and state. One British delegate noted that the "solemn phalanx" of Germans at Stockholm "seemed almost drilled."[21] Siegmund-Schultze criticized the German delegation as too official, too dominated by members of the church hierarchy, who were too conscious of their duty to represent conservative authority rather than the diversity of opinion found in Germany. He concluded: "The Germans were sent to Stockholm like couriers with sealed orders."[22]

The *Kirchenausschuß* continued to dominate German participation in Life and Work after the Stockholm conference. However, because the entire European section at Stockholm elected the

European members of the continuation committee from the floor, a
few moderate and liberal Germans such as Deissmann, Simons,
and Siegmund-Schultze managed to get positions as a result of their
popularity with delegates from other continental countries. Thus
they were able to continue voicing their minority opinion until the
continuation committee was reorganized into the Universal Christian Council in 1930.[23] The other Germans who attended Life and
Work meetings through the rest of the decade were consistently
members of the church government. Hermann Kapler played an
increasingly large leadership role in the later 1920s, becoming vice-president of the European section of Life and Work at Stockholm.
Söderblom was president, but as his health failed in the later 1920s,
Kapler took over his duties, finally replacing him when Söderblom
resigned in 1928.[24] J.R.C. Wright portrays Kapler as a pragmatic
bureaucrat who came to terms with the Weimar Republic. He was
nevertheless a patriot who saw the Stockholm movement as an
opportunity to bring the German point of view before world opinion.[25]

The *Kirchenausschuß* sent Hans Schönfeld to Geneva as a
German collaborator, as they called him, almost as soon as the
Social Institute of Life and Work opened its doors. Schönfeld, a
young theologian whose doctoral training was in economics, had
spent a year working in the *Reichswirtschaftsrat,* the German
Industrial Office, before coming to Geneva. Jacob Schoell of the
Kirchenausschuß personally ordained Schönfeld as a clergyman of
the German church after his move to Geneva.[26] Schönfeld's ordination was a symbolic statement of the *Kirchenbund*'s official representation in the Social Institute. The *Kirchliches Jahrbuch* reassured any doubtful readers that Schönfeld, as an employee of the
Kirchenbund, had been sent to keep an eye on the actions of the
Social Institute.[27] The Germans somehow remained involved in
Life and Work, in their somewhat suspicious way, to the end of the
decade.

Therefore, the Life and Work movement managed successfully
to attract German and British Christians to one limited arena for
discussion of the social question. On the British side, the movement
absorbed the work of Copec and involved the key individuals and
church-social agencies concerned with social questions. The German participation showed the domination of the conservative
Kirchenausschuß, with some dissent by prominent liberals. It in-

cluded no representation of the Christian socialists on the left, who probably had the most to say on social issues—perhaps a measure of their isolation on the fringes of German Protestantism. With the extensive preparatory studies for Stockholm, the conference speeches, and the various activities of Life and Work from 1926 to 1929, the movement created a wealth of materials that reveal the great difference in outlooks between British social idealism and German social conservatism in the 1920s.

Although British Life and Work leaders tried to avoid theology, a coherent theological perspective emerged that underlay all their criticisms and suggested reforms. The Life and Work movement intended to discuss practical matters of ethics and society. In the nascent ecumenical movement another organization—Faith and Order, begun with the Lausanne conference of 1927—dealt with theology. Theology was divisive. As the president of the German Church Federation, Hermann Kapler, put it: "Doctrine divides, but service unites." [28] Nonetheless, the British optimism and call for social reform rested upon their theological asssumptions.

A theology is a conception of God and His relationship to humanity and the world. The views of God and man expressed by British participants in Life and Work were clearly influenced by Protestant liberalism. The first Copec report, condensed to become a contribution to Stockholm, laid a theological basis for the practical suggestions of later reports.[29] Consistent with liberal views, the report emphasized even in its title that one knows "the nature of God and His Purpose for the World" through His son, Christ: "We go to Jesus for our guidance in religion. Finding God present in him, we learn to see God everywhere, and to see him as the father." [30] Through Christ, the divine became the human: "The incarnation . . . means that God's fullest self-revelation was made to us through and in the material world." [31] British churchmen emphasized soteriology, Christ as the redeemer of mankind, at the Anglo-German study conference sponsored by Life and Work in 1928. British theology had always stressed the incarnation, God as man, said John Martin Creed, an Anglican theologian at Cambridge. A.E.J. Rawlinson reasserted the Anglo-Catholic view of sacramental community by the multireferential symbol of Christ's body, which signified Christ's person, the eucharistic meal, and the Christian community.[32] Thus the emphasis on the humanity of

God brought British churchmen back down from the heavens to the material world, the subject at hand.

The British successfully trod a narrow path between Christocentrism and assimilation of modern scientific thought. The reports for Stockholm emphasized that one knows Christ primarily through the pictures of Him in the gospels. The challenges of scientific criticism did not lead most British writers, unlike some liberals, to doubt the historicity of Christ. "The testimony of the eye witnesses," they concluded, "has been confirmed."[33] In the debate on Christology in 1928 the British theologians portrayed Christ's human life on earth as real and concrete. Edwyn Hoskins, an Anglican theologian from Cambridge, attacked such critical methods as those of the *Formgeschichte* school, which questioned the traditional picture of Christ. He argued that the Old Testament—not the Roman Empire or the Hellenistic world—was the setting against which the gospel must be judged.[34] Yet the British seem to have adopted what they wanted of modern science, such as Darwin's theories of natural selection and his denial of a sudden creation.[35] It was the view of a mechanistic, purposeless natural order that the reports rejected. Evolution for the Christian meant "a prolonged development through individuation, self-consciousness, self-mastery and self-surrender."[36] Like liberal theology in general, British thinking transformed the theory of evolution, the greatest intellectual challenge to faith since Copernicus, into a new myth of gradual progress through Christ. Yet their acceptance of scientific criticism did not extend so far as to question the historical bases of faith.[37]

This acceptance of modern science was consistent with the optimistic British emphasis on man and his reason. The reports for Stockholm stated that man knows God through nature, by applying his own intellectual faculties and learning about the world: "God reveals Himself progressively in Science, History, Art, and Literature." The reports called the adventures of the human intellect "channels of revelation."[38] Again, Christ was the connection between God and man: just as God became like man in Jesus, so does man become like God through Christ. Alfred Garvie summed up the idea at Stockholm: "Christ as the divine-human Son is the first-born among many brethren, the beginning of the divine-human family of the redeemed race of man."[39] The reports for Stockholm emphasized that individuals must recognize their own true worth and goodness; the church must "achieve her Master's faith in the possibilities of human goodness." [40] The reports did not discuss man as fundamentally flawed. Original sin was not a popular term. Instead, flaws and failures were seen as obstacles that could be overcome. Reports preferred the term "ignorance" to "sin," because ignorance could be a temporary condition. Becoming a Christian meant a total transformation, a "remaking of the whole of the human life in accordance with the spirit of Christ." Man could escape any kind of sin by conversion, which turns "the whole personality to a right attitude toward the purpose of life— toward God." [41]

All this Christocentrism and the inflated view of man worked to synthesize the transcendent with this world, to minimize the differences between God and man. According to the British churchmen, one cannot separate God from this world; God's concern *is* this world. At the Anglo-German conference in 1927, Edwyn Hoskins argued that Judaism is a religion of another world, one that keeps a veil between God and man so that man is without knowledge or access to God. Christianity is the rending of the veil, he said: "The two worlds of the Flesh and of the Spirit, of this world and of the world beyond, remain no longer two periods of history, but are merged into one mystical ethical living whole." [42] This denial of a chasm between God and nature was a presupposition necessary to a call for the organization of this world according to divine principles.

The British used two symbols continually to reinforce the integration between the transcendent and the temporal world: the idea of family, and the metaphor of the Kingdom of God. British rhetoric constantly referred to the world of God and man as a family situation. God was the father whose will should prevail. The father provided guiding principles, the model toward which the family should work. The world of humanity was a community of brothers in God's family. All were children of one father. "Brotherhood" was a key word invoked by British participants rhetorically to overcome oppositions within humanity. At Stockholm, W. Moore Ede, Bishop of Worcester, called on a sense of brotherhood to bridge the classes in industrial society, and Lord Parmour expected brotherhood to overcome the problems between nations.[43] The spiritual experience of brotherhood meant acceptance of all humanity as the children of God: "This alone leaps the barriers of class and race."[44] The idea of family brought God and man into close association; brotherhood united all mankind in common purpose and spiritual inheritance.

The most significant symbol used by the British participants was the Kingdom of God. Commonplace among liberal theologians such as Maurice and Ritschl, the Kingdom metaphor identified those who had liberal expectations for a perfected social order.[45] References to the Kingdom appeared on almost every page of the Stockholm preparations and in almost every British speech given at the conference. A conference of British and German theologians even met in 1927 to discuss their varying views on this theme. Throughout the history of Christianity, theologians have argued over the meaning of the Kingdom of God. The British use of the term in the 1920s was somewhat ambiguous, but there was general agreement that God intended Christianity to be a new world order. The reports for Stockholm, statements representing the views of various church groups, agreed that earthly life came within the domain of Christian ethics and guidance. The Kingdom of God not only was transcendent but also embraced humanity and the physical environment. The Kingdom, then, was both heavenly and earthly. "Like Christ Himself," said Bishop Woods, "the Kingdom is natural, living its life in human circumstances, taking human society as it is, and introducing the leaven by which it may gradually be raised to a new level. But like Him it is supernatural. It is God breaking into the world order."[46] So while the British recognized the supernatural nature of the Kingdom, they emphasized the Kingdom on earth: "Eternal life begins here. . . . Our immediate task while on earth is to realize the purpose of God within this world with ever increasing fullness."[47] Consistent with the liberal views of God and man, the Kingdom metaphor worked to destroy the dualism of heaven/earth, God/man, and eternity/physical life.

For some, the Kingdom meant the expectations of a social utopia, where heaven comes to earth. Several of the British speakers at the Stockholm conference referred to the Lord's Prayer—"Thy Kingdom come, Thy will be done *on earth* as it is in heaven"—as direct evidence that God meant for his Kingdom to be an earthly reality.[48] Theodore Woods made perhaps the most vocal call for the Kingdom of God on earth. Using as his text Matthew 4:17,

"Repent ye, for the Kingdom of Heaven is at Hand," Woods preached that a Christian utopia was just around the corner: "When once a man or a community is redeemed there is no limit to what they can become. . . . In Christ we can do the impossible." [49] Woods was speaking in 1925 after the Locarno Treaty had brought a new spirit in diplomacy and during the temporary respite in the British coal crisis. With unbounded optimism he uttered his expectations that this utopia was coming in the 1920s with the League of Nations, better labor conditions, and improved education. Even three years later, after the General Strike of 1926, Woods wrote in the first issue of the *Stockholm* journal that the Life and Work movement was setting up God's Kingdom in the world: "Christ heralded the coming of a new order; it was to come here and now— the Kingdom of God is *at hand*. It was not to be fulfilled in some other world, at some other time, but in this world, in the personal lives and social relationships of ordinary men." [50]

Other British participants in Life and Work were less utopian than Woods. At the Anglo-German study conference on the Kingdom of God, learned biblical scholars such as C.H. Dodd admitted that the Kingdom was transcendent: "The harvest is not here." Dodd argued nevertheless that the Kingdom was not eschatological. It did not await the end of the world for its coming, but was "a process working itself out through a community." There is, he said, a "progressive revelation of the Kingdom of God within this historical order." [51] Dodd's colleague A.E.J. Rawlinson quoted St. Paul's statement that flesh and blood cannot inherit the Kingdom of God. Yet he argued that the Kingdom is on earth in anticipation of the end times. It is as yet incomplete, he added; there are still enemies to be subdued. [52]

While socially minded activists looked for the Kingdom on earth to be a future utopia, biblical scholars involved in Life and Work used the term more guardedly. However, for all the British spokesmen there were common themes. The British view of the Kingdom had implications for earthly creation. It assumed that the nature of creation was not irreparably flawed. For example, Will Reason explained that nothing in creation made the coming of the Kingdom impossible. The Kingdom was not contrary to the nature of the earth. It meant the "development of that human society according to its true nature, from which it is somehow perverted."[53] Also the idea of the Kingdom demanded action. It was the church's role to present this Kingdom to the world.[54] For Bishop Woods, Life and Work itself was incorporating the Kingdom.

Finally, the British churchmen agreed that there must be changes to effect the Kingdom of God. Scott Lidgett, a Methodist clergyman in London, wrote in *Stockholm* that British local government, the institution that brought meaningful human services to the public, must work to advance the Kingdom if it were ever to reach the height of its power to serve mankind.[55] Even the theological report prepared for Stockholm, general though it was, stated that the "Christianizing of society implies a more equal division of worldly goods."[56] The ten reports that followed the *Nature of God* were guidebooks to instruct Christians on how to build the Kingdom of God. Reports on war, crime, education, industry and property, and so on, explained changes necessary to build the Kingdom. In their Life and Work studies the British participants thus described a theological justification for Christian reform and social action. The Kingdom of God concept brought the socioeconomic environment into the domain of the churches.

The British churchmen therefore felt justified in challenging the theoretical bases of capitalism. With R.H. Tawney on the committee that wrote the original Copec report, the work titled *Industry and Property* reads much like the denunciation of capitalism in *The Acquisitive Society* or the Collegium's *Competition*.[57] The report even questioned the principle of property rights: "The moral justification of the various rights which constitute property depends on the degree to which they contribute to the development of personality and to the good of the whole community. If such rights subserve those purposes they deserve the approval of all Christians; if not, they should be modified or abolished."[58] At Stockholm the Bishop of Worcester described Adam Smith's *Wealth of Nations* as "a congenial gospel for the fortunate," a gospel that had kept the church out of politics and business by promulgating the myth that the economy runs according to autonomous natural laws of its own. The philosophical principles of capitalism were contrary to those of Christianity, argued the Congregationalist Alfred Garvie. *The Wealth of Nations*, Garvie said, could not be an economic Ten Commandments for all lands and all ages. He challenged the idea that economic forces are natural and constant and that the pursuit of self-interest necessarily results in the common good.[59]

The British consistently criticized the social consequences as well as the theory of capitalism. Garvie and others writing in *Stockholm* praised the writings of Fabians, such as J.L. and Barbara Hammond, Sidney and Beatrice Webb, G.D.H. Cole, Harold Laski, and John A. Hobson, who demonstrated the misery and inhumanity of industrial capitalism.[60] The Stockholm reports condemned the divisive class stratification of contemporary society: "It is repugnant to Christian principles that a small class, of which the individuals are not necessarily distinguished above their fellow citizens for virtue or ability, should command more money than they can spend rationally or profitably, while by far the largest class in the same country has no security for a good life on the simplest lines, and a substantial portion of this class is living permanently below the line at which a sufficient minimum of human needs can be satisfied."[61] The Bishop of Worcester, speaking at Stockholm, decried the discontent and injustice resulting from a system in which rewards were not distributed according to work or merit. The reports particularly criticized the existence of an idle wealthy class. They argued that a good home life was not possible in many wealthy households because luxury and self-indulgence had destroyed a spiritual atmosphere. The very poor and the very rich, according to the report *The Treatment of Crime,* were most likely to produce undisciplined children criminally inclined. The report called *Leisure* described the absurdity of maintaining a leisured class that engaged in sport and extravagant living.[62] The speeches at Stockholm and articles in the quarterly review made many of the same points, identifying crime, ill housing, class polarization, and poverty as products of competitive capitalism.

Industry and Property graphically pointed out many evils in the present state of industrial capitalism: it had destroyed much beauty in the land; it allowed no freedom for workers to develop their own interests, skills, and personalities; it created hostility, strife, and mistrust between people. Finally, industrial competition caused strife between nations, which often led to war. The report especially condemned unemployment, job insecurity, and industrial conflict. Yet these problems were not insoluble, the report insisted. They were flaws in a system that could be perfected: "Human intelligence, directed by moral conviction, can find the solution."[63] Therefore, a denunciation of capitalism's social and economic sins did not mean the embrace of socialism or a call for revolutionary change. Capitalism was not intrinsically un-Christian. The present system should not be destroyed, said the Bishop of Worcester, but it should be transformed by making it more Christian. Progress would not come through revolution, added William Ashley, the noted economist of the University of Birmingham. The church should work toward improving, not rebuilding, the economy.[64] "The Christian method is not revolutionary but evolutionary," wrote Alfred Garvie. "The realization of the ideal indicated by the Golden Rule must be gradual."[65] Even though it called for reorganization of industry into a cooperative effort for the good of all, *Industry and Property* added: "This does not involve one particular type of organisation universally applied."[66]

The British churchmen decried class stratification and suggested some redistribution of income. Yet they did not want truly to eradicate class distinctions. The reports for Stockholm recommended raising the incomes of the poor and talked of a "juster redistribution," but they attacked only the extremes of wealth and poverty. They provided no plan for thorough equalization of income. Private property was morally justifiable to the degree that it contributed to the good of the community. The reports supported Christian uses of private capital. The wealthy should endow housing schemes or public utility societies and use their leisure time for service.[67] The reports did not criticize the employment of domestic servants, just the lack of respect for household duties. Prosperous citizens should voluntarily choose a simpler life-style.[68] The report headed *Education* criticized class distinctions in education, but it concerned only those who attended only primary school, skipping secondary education. It did not broach the subject of the English public or fee-paying school that was so central to class distinctions in Great Britain. The divisions of race, nation, and class would and "even must remain," said Alfred Garvie at Stockholm. Common friendship, however, must be closer than class bonds.[69]

British church leaders' recommendations ranged from vague platitudes to demands for charitable work and suggestions for specific changes possible only by state action. They called at length for the substitution of cooperation for competition and of service for self-interest in industry. Among other nonsubstantive rhetoric they asked that a sense of brotherhood and common purpose be instilled among the classes, that the Golden Rule be applied to industry. But they also called for specific actions by the church. The

British devoted one entire report in their preparations for Stockholm, *The Social Function of the Church,* to an eloquent justification for Christian activism in social matters. It was the duty of the church, the report argued, to preach the social implications of the gospel of Christ and biblical hope of the Kingdom of God. Church members must be educated to the social realities of the present, their level of social consciousness raised. Specific pronouncements must be made on the morality of certain situations. Clergy should be trained in "Christian Sociology." On the local level, churches should organize united councils to discuss social questions; recruit volunteers for all varieties of social service; investigate local conditions of housing, unemployment, and similar problems; and lobby to gain public support for philanthropic and political measures to redress the problems.[70] A new united Christian social bureau should do research in social questions, distribute information, and coordinate social activity among the churches. This last recommendation eventually became a reality when the Christian Social Council replaced the Copec continuation committee in 1929.

The British made many demands for reform that went beyond the capacity of the church. A "juster distribution" of wealth and "living wages" obviously required state intervention. The reports for Stockholm praised past legislative reforms—factory acts, old age pensions, unemployment insurance, local health and welfare schemes—as steps in the right direction. Such great reforms, emphasized A.J. Carlyle of Oxford, had come from the state, not from individual action.[71] Moving toward the Kingdom of God meant more such changes requiring state intervention. One report for Stockholm called for government to take over the sale of alcohol. Others recommended that wage boards be established to ensure that industries paid living wages and that yearly paid vacations were made available to all workers.[72] Alfred Garvie called for a minimum wage and a maximum profits scale. F.S. Livie-Noble urged legislation to raise the school-leaving age and to reduce working hours for youth.[73] Declaring British housing conditions deplorable, the reports for Stockholm recommended that at least a million new houses be constructed. At Stockholm Mrs. George Cadbury, wife of the humanitarian industrialist, praised the housing legislation of the nineteenth century and early 1920s and recommended that housing measures already on the books be put into practice to the fullest extent. The report called *The Home* even described the minimum standards for an acceptable home: a large living room, separate sleeping accommodations for children of different sexes, a back garden, and sufficient light and air. The report called for slum clearance and for construction of new planned towns. Other specific programs recommended by the Stockholm reports were government allowances for children, child welfare centers, and a "home helps" program whereby women employed by local authorities would assist sick and pregnant women with household and child-care duties.[74]

Since British Christian activists called for so many reforms requiring political action, some thought had to be given to the nature and purpose of the state and the church's relation to it. According to the British reports for Stockholm, the purpose of the state was not secular but inherently moral. It existed not only to keep order and maintain peace but to ensure a just order and a "righteous system of life."[75] Although much of the day-to-day business of the state might seem morally indifferent, the essential function was indeed moral. No society had achieved a truly just and moral social order, but a state should be judged by its movement toward a moral ideal. The reports advocated that Christians work with the state. Since the state derives its authority from God, its authority is the expression of righteous principles. Therefore the Christian's role is to obey and cooperate with the government for these moral goals. The church should work through, not outside the state. In the past the church had exercised welfare programs of its own. The modern organization of social life meant that Christians must be ready to work through state and civic welfare agencies. The reports instructed Christians individually to use their support and influence with Parliament and local authorities and even to involve themselves in government.[76] The Christian's duty is to make moral judgments in politics. Should the state stray from its moral purpose and righteous principles, then the Christian may even challenge the state as going beyond God-given authority. J.A. Kempthorne, the Bishop of Lichfield, emphasized at Stockholm that the church could not take a hands-off attitude toward politics. He quoted Cardinal Newman: "The Church was formed for the express purpose of interfering or (as irreligious men will say) meddling with the world."[77]

The Stockholm reports did not portray the primary task of the church as being political or social. The purpose of the church, they declared, was to point out Christian principles and preach the gospel. Certainly the church should not identify with political parties or with partisan political programs.[78] However, the reports made many directly political statements about a variety of questions. The specific socioeconomic reforms recommended by the churchmen dealt with subjects that were unavoidably matters of party politics. This contradiction underscores the rhetorical nature of the reports. By calling for reform without endorsing a particular program for carrying it out, British activism stopped somewhere short of genuine action.

Further, though British churchmen claimed to avoid matters of domestic partisan politics, they freely expressed opinions on international political affairs. For example, Life and Work leaders favored disarmament, opposed tariffs as provoking ill will among nations, and called for the resolution of problems in the Baltic, Balkans, Armenia, and North Africa.[79] They displayed ambivalent attitudes toward imperialism and its concurrent problems. The report *International Relations* declared that the age of "grab" was over. Europeans should now teach natives to manage their own affairs. When sufficiently experienced in self-government, they should have complete independence. But, the report added, the interests of the different parts of the world must be subordinate to the whole: "From this it follows that in territories possessing valuable supplies of raw materials which their own people are unable or unwilling to develop to their fullest extent, this inability or unwillingness should not be regarded as an absolute reason for preventing European or other nations from developing them." While the natives were being taught to manage their own affairs, "matters connected with the development of the country should be administered under the supervision of an international authority." Part of the purpose of the League of Nations was to serve as such a supervisory body.[80] Apparently, the British churchmen's vision for the Empire was that its members become like the mandates and independent states of the Middle East. The mandates, which were theoretically supervised by the League of Nations and moving toward independence, were in actuality, of course, new colonies under new names. In "independent" states such as Iraq (after 1932), Egypt, and Iran, the British exercised enormous political influence, while their companies controlled the newly discovered oil fields.

Just as British church leaders looked to the League of Nations to supervise its post-grab imperialism, they also expected the League to solve every other international problem. The British unequivocally endorsed the League and other international agencies in all the reports, speeches, and discussions of the 1920s. For example, Constance Smith suggested at Stockholm that the International Labor Organization (ILO) stood for Christian goals. The Bishop of Lichfield praised the ILO and the League for promoting fellowship among the nations. He argued that such work of secular experts was sacralized by the church's vision of God's purpose for the world, setting forth the Kingdom. For Lord Parmour, Christ was the inspiration for internationalism; a League of Nations was essential as a mechanism for such Christian goals as disarmament and the reduction of national competition.[81] Speeches on education emphasized the need for teachers to praise and publicize the League to students. The only criticism of the League uttered by the British came from Harold Buxton, who expressed hope that someday the League would be "freed from its embarrassing relationship to the Allies." *International Relations* called also for the entry of Russia, Germany, and the United States into the League.[82]

The British staked their hopes in the 1920s on the League of Nations. When the continuation committee of Life and Work established the Social Institute in 1926, the British—along with the French and the Americans—insisted that it be located in Geneva to associate and cooperate with other international organizations there.[83] They even linked the League to the coming of the Kingdom of God: with it, "the Kingdom of God is within our reach, is at hand. . . . We have no other hopeful means of averting the horrors of war or of promoting international friendship and the coming of the Kingdom of God on earth."[84] Like the domestic socioeconomic environment, the international order was perfectible through the coming of the Kingdom of God.

Within the Life and Work movement British church leaders articulated a surprisingly confident interpretation of the social reality of the 1920s. With Protestant liberalism as its theological basis, this British social gospel simply agreed that some change must take place in the conditions of contemporary society and that the church should point the way. With the application of Christian ethics to society, the economy, and the world order, justice could be achieved and the Kingdom of God made an earthly reality. The

British participation in Life and Work shows that this liberal world view went into operation in the 1920s to identify problems, assume responsibility for them (at least rhetorically), and describe appropriate solutions. That this confidence and optimism could have survived the Great War and the social unrest of the 1920s is evidence of the tenacity with which church leaders held these views.

German involvement in the Life and Work movement, by contrast, revealed a social quietism that put church leaders at odds with the rest of the ecumenical community.

> Sit down, O men of God.
> His Kingdom he will bring
> Whenever it may please his will;
> You cannot do a thing.

Such, joked Americans at the time of the Stockholm conference, was the German version of the popular hymn, "Rise Up, O Men of God." [85] The Germans awaited no Kingdom of God on earth. In contrast to British views, German pessimism about human nature and lack of hope for the future disallowed any call for church-social activism.

As with the British record in Life and Work, basic theological presuppositions about God and humanity underlay social ethics and policy. The Germans viewed God as wholly other than man. For example, Heinrich Frick, a professor of theology at Marburg University, declared at the Anglo-German conference on Christology that Christ was incomprehensible; He could not be rationalized: "His glory is hidden as far as we are concerned." Gerhard Kittel, a New Testament scholar from Tübingen, maintained that Christ historically was vague; one does not know Him rationally or empirically but only by faith. [86] While Germans viewed God as mysterious, elevated, and far from man, they described man as debased and sinful. In the preparatory reports for Stockholm, Jacob Schoell, for many years chairman of the social subcommittee of the *Kirchenausschuß*, condemned Christian socialism as based on a false confidence in human nature. German writers spoke of sin not as something temporary that could be overcome but as a trait embedded in human nature since the fall of mankind with Adam. [87] The problems of society, such as crime, poor relations between the sexes, and so on, were rooted in this sin. The free will of man led to evil. The German report on crime explained criminal activity as the result of this unrestrained free human will. The task of Christian culture was to strengthen and enlighten man's free will, which tended so naturally toward sin.[88] Human sinfulness was responsible for the evils in the social, economic, and political systems, not the other way around. At Stockholm the Germans reacted to the optimistic and idealistic tone of the conference by reemphasizing man's evil nature. In the opening speeches Hermann Kapler stressed that the conference must account for the "perverseness of the world and the hardness of the natural man." Ludwig Ihmels, Bishop of Saxony, also criticized the assembly for presupposing that one could reason out God's purpose for the world. The scriptures, he emphasized, present a different view of humanity; they show a sinful and lost man, doomed to eternal death for his sins.[89]

With such a dark view of human nature, the Germans were pessimistic about possibilities for improving the temporal order of creation. They assumed that sin and injustice were here to stay. Kapler called the world's perverseness and man's sin insuperable obstacles to the work of Stockholm. He awaited no social utopia: "We do not know what the results of our work will be." Bishop Ihmels had no hope that human beings could perfect the social order: "We can do nothing, we have nothing, we are nothing." In a keynote address Friedrich Brunstäd, a professor at Erlangen, lambasted liberalism for perverting Christianity into evolutionary optimism and mere humanitarianism, a view out of touch with the realities of the world: sin and death.[90] Similarly, Jacob Schoell maintained that Protestants must not hold to the unbiblical dream that some day the world would become fully Christian. The proper Christian attitude to the problems of contemporary society was not false hope for a social paradise but resignation to God's will. The Social Message of 1924 praised the German middle classes for weathering the Great War and its bitter aftermath, saying that their strength and character in these difficult times were possible only because of an unshakable trust in God and resignation to his will.[91] According to the German churchmen, suffering and injustice were part of a divine plan that human beings must trust but could not understand.

Given this pessimistic view of man and the possibilities for human society, it is not surprising that the Germans instructed believers to concentrate on saving souls, not bodies. In the preparatory studies for Stockholm, Schoell reminded readers that rescuing souls was the ultimate goal of Christianity. One human soul was worth more than the entire world, Ihmels stressed. The gospel stressed the worth of the human soul over any earthly good, admitted Wilhelm Schneemelcher, general secretary of the Evangelical Social Congress.[92] To deal with a corrupt social order, the church must convert individual sinners. Without Christ, Schoell said, the soul would die and the social order dissolve. Only by converting the souls who constituted it, argued Ihmels, could the church change society.[93]

The otherworldliness of German Protestantism came across clearly in the reports and speeches. The Germans dwelt on life in the next world rather than in this one. At the Anglo-German theological meeting of 1927 Wilhelm Stählin, a young theologian from Münster, asserted that Christ's teachings were negative concerning all forms of human association such as economics, the state, and the family. All these, he said, were the social forms of a transitory world ruled by sin. The president of the *Kirchentag* from 1921 to 1930, Wilhelm von Pechmann, reminded the assembly at Stockholm that sin and transitoriness were the curse of human relations: "It is not the ennobling or elevation of this life that we seek but we believe instead in a life of a higher order."[94] Bishop Ihmels praised the Social Message of 1924 for bringing the reader's mind to the subject of eternity, where the ultimate worth of the human life would be decided. Any work on earth must be in reference to the life to come. The motto for German social work, he proposed, should be "Im Licht der Ewigkeit" (in light of eternity).[95]

Other Germans maintained the Lutheran distinction between things temporal and transitory and things spiritual and eternal. In a thinly veiled attack on Protestant liberalism, Friedrich Brunstäd argued that European Christianity since the Enlightenment had sought to reduce Christianity to "a purely human phenomenon, but without mention of God and his revelation in history." Brunstäd denounced this secularization of religion, this accommodation of Christianity to a society in which the Kingdom of God becomes the product of cultural progress. Similarly, Ihmels asserted that the church must not forget that "Christianity is religion and nothing but religion." [96] Instead of the synthesis between Christ and culture of the liberal tradition, Heinrich Frick admitted in 1927 that German thinkers—from Luther to Leibnitz, Kant, Hegel, and Fichte—had envisioned an irrevocable tension or dialectic between the transcendent and the temporal. The synthesis would come only in the afterlife.[97]

The German view of the Kingdom of God summed up these theological positions that underlay German social ethics. Protestant orthodoxy in Germany had never accepted Albrecht Ritschl's definition of the Kingdom of God as the organization of humanity through action inspired by love. In the preparatory studies for Stockholm the German usage of the term *Gottes Reich* implied a spiritual kingdom, never a possible physical reality on earth. Some Germans even explicitly denied that the Kingdom could be earthly.[98] At Stockholm the differing views of the Kingdom created a major controversy. After the Anglican Bishop Woods's bold call on Stockholm's opening day for the Kingdom of God on earth, Bishop Ihmels followed immediately with the Lutheran explanation of the Kingdom.

Ihmels was an authoritative spokesman for the German theological position. An enormously respected Lutheran confessionalist, he had written many scholarly theological works as he climbed the church hierarchy to the historic and prestigious post of Bishop of Saxony. A German delegate to Stockholm recalled many years later that although Kapler was the head of the German delegation, Bishop Ihmels was the true representative of German Christianity, one who made a deep impression on those who heard him.[99] Ihmels explained that the flawed nature of humanity would prevent the building of the Kingdom. The Kingdom of God existed already on earth in the hearts of redeemed believers. It was not a future state. The cross established the Kingdom among believers. In the Lutheran view it was the kingship of God over the hearts of followers: "The Kingdom of God, however, means the Kingship of God. It is not an Ethical Society . . . it originates in the purpose of redemption, is something quite different from the natural and social order by which it is surrounded. It is not a world that has been elevated by moral education, but a world which is an entirely new creation." [100] This Kingdom, Ihmels maintained, would remain incomplete until the end times, the second coming of Christ. Because of sin, the Kingdom of God could never be complete in our

own age. Other Germans supported Ihmels' eschatological interpretation. Church superintendent Karl Viktor Klingemann noted
that "Luther taught us four hundred years ago to separate the idea
of God's Kingdom from all earthly endeavors." Von Pechmann
explicitly denied that "it is possible to transform this world and
bring in the Kingdom of God by human action and effort." [101]

The controversy over the contrasting views of the Kingdom of
God continued long after the conference adjourned. Polite articles
appeared in Britain shortly afterward, noting the grave differences
between what all called the Anglo-Saxon (British and American)
and German views of the Kingdom. [102] On the German side, angry
literature denounced the Anglo-Saxon views as childish, naive,
evolutionary, and unbiblical. An important church periodical complained that Anglo-American Christians seemed to know God's
plans as well as if they were sitting in His counsel; they forgot that
the Kingdom was not of this world. Other writers agreed, including
several returning delegates from the conference. [103] President von
Pechmann argued that "the present world is not advancing to the
gradual transfiguration into the Kingdom of God, but to the
judgment." Only the moderate Adolf Deissmann tried vainly to
reconcile the differences between British and German views of the
Kingdom. [104]

The controversy was so problematic for Life and Work that the
first study conference organized after Stockholm was the 1927
conference of German and British theologians on the subject of the
Kingdom of God, held in Canterbury. At this conference theologians offered a sophisticated German analysis of the meaning of
the term. Karl Ludwig Schmidt, a professor at Jena, argued that the
Kingdom of God was beyond all ethics; it would come far in the
future without any assistance from man. The Kingdom could not
be both present and future, as the English would like to have it, Paul
Althaus said. The righteousness of the Kingdom would come only
in the end times. [105] Although Judaism expected an earthly Kingdom of God, Gerhard Kittel emphasized that Christ had destroyed
this expectation. The human physical world was the antithesis of
the Kingdom of God, emphasized Wilhelm Stählin. As Schmidt
said, the Kingdom was *ganz andere* (entirely other). The phrase
became a slogan for the German position at Canterbury. [106] Likewise, Heinrich Frick, who had written a book comparing German
and American views on the Kingdom, emphasized the Germanic

dialectic between the spiritual and the physical. The Germans accused the British of confusing the Kingdom with the church. The Germans even made a dualistic distinction between the church on earth and the invisible church, with Althaus stressing that the ultimate church was *ganz andere;* what was seen on earth was the mere scaffolding for the building of the church.[107]

The German view of the Kingdom of God illustrated the theological restrictions on a dynamic social ethic. Into the 1920s Germans retained their dualism between spirit and matter, between this world and the next, between God and man. The German churchmen participating in Life and Work were careful to keep the separation intact. At Stockholm, *Kirchentag* President von Pechmann reasserted the dual morality: "There are laws that determine the natural life and there are laws that determine the spiritual life." The autonomy of natural life thus disallowed church intervention. The Social Message argued also that the economic order follows its own laws. Bishop Ihmels praised the message for skillfully avoiding technical instructions for public life. The church had no right, he said, to speak on technical economic questions.[108] For example, one pressing question facing Germans in 1924 during the preparation of the reports for Stockholm was the eight-hour day, one of the first acts of the socialist-led Weimar government. In 1924 industrialists and businessmen argued that the work day must be lengthened to end Germany's economic slump after the recent inflation. Both Friedrich Mahling of Berlin University and Schoell mentioned in the reports for Stockholm that the church should issue no opinion on the eight-hour day; such matters lay beyond its competence.[109] At the 1927 Canterbury meeting Stählin and Frick repeated this warning. Althaus emphasized the danger of the church's becoming a dilettante in social questions. Instead, asserted Ihmels, the church should teach Christians to preserve their faith in God and live within the natural and social order to which they belonged.[110] Like the middle classes during wartime and after, one must trust God and be resigned to his will.

Consistent with their emphasis on conversion and salvation, the Germans continually appealed to individual efforts. Their reports stressed that the renewal of the social life of the nation would come through individual, not corporate, action. The duty of the church was to train and equip individuals spiritually to renew the social system of Germany. Thus the family became a matter of great concern, the center where individuals were trained and nourished.[111] The German churchmen called on individuals to carry a sense of brotherhood and responsibility into the workplace. Ihmels stressed that Christianity must teach its followers to exhibit Christian fellowship in all areas of their lives. The Social Message urged them to treat workers as individuals, as brothers, as fellow children of God. Ihmels advocated renewing the idea of noblesse oblige.[112] The reports stressed such key words as service, responsibility, and sacrifice. They emphasized that Christians should exercise these virtues individually, not publicly.

The German church leaders also encouraged charity as the appropriate social action for Christians. Several Germans enunciated a litany of charitable endeavors, from Wichern's onward, as evidence of the vitality of social concern in Protestant Germany. Articles in the journal *Stockholm* praised relief work performed by the churches during the hunger crisis of 1922-23 and continuing work with the sick and aged in Berlin.[113] In the preparatory reports and at Stockholm, Secretary Johannes Steinweg argued for an expanded role for his Inner Mission to ease social pressures in the 1920s. Somewhat less Victorian than Bishop Ihmels, he recognized that the basis of social problems was not personal moral guilt but damaged social relations. Yet his solution still was not reform but "acts of love." Writing about the expanded welfare programs of the Weimar government, he suggested that the church should establish its own welfare system for church members while financially supporting the public system.[114]

Finally, the German churchmen declared that the church must raise the level of public consciousness to social problems. Without suggesting specific changes or reforms, the church could legitimately point out problems in society and educate the public so that citizens could make their own decisions. The church itself should speak out only on broad moral issues, such as hunger, excessive usury and profiteering, ruthless competition, and gross exploitation in the workplace.[115] Despite its avoidance of technical matters, the church could publicize the work of experts without endorsing it. Hence the churchmen could allow as statements by experts in the reports for Stockholm a barrage of statistics concerning inadequate housing, abortion, illegitimate children, and working women, as well as a trade unionist's call at Stockholm for legal regulation of unemployment.[116] German articles appearing in

Stockholm later in the decade were often highly technical analyses by engineers, economists, and members of the German industrial office. For example, one article discussed the physical and psychological damages associated with Henry Ford's assembly line and recommended a new system replacing Ford's vertical lines with horizontal ones. Another discussed housing problems that could be alleviated by importing cheap foreign credit.[117] With his doctorate in economics, Hans Schönfeld, the German collaborator sent to Geneva by the *Kirchenbund,* viewed his position as that of a scientific researcher. Almost immediately he began a study of unemployment, which he pursued into the 1930s. Unlike R.H. Tawney, for instance, he never claimed to present a Christian view of unemployment. Throughout his long career with Life and Work he rarely made a recommendation for any practical action by German churches. Leaving technical matters to the experts, the Germans maintained the dualism between laws of nature and laws of God.

But if German church leaders clung to this dualism in social and economic matters, they violated it freely when it came to political questions.[118] Although they claimed no party affiliation, they continually passed judgment on the socialist parties. Secretary Schneemelcher of the Evangelical Social Congress proudly claimed that the congress promoted no politics but then called the SPD a dangerous and destructive organization. Mahling lamented Stöcker's failure in the 1880s to prevent workers from identifying with the Marxist Social Democratic Party.[119] Stöcker's son-in-law Reinhold Mumm, who inherited the leadership of his conservative Christian Social League, noted in his speech at Stockholm, that 140 of the 170 communist and socialist deputies in the Reichstag had cut themselves off from any religious community and remarked that no German socialists had sent greetings to the conference.[120] The churchmen feared socialism's revolutionary tendencies. Schoell spoke of the "wild passion of the masses." The Social Message condemned materialistic mass movements in which individualism served the will of the masses. Although Jesus stayed with the poor and downtrodden, Ihmels assured readers, he was no proletarian king.[121] Ihmels and Schoell consistently justified the preservation of private property against socialist threats; both upheld the moral value of property ownership. The Social Message called property "a trusted good." [122] The churchmen used Luther's idea of the calling to legitimate the preservation of classes. Mahling explained at

Stockholm that God-given callings created social distinctions within humanity; the classes should cooperate rather than fight with one another. President Heinrich Tilemann of the Oldenburg Church Council emphasized that Christianity was interested not in destroying social differences or tensions but in leading people to a fuller life.[123] Without hesitation, qualification, or seeming awareness of any contradiction, the Protestant leaders negated the political goals of socialism.

Likewise, the Germans in Life and Work glibly spoke out on political issues of war and peace. When the Stockholm conference considered the subject of the Church and international relations, a second controversy developed which, like that over the Kingdom, threatened to dissolve the ecumenical movement in its infancy. The German delegates realized that they would be misfits at Stockholm. Siegmund-Schultze and his liberal colleagues of the World Alliance had met in 1924 to discuss how to deal with the question of German war guilt at Stockholm, deciding they would avoid it if possible. Just before the conference in 1925 the *Kirchenausschuß* met in Eisenach, and then the delegates met in Berlin to ensure solidarity at Stockholm.[124]

As the Germans expected, the conference speakers, who were mainly from Allied and neutral nations, overwhelmingly lauded the League of Nations and condemned the recent war. Hermann Kapler, head of the German delegation, responded with what he called the unanimous opinion of the German delegates, condemning the conference's simplistic treatment of international problems. Karl Viktor Klingemann, superintendent of the Rhine Province and DNVP member of the National Assembly of 1919, followed with a scathing attack on the League and the postwar settlement. Germans did not share the optimism of other countries, he said; they lived under heavy burdens in a land torn to pieces, where wealth was destroyed and industry fettered. The war-guilt clause and enforced German disarmament were unjust and unrighteous. Germans were convinced that the war had been a good and holy cause. The League of Nations endangered the liberty and independence of individual countries. Especially, he resented British attempts to link the League to a Christian purpose: "In the present state of the League we cannot find religious power or any communion with the Kingdom of God."[125] Several Germans repudiated pacifist sentiments expressed by other conference members. Walther Wolff of

Aachen criticized speakers who called for outlawing the use of force in international affairs. Justice, he argued, was based on and maintained by force. God himself used force executed by man. Klingemann agreed: "There may be complications in the life of nations that only war can solve. . . . Questions of war and peace follow their own laws which we cannot change." [126]

Besides disrupting the conference, this intransigence further divided German liberals and conservatives. Also on the program on international relations were Siegmund-Schultze, Deissmann, and Richter, none a member of the official German delegation. Trying hard to steer a middle course, Adolf Deissmann stopped short of endorsing the League of Nations, but he expressed sympathy with its goals. From Kant to Schiller, he concluded, German thinkers had been key prophets of the League idea. The conservative German press later ridiculed him for these remarks.[127] Although finding most of its decisions concerning Germany unjust, Julius Richter similarly supported the covenant of the League. When German delegates criticized his speech, he angrily left Stockholm the same evening. Finally, the official German delegates threatened to leave the conference if Friedrich Siegmund-Schultze took the podium. When he voluntarily abstained from giving his speech, Söderblom told him: "You have saved the conference." [128]

The official German stance articulated at Stockholm—anti-League, anti-Versailles—certainly undermined the cause of ecumenical unity and strained German participation even more than before. Several conservative German delegates returned home to write articles ridiculing the conference. Klingemann wrote that the motto of the German church after Stockholm should be "Work in the homeland and for the homeland." [129] Other German delegates—Erich Stange, Johannes Herz, Bodelschwingh, Steinweg—praised the conference but noted the grave differences between Germans and foreign nationals.[130] Only the liberal and socialist press, such as *Vorwarts, Die Christliche Welt*, and Siegmund-Schultze's *Die Eiche*, criticized the nationalist German view articulated there.[131]

Before leaving Stockholm the German delegation presented a letter to the conference denying the concept of German war guilt and demanding that the issue be resolved before they participated further in Life and Work.[132] The executive committee appointed a subcommittee—chaired appropriately by Alfred Garvie, whom the

Germans respected—to prepare a response for the next year's meeting of the continuation committee in Bern. When presented the following summer, the committee's report was very noncommittal. It recognized that the causes and conduct of the war needed study, but it took no position, settling for pious rhetoric calling for the transformation of international relations through the cross of Christ. Although there was some controversy over differences in the English and German translations of the war-guilt statement, the *Kirchenausschuß* reported that it opened the road for further ecumenical work for the German churches. Kapler announced that several cabinet ministers and even the chancellor had approved the statement. The continuation committee then declared the matter "duly dealt with" and moved on to other business.[133]

The next political row for the Germans centered on the location of the Social Institute in 1926. English and French speakers wanted it in Geneva near other international organizations. Söderblom preferred Bern, close to Geneva but far enough away that the other international agencies would not overwhelm it. The Germans argued for Zurich; they strongly opposed the move to Geneva. Even the moderate Walter Simons, the Weimar functionary and president of the Evangelical Social Congress, warned against the possibility of excessive influence by the League of Nations and the International Labour Organization (ILO). The Germans lost. The Geneva office opened its doors 1 April 1928 at 19, rue de Candolle.[134] The Social Institute's move to Geneva may have inspired the German church authorities to send Schönfeld, whom they employed, to observe its actions. The yearbook of the German churches assured its readers that Schönfeld's task would be "especially to make sure that the Social Institute presents to Germany's satisfaction an independent line in contrast to the ILO."[135] Nevertheless, the Germans were still complaining about the Geneva location as late as 1929.[136]

With the League of Nations located there, Geneva was just too much a reminder of Versailles for the Germans to stomach. Arthur Titius, the German editor for Life and Work's journal *Stockholm,* wrote an editorial on the anniversary of Versailles in 1929 describing the immeasurable political and economic misery resulting from the treaty. He noted the proclamation by the *Kirchenausschuß* of 28 June 1929 as a *Trauertag* (day of sadness). Garvie and Elie Gounelle, the other editors, added a footnote in French denying

any association with those editorial statements.[137] These developments only echoed the growing conservative nationalism of the
German church in the later 1920s. For example, the 1924 *Kirchentag* had met in Bethel, the site of Bodelschwingh's famous social
ministries, and produced the Social Message of the German Evangelical Churches. But the next *Kirchentag* met in 1927 in Königsberg in East Prussia. The journey to Königsberg, on the other side of
the hated Polish corridor, would painfully remind delegates of the
effects of Versailles. Instead of a Social Message, Königsberg produced the *Vaterländische Kundgebung* (Patriotic Proclamation)
which stated that although they took their Stockholm work seriously, "We are Germans and want to be Germans. Our nationhood
has been given us by God. To uphold it is our bound duty. . . . Such
service to the fatherland is also service to God." [138] The *völkisch*
speeches and the *Vaterländische Kundgebung* were enthusiastically received and widely publicized in the German church
press. The Königsberg *Kirchentag* has been widely perceived as
marking a pronounced shift to the right for the German
churches.[139] The Königsberg speeches and proclamation revealed
a willingness of German churchmen to make clear political statements when it came down to matters dear to their hearts.

By the time the depression arrived in Europe in the 1930s,
German Protestantism had offered no idealistic social gospel to its
adherents. From the rhetoric generated by the Life and Work
movement it is evident that German Protestants had no other
analysis of social problems than the schema of the sinfulness of
man, no solution for problems beyond an appeal for Christian
charity and hope to change the hearts of individuals through
conversion. However much the Germans tried to keep separate the
kingdoms of God and man, they occasionally themselves trespassed into the temporal kingdom with their frequent political
statements. Moreover, their worldly activism was a dangerous mix-
ture—antisocialist, anti-Versailles, and antiinternationalist.

4. RESPONSE TO THE ECONOMIC CRISIS
1930-1933

THE Great Depression provided ample fuel to keep the Christian social debate going in the early 1930s. By 1930 Life and Work was well organized with its bureaucracy in place and networks of communication established. The depression, of course, magnified the problems its members had already been discussing: the flaws of capitalism, unemployment, class conflict, and the like. But the heightened tension and perception of a crisis in the making gave the discussions a new sense of urgency.

In 1930 the Stockholm movement became officially the Universal Christian Council for Life and Work (UCCLW). The old continuation committee became the UCCLW's executive committee and continued to meet yearly, as before, for pious speechmaking and routine business. The administrative office moved from London to Geneva, and the Social Institute became the council's research department. The Geneva office was the nerve center of the growing ecumenical movement. Headed by the German collaborator Hans Schönfeld, the research department studied a variety of questions such as nonindustrial child labor, reform of the calendar, and the welfare of seamen. But the primary focus in the early 1930s was unemployment.

The UCCLW sponsored a conference in London in 1930 on the topic "The Churches and Present-Day Economic Problems." The next year there was a week-long study meeting in Geneva concerning unemployment. Throughout the fall of 1931 and 1932 the council prepared for a large conference on unemployment at Basel, which was followed by conferences concerning Christian sociology and unemployment in Geneva. Finally, in March 1933 another major conference convened in Rengsdorf, Germany, on "The Church and the Social Order." The Rengsdorf conference, coming on the heels of Hitler's accession to power in Germany, closed a chapter in Life and Work's history. Its leaders came to the realization that they could no longer consider the social question apart from political and theological questions. Thereafter Life and Work turned its attention away from socioeconomic matters to the still more urgent questions of church and state and rising totalitarianism, culminating in the 1937 Oxford conference on "Church, Community, and State."

Representing England in the Life and Work movement was the Christian Social Council (CSC), organized in London in 1929. Because the Life and Work meetings of 1930-33 were not large assemblies like the Stockholm and Oxford conferences, British participation was less broadly based, less individualistic, less contradictory, and less diverse than before—and thus also less representative of the gamut of British church opinion. In theory, however the CSC was quite representative, half the sixty members being Anglicans, and the other half coming from other Protestant denominations.[1] The chairmen were the two key British Life and Work leaders of past years, Alfred Garvie, president of the National Council of Free Churches, and Theodore Woods, Bishop of Winchester. The administrative officers who did the actual work of the CSC were the Congregationalist clergyman Malcolm Spencer and P.T.R. Kirk, president of the Anglican Industrial Christian Fellowship. Spencer and Kirk had been leaders on the Christian social scene since Copec. Both had attended the Stockholm conference in 1925.

The CSC's full-time director of research was a young Anglican curate named Vigo A. Demant. Born in industrial Newcastle and educated at the University of Durham and Oxford, he was much involved in Christian socialist groups such as the League of the Kingdom of God. By the 1930s Demant was on the editorial board of the Anglo-Catholic Christian Socialist journal *Christendom*. He was a tireless and enthusiastic propagandist for the Christian social movement throughout the 1930s. Under his direction, the CSC launched a study of unemployment, which continued through 1933. It also sponsored study meetings, night classes, and lunch lectures on Christian sociology. A prolific writer, Demant sat on

Life and Work's Research Commission, which planned research topics for the Geneva staff and the international study conferences. Wishing to remain in England, in 1930 he declined the UCCLW's offer to become research director in Geneva.[2] But Demant was constantly traveling throughout Europe to represent Britain in the many Life and Work gatherings of the 1930s. The CSC forwarded his writings and those of other British leaders to Geneva, where they became part of the growing Life and Work collection.[3] In 1933, when the stipend underwriting Demant's research expired, he accepted a vicarage, considerably reducing his involvement with the CSC.[4] The next year the focus of British involvement in Life and Work shifted from Demant and the CSC to a circle around Joseph Oldham of the International Missionary Council, who began to direct preparations for the Oxford conference of 1937.

The Germans had no constituent body for the UCCLW within their own country equivalent to the Christian Social Council. German participation in Life and Work from 1930 to 1933 was coordinated by Hans Schönfeld, in Geneva and in the *Sozialausschuß* (social subcommittee) of the *Kirchenausschuß*, led by the conservative clergyman Jacob Schoell. Schoell, a former gymnasium teacher and church official in Stuttgart, was a member of Reinhold Mumm's ultraconservative *Christlich-Sozialer Volksdienst,* a party that had split from the DNVP in 1930.[5] Under Schoell's direction the *Sozialausschuß* organized German national study conferences to prepare for Basel and Rengsdorf and chose the German delegates to these major ecumenical conferences of the early 1930s.

Although Hans Schönfeld became director of research of the UCCLW, he was employed in Geneva by the *Kirchenausschuß* and clearly subject to the supervision of Schoell and President Kapler.[6] However, as a key person on the UCCLW staff, Schönfeld did not follow a trenchant, dogmatically conservative line. In his presentations he exhaustively described the problems of the depression, discussing everyone else's analyses and conclusions, but he never revealed his own views. The reticence of this faceless man enabled him to maintain his precarious position as bridge between conservative Germans and the UCCLW. Throughout his association with Life and Work, Hans Schönfeld was torn between his loyalty to the conservative German church and his ties to colleagues in the ecumenical movement. Noncommittal though he was, he was a moderating influence on German participation. On those occasions when the *Kirchenausschuß* did not choose the German representatives to Life and Work meetings, Schönfeld invited both liberal and conservative Germans.[7]

As German editor of *Stockholm*, Arthur Titius also provided moderate German participation. Titius had studied under a liberal scholar, Julius Kaftan, and was deeply influenced by the theology of Friedrich Schleiermacher, the early prophet of Protestant liberalism. A member of the *Kirchenausschuß* but also of the Evangelical Social Congress from its early days in the 1890s, Titius was a theologian more open to free expression of opinion than most in the German hierarchy.[8] As a result, some German liberals and even a socialist published articles in *Stockholm* in 1930 and 1931.

German participation in Life and Work from 1930 to 1933 became increasingly strained. In 1931, 282 German subscriptions to *Stockholm* were canceled, and the journal ceased publication after the fourth issue of that year. Financial difficulties partly explain these cancellations, but they also point to a growing German opposition to the ecumenical movement. The depression-stricken United States had only thirty-five cancellations that year.[9] As early as January 1931 a *Kirchenbund* official, Hans Wahl, expressed concern to Schönfeld over the growing German opposition to the ecumenical movement, opposition which was theological as well as political.[10] Preparations for the World Disarmament Conference in Geneva in 1932 brought attention back to the problematic postwar settlement. Germans used the opportunity to bring up again the war-guilt issue. At the executive committee meeting of the UCCLW in Cambridge, German representative Jacob Schoell asked that war guilt be reconsidered. French and British members refused to discuss the question, arguing that it had been settled at Bern in 1926.[11] The next summer in Geneva, President Kapler declared to the executive committee: "The German people find it no longer tolerable that still today, fourteen years after the end of the world war, discrimination against Germany still arises."[12] The German leaders were greatly displeased with the continual lobbying of ecumenical leaders for disarmament. Throughout 1931 they complained about "Anglo-Saxon" domination in Life and Work and the great need for the German position to be voiced.[13] In August 1932, Kapler warned the UCCLW that many Germans now favored German withdrawal from the ecumenical movement because of the discriminatory reparations and disarmament. Wilhelm Menn, a German member of the Advisory Commission for Research, gave Schönfeld a similar evaluation.[14]

By 1932 Schönfeld was clearly losing favor with the German authorities. Jacob Schoell's conservative *Sozialausschuß*, which increasingly dominated German involvement in Life and Work, thought Schönfeld's research too theoretical and insufficiently German. Although Schönfeld reassured the committee that he had stood up to the American position and kept his German identity clearly in mind, the *Kirchenausschuß* informed the UCCLW that it was reducing his salary. By summer the committee announced it would cease paying Schönfeld entirely.[15] Ironically the date set for Schönfeld's termination was February 1933, the month following Hitler's accession to power, when the political situation of the German church would be transformed entirely. A swing to the right thus preceded Nazi control of the German church.

The difficult circumstances of the early 1930s merely exaggerated both the British and the German tendencies of the previous decade. While British participants in Life and Work retained their idealism, the tenuous German involvement of the 1920s became even more strained as international tension heightened in the wake of economic crises. Moreover, in their social analyses, Germans tended increasingly to hand over social problems to politics, in some ways intellectually preparing the way for the Nazi revolution.

The British attempted to explain the causes and nature of depression problems and call for specific reforms to conquer them. They still looked optimistically for the coming of the Kingdom of God on earth. In 1932 the CSC reminded Christians that "economic sufficiency can only be gained when the realisation of God's kingdom is preferred to economic success."[16] A report on unemployment presented to the Church of Scotland Assembly in 1932 proclaimed that the Kingdom of God was at hand. Similarly, E.J. Hagan's report on the social ethic of Scottish Calvinism, given at the 1932 Geneva study conference, emphasized the expectation of and work for the coming of the Kingdom in Scotland.[17]

Such expectations could survive into the 1930s because the British did not blame the depression problems on human nature. British church leaders were more ready to admit original sin than they had been in the 1920s: the world order, including human society, was perverted and under sin, argued Demant at Rengsdorf. Yet sin had not caused the present crisis. Demant thought it was erroneous to blame the situation on human nature, as if man were so stupid, greedy, and bad that he could not run his economy efficiently. This view, Demant continued, was a "measure of human depravity which has no warrant in any Christian theory of human nature." Blaming human depravity for the depression was untenable on both rational and Christian grounds. The Bishop of Woolwich agreed in *Stockholm* that Christianity could not accept a low view of human nature.[18]

In a veiled attack on German Christianity, the British suggested that false theology was the basis for the social quietism displayed by churches in some lands. Attributing the economic slump to sin or human nature, Demant emphasized, led only to hopeless psychological depression. The Bishop of Lichfield wrote in *Stockholm* that the church must emphasize the incarnation of God in Christ; false teachings of God as only otherworldly led to secularism. Contemporary society, Demant agreed, denied the promise of incarnation, which removed the spiritual significance from life, resulting in purely personal, transcendent, wholly other forms of religion, like that of the rising Barthian school.[19]

The concepts of the Kingdom of God on earth, a this-worldly God in Christ, and an inculpable human nature remained necessary theological bases for Christian responsibility for the social and economic crisis. British theology continued to assert the primacy of God over all dimensions of life. As the Bishop of Lichfield said: "He is Lord of our Industry; He is Lord of our politics. . . . Everything comes within the Kingdom." Demant needed the argument that "human society is part of God's created order" to justify his extensive theoretical analysis of the Christian economy.[20] The British retained the view of the 1920s that criticism and action in social and economic matters were the duty of the church. According to Ruth Kenyon's paper for the Geneva conference of 1932, the archbishops' 1918 committee report with its principle of judging economic activities by moral standards remained the authoritative view of the Church of England.[21] Articles by British church leaders in *Stockholm* read like the Copec reports of 1924; they discuss the standard topics: the infinite value of the human soul, the idea of the calling and duty in industry, and the fatherhood of God and brotherhood of man. Starting from the same theological premises, British social statements of the early 1930s rehashed the generalities and moral criticism of the previous decade.[22]

The British Life and Work rhetoric echoed the message in the important book *Christianity and the Crisis,* which appeared in 1933. Edited by the Anglican canon Percy Dearmer, the volume contained contributions from the likes of Archbishops Temple and Cosmos G. Lang, and Alfred Garvie, the president of the National Council of Free Churches. Displaying a vivid perception of a crisis that Christianity must solve, the message was the same as that of the 1920s. Wrote Dearmer: "We stand at this moment of writing on the brink of irretrievable disaster. It is in a very real sense true that only Christ can save the world from ruin to-day." For the Bishop of Ripon the choice in this crisis was between Christ and chaos; for another writer, between secular communism and a rebaptized church.[23] Vague terminology abounded: moralizing the "motives and methods of human life," asserting the "supremacy of the moral factor in politics, in economics, in finance, and in every field of human activity," and, of course, bringing the Kingdom of God to earth. John Oliver argues that the book was a fair reflection of Christian social thought in Great Britain in the early 1930s.[24]

British Life and Work participants continued to call for the standard church actions to deal with the suffering of the depression. In 1932 the CSC published a pamphlet, "For the Unemployed," which recommended the formation of clubs where the unemployed could meet for social activities, recreation, and lectures; workshops where useful handicrafts such as carpentry and shoe repair could be practiced; allotments where the poor could grow their own food; and a variety of voluntary personal assistance ranging from sharing material goods to organizing discussions between the unemployed and labor exchange offices.[25] Yet the British churchmen did go beyond the standard social gospel of the 1920s. Such programs, they emphasized throughout the depression years, were insufficient. The CSC report admitted that such measures were at best palliative; the church must deal with the causes of the problems. The church, agreed Ruth Kenyon, could not be satisfied with mere relief: "Mercy is not enough; behind it lies the claim for justice." Clubs and unemployment centers, Chairman Kirk warned, should not be allowed to distract attention from the roots of the unemployment problem. The church was not just a salvage corps; it also was called to remove the causes of the disablement of society.[26]

Nor would the moralization of the population alone be sufficient to solve the depression problems. Sacrifice and self-improvement would not change things, Demant repeatedly argued. When the church encouraged only heroic supernatural virtues, he said, it tended to deify conscience, making moral gestures the entire content of religion. For generations, Demant added, the moral teaching of the church had instructed the poor to be thrifty and productive. In an age of excessive production and insufficient consumption, these virtues had become obsolete. The nineteenth century's social virtues had become the twentieth century's social vices.[27] Prayer and conversion would not solve social problems. In Demant's view, the Christian ideal for the twentieth century was not a social order where all were Christian but one that provided a framework of social law and custom in which a full life could be lived. The Scottish churchman William Watson agreed. A change of heart was not good enough: "The consequences of bad economic theory and practise cannot be evaded, though the theory is operated by good people. . . . Neither prayer nor good will, in themselves, matter until we mend the defect."[28]

What then besides relief work must the churches do about the depression situation? British churchmen in Life and Work answered that the church must provide a Christian interpretation of the causes and conditions of the economic crisis and solutions to it. The first step was taking a stand. The church, wrote Garvie in 1930, must declare unemployment intolerable. Kirk agreed: "Where we find evil causing suffering, where we trace any signs of oppression, we must make our protest as Christians."[29] Blame must be put in the proper place, Spencer and Demant added. The CSC argued that the church must study the problems and make specific Christian judgments. Garvie emphasized in Stockholm that a Christian sociology was needed to understand and interpret social reality. Christian sociology, said Demant, should reaffirm man's faith that there is meaning in the madness and that God is ultimately in control.[30] What the CSC meant by the phrase "Christian sociology" was, of course, not sociology at all but an attempt to define Christian principles for society.

Beneath a veneer of facile, pious generalizations and calls for alleviative actions, the CSC between 1930 and 1933 undertook a definitive Christian explanation for the economic malaise. Ruth Kenyon listed several generally accepted culprits: the deflationary policies of the early 1920s, the return to gold in 1925, and postwar peace terms that created indemnities and new nations without regard to economic unity. The unemployed themselves, the CSC emphasized, were not to blame. The depression was not merely the result of the war. Nor was it a normal trough in cyclical capitalism that would soon right itself.[31]

The explanations generally repudiated orthodox capitalist assumptions. The CSC's message on unemployment called on the Christian community to "think again whether society has not allowed some false theory to be incorporated in the foundations upon which our present industrial civilisation is reared."[32] Adam Smith's economic laws came in for ridicule. Kirk wrote that "economists invent a vocabulary of their own, string the words together in a semblance of grammatical order, and thus proclaim a 'law' by which all the intricacies of supply and demand are governed." The Scottish report of 1932 charged that "many so-called 'economic laws' are now exploded theories. . . . The principle of laissez-faire has disintegrated." David Ricardo's iron law, said William Watson, "has simply melted into thin air." Not iron laws, concluded the Bishop of Woolwich, but human thoughtlessness and greed underlay the crisis.[33]

The chief evil to which the CSC analysis pointed in the depression was the paradox of poverty and plenty, of overproduction and dire need. Nearly all the British Life and Work participants focused on this absurdity. Demant's speech and the CSC's memorandum to the London conference of 1930 had already noted the waste in a system where foodstuffs and raw materials were deliberately held off the market or even destroyed in the midst of massive unemployment.[34] "There must be something fundamentally wrong, morally unsound, and socially insecure," wrote Kirk, "in such a condition as this." The contradiction of overproduction and human want, argued the CSC memorandum, led to the conclusion that existing theories of industry and commerce must contain some fundamental fallacy.[35]

Demant particularly repudiated the old way of economic thinking. In the past, he said, people regarded production as an absolute goal in itself, but increasingly large outputs for forced export were not achieved in response to human need. In his view, a society should not consume to produce but produce to consume. The age of mass exports had ended. Now that everyone believed that exports must outweigh imports, Demant continued, all could not win. The world was overtraded and overindustrialized.[36] The root of the overproduction problem, according to the CSC, was underconsumption: a weak internal market resulting from the inadequate purchasing power of the home population. For centuries, market surpluses had gone to supply foreign markets, not to improve the standard of living. As Demant put it: "This defect can only be diagnosed as the failure of each process of production automatically to distribute enough purchasing power to market its product." Wealth had become concentrated in ever fewer hands. The world crisis, according to Demant, was the result of this internal situation multiplied by many individual nations worldwide.[37]

This explanation of the depression by British Life and Work associates was obviously influenced by the economist John Maynard Keynes. As early as 1929, *Stockholm* published a series of articles by Spencer and Demant that anticipated a Keynesian view of the capitalist economy. For example, Spencer argued that in a recession like that of the 1920s, unregulated capitalism choked the flow of buying and selling by failing to place money in the hands of consumers who could buy up the oversupply of industrial products. By piling up capital in the savings of those who would not spend, the system only created more supply, when the problem was not enough demand. The solution, according to Spencer (and Keynes), was the violation of Adam Smithian principles—artificially stimulating demand by redistributing wealth, regulating the money supply, and fixing prices.[38]

The Great Depression only confirmed their Keynesian analysis. Demant and the research department blamed the economic crisis on the monetary system. Overproduction and underconsumption, claimed the CSC, stemmed from a radical defect in monetary organization which, in return, determined the purchasing power of the community and the distribution of wealth. The present system intrinsically engendered chronic poverty because it could not adequately distribute purchasing power.[39] The system sacrificed a higher standard of living for all to maintain artificial material scarcity. Chairman Kirk criticized the small, unelected oligarchy of rich men (the Bank of England) who controlled the nation's elected officials. Developed when the economy was primitive, the monetary system had now become obsolete.[40]

The British council rejected traditional remedies as inadequate. It criticized cutbacks and economies as an un-Christian policy of despair. The greatest wrong was the reduction of social services and welfare at a time of the greatest need, violating the Christian law of love.[41] Nor was rationalization in industry an acceptable remedy. The first consequence of such cost cutting, amalgamation, technological improvement, and efficiency in industry would be a rise in unemployment. At best, rationalization would be a quick fix, leaving fundamental economic problems untouched.[42] Tariffs and trade barriers were merely stopgap remedies that might benefit some quarters at home by exporting misery abroad. In any case, tariffs were contrary to the Christian ethic because they upset world harmony and violated ideals of Christian brotherhood.[43]

The council's positive recommendations were more muddled and sometimes contradictory. Some insisted on cutting British military expenditures. Ruth Kenyon suggested reducing the work force by raising the school-leaving age and pensioning off older workers.[44] All agreed that purchasing power must rise and domestic consumption must replace the forced export of production. But the churchmen offered few real plans to accomplish any of these goals. One British writer in *Stockholm* recommended supplementing wages to distribute purchasing power.[45] Others advocated loosening credit to provide a continuous flow of funds to consumers. Still others suggested that tight control of credit would avoid cyclical fluctuations in the capitalist economy. One report advocated a system of national credits to rejuvenate agriculture and revive industry.[46] Was it not easy enough, asked William Watson, to issue seven million pounds a day in credits to fight a war to destroy things? However, another CSC publication argued that piling up debt was intolerable, since repayment would cancel all the good effects of credit.[47]

British churchmen were groping toward a new economic theory, Keynesianism, without knowing where it would lead them. What was needed, they agreed, was a "new economic system." Many reports talked about the "fundamental changes necessary." A council of clergy including ten Anglican bishops stated emphatically that restoring the past was not the answer: "Our social life has to be re-built." The British Life and Work associates rejected laissez-faire capitalism in favor of the planned economy. The CSC warned that current planning measures were "desperate and impossible attempts to save a situation which never ought to exist." The report for the Scottish Church emphasized that the laissez-faire system had disintegrated. The logical alternative was conscious direction, planning, and control.[48]

It is not surprising that these British proposals were fragmentary. The CSC people were trained in theology, not economics. Even Keynes had not yet clarified and systematized his ideas; his *General Theory* did not appear until 1936. Keynes had abandoned laissez-faire capitalism in the 1920s. During the 1930s he advocated currency management through manipulation of the interest rate, government-stimulated domestic investment, large public works projects, and raising mass purchasing power to remedy unemployment.[49] The Christian sociologists of the CSC clearly respected Keynes and invited him to speak at their October 1931 meeting.[50] While the CSC generally agreed with Keynesian ideas on monetary policy, credit, and purchasing power, no one came to the point of calling explicitly for deficit spending. Chairman Kirk, for example, who condemned cuts in welfare as un-Christian, privately admitted in 1931 that Ramsay MacDonald was right in balancing the budget. Nor were public works accepted as a solution for unemployment. Holding to the idea that unemployment should be distributed over the population as leisure time, the CSC's memorandum for London 1930 opposed public works as "making work" for the unemployed as if man's value came only through production. In Kirk's view the public purse would have to pay for public works: workers would end up paying higher taxes.[51]

Though these churchmen preferred to think of it as a new system, the muddled Life and Work analysis was stumbling toward the idea of a planned capitalist economy. It certainly was not socialism. A few suggestions were made for national boards to direct industry, and one Christian socialist recommended in *Stockholm* that industry be reorganized as a public trust.[52] But no calls came for communal ownership or the abolition of private property. The church must insist on the right of private property, Demant argued, and condemn the allocation of property to a minority. Property ownership contributed to the development of personality. The "complete social reorganization" he advocated was one in which private property could be enjoyed by the entire community.

The fatal error of socialism, he added, was its supposing that private property caused capitalism.[53] The intent of Demant's and the CSC's Christian sociology seemed to be to remove the evils of capitalism—and this would prevent the coming of socialism. The unreformed economy, warned the CSC, posed the threat of either ungodly individualism or ungodly collectivism. Both were responses of despair. The alternative to its economic recommendations, warned the council in 1931, would be complete social and international breakdown.[54]

Although clearly not socialist, the CSC's innovative, unorthodox economic analysis put them to the left in the spectrum of church opinion. It took the council beyond the simplistic moral criticism and generalities of Percy Dearmer's *Christianity and the Crisis*. Some quarters criticized the CSC as a group of idealistic social theorists whose work cut no ice in Britain. Even the rest of the council, Demant admitted pointedly, were not so keen on his ideas.[55] Several CSC publications included a footnote stating that the council did not hold itself responsible for all the opinions expressed by the research department; the CSC, particularly Demant, did not therefore speak for British Christianity on social and economic issues. Yet it is significant that this degree of social criticism and economic analysis was encouraged and supported by the British churches, even though they may not have endorsed all the conclusions reached. Demant did his work as part of a council of representatives from the major church bodies of Great Britain, under the presidency of an Anglican bishop appointed by the Archbishop of Canterbury and the head of the National Council of Free Churches. With his theoretical and somewhat visionary studies, Demant may have been a step ahead of most English churchmen, but he was still closer to center than were his critics.

Hensley Henson, Bishop of Durham, was the chief Anglican spokesman for economic individualism and the competitive system. He had denounced Copec in 1924, complained in the General Strike of 1926 of clergy who were "tools and toadies of Labour," and denied the possibility of a distinctively Christian economic system or social policy. By 1931 he was complaining about his isolated position in the church. He had earlier said, "I am too far out of sympathy with the methods and ideals of the clergy to be able to influence them." [56]

With the work of Demant and the CSC, the British Life and

Work movement signified confidence that the depression problems were not beyond human understanding or control. The CSC constantly offered a message of hope: "It is a vital function of the Christian church to keep alive in the world the spirit of hope. It is equally its duty to declare that there is always a way, if men rightly seek it, by which society can offer security of life and responsible freedom to all its members." Christianity could remove all fear, declared Kirk. It could inspire men to attain truth, happiness and justice in this world.[57] Recent events were not beyond man's power to remedy. These confident assertions were based on the view that unemployment and economic disruption were irregularities in a rational world. The churchmen often spoke of the depression problems as irrationalities.[58] Human reason, then, if properly applied, could solve the problems. Christians needed more than good will; they needed good reason: "A Christianity which does not think will never convert."[59] Despite candid descriptions of the grave depression problems, optimism dominated the council's work. Christian sociology could find the right solutions where secular experts had failed.

The British participants in Life and Work, therefore, met the depression head on. The unemployment, poverty, and resulting social tensions brought a perception of crisis to British church leaders. They responded by expressing concern for the depression's victims and prescribing actions to alleviate distress. They analyzed the problems as this-worldly phenomena controllable by human reason and effort. The theological liberalism, social idealism, and criticism of the 1920s survived into the depression years to maintain optimism and psychological equilibrium among these British church leaders. Such was not the case for Germany.

The German analysis of the origin and nature of the economic crisis differed markedly from the British view articulated by the Christian Social Council. As one would expect, the Germans strongly emphasized the war and reparations as major causes of the depression. In fact, German church officials wanted a strong representation at the Basel conference to present the German view that the causes of unemployment were reparations and the war guilt problem.[60] The Germans prepared for Basel with their own conference in Berlin. The report of the preparatory conference emphasized the economic damage resulting from territorial losses in the peace settlement. It noted the ill effect on German industry of the loss of three-quarters of the country's iron ore, two-thirds of its zinc, and its monopoly on potash. The report also lamented that the loss of territory at the war's end was greater than the loss of population: a proportionately larger population had to be supported in a smaller Germany.[61] A survey of clergy in the Hanover area in 1931 showed that many Protestant pastors in the region generally blamed the war as the single independent cause of unemployment. In particular, many mentioned the loss of territory and industrial resources and the restricted living space resulting from Versailles.[62]

The most significant result of the war and the treaty, the Germans emphasized, was the financial chaos they engendered. The report for Basel estimated the cost of the war for Germany as 310 billion marks, or half the total national wealth, constituting an enormous, unproductive exhaustion of capital. The peace settlement only perpetuated the capital loss through reparations payments, which were blamed for the unstable budget and inflation of the postwar years. Inflation in turn wrote off assets, savings, and the wealth of the middle class. With German capital depleted, the economy thus became dependent on foreign capital. The German economy was making good the war losses of other countries, then receiving back its own capital payments in the form of high-interest loans. In short, "the consequences of the war and the nature of the peace settlement have resulted in the impoverishment of the German economy."[63] Whereas Demant and the Christian Social Council emphasized insufficient demand resulting from inadequate mass purchasing power as the root cause of the problems in postwar capitalism, the Germans emphasized lack of capital. The Basel report quoted statistics and expert economic reports in support of its attribution of the dearth of capital to the war. Even the moderate Schönfeld saw a shortage of capital as the root of the depression problems.[64] To all his connections in Germany and foreign countries he recommended the more sophisticated German economic analysis of the capital problem of Kuno Renatus.[65] Renatus argued that the reparations alone did not explain the shortage of capital; internal debts from the war absorbed a much greater portion of available capital. Any new capital was only thrown into unproductive debt service. The transformation of this dead to live capital, Renatus concluded, could come only by writing off debts (as Germany had done in the great inflation) and by balancing the state budget.[66]

The emphasis on capital shortage signified a German version of orthodox supply-side economic analysis, placing blame for the entire mess on the unfavorable outcome of World War I. The Germans dismissed Demant's monetary analysis as simplistic, theoretical, and obsessive. Wilhelm Menn, a social pastor from Andernach who had encountered Demant at the London conference of 1930, thought the Englishman was so obsessed with his theories that he had lost an unprejudiced view of the facts.[67] From this orthodox economic mentality, Schönfeld suggested that current state policy in Germany only aggravated the capital shortage, particularly with excessive public spending approaching half the national income. He rejected public works as a drain on capital. He and others argued that the labor force simply had too many workers.[68] Schönfeld, with his doctorate in economics, echoed the remarks of the untrained pastors of Hanover, who suggested that high wages, high taxes, and high social expenditures all contributed their part to the unemployment.[69]

This standard German analysis of the depression did not offer much hope. Just as Germans blamed the ultimate cause of the depression on foreign economic and political powers, so they saw an independent German solution as impossible. In such a situation the state, by sharing in relief work, must simply make sure that no one starved. The churches had indeed expanded their charitable work during the crisis. Stressing the teaching of farm skills, the Inner Mission operated forty-four workers' colonies with places for nearly five thousand unemployed workers. Bodelschwingh's program at Bethel for unemployed vagrants also expanded, emphasizing training in agricultural occupations.[70] The report for Basel supported the land settlement program, even though it reached only a handful of the masses of unemployed and could never become a large-scale movement because of the capital shortage.[71]

Although the Germans viewed rationalization as a contributing factor to unemployment, they saw it as a partial remedy for the crisis. Some short-term unemployment might occur, but the end result of rationalization would be more employment.[72] At the London conference Demant called rationalization a quick fix that ignored the fundamental problems. Schönfeld answered that rationalization would stimulate employment by raising consumption with lower costs and prices. The other German at London, Wilhelm Menn, seconded Schönfeld's view. Schönfeld blamed ineffective rationalization on "the interference of State social policy." Menn agreed that the involvement of the state in rationalization frequently meant an irrational factor.[73] Again, the German and British spokesmen were speaking right past each other, the Germans emphasizing supply and the British focusing on demand.

Besides charity and rationalization, the German churchmen offered few solutions to the depression. The report for Basel outlined only two possible alternatives for the future. Either the German economy would continue to be involved in a capitalist world system and a global crisis beyond its control, or it would break with the international economy and move toward self-sufficiency. The first alternative meant laboring on hopelessly; the latter opened possibilities for frightening changes. The report added that the second choice, a policy of autarky, would entail the growth of state control over the economy and lead inevitably to "severe internal disturbances and a strong Bolshevist movement."[74] The Germans did not endorse the policy of autarky, evidently assuming that state control must lead to socialism. But they had closed all the other doors. Given this mental paralysis, Hitler's version of autarky and state control combined with his violent anti-Bolshevism would become the obvious alternative.

The German socioeconomic analysis therefore differed greatly from that of the British church leaders. The international Basel conference took up the question of autarky in its sessions of April 1932 and adopted a strong statement favoring world cooperation over national autarky.[75] The Germans consequently criticized the Basel message for establishing concrete goals to direct political affairs. This was more than a proper moral admonition, the official *Kirchliches Jahrbuch* asserted; it was meddling in affairs of state.[76] The British too had reservations about the Basel message but for very different reasons. Bishop George Bell, president of the British section of Life and Work, said that although he was in general agreement with the message, he did not know whether he could sign it, because it was not linked with any action that the churches should take.[77]

The contrast between British and German church-social policy became more and more striking as the years went on. In matters of practical economic analysis, the British explained the depression's causes and nature as rational, not beyond man's understanding and control. They prescribed optimistic, somewhat idealistic remedies such as redistributing mass purchasing power. The Germans saw the causes of the depression and the solutions to it as lying outside the control of the German people. The only recourse seemed to be autarky, which only brought fears of revolutionary socialism. One German report explained the rapid growth of public support for autarky: "It is symptomatic of the complete loss of belief in the economic and political reasonableness of the world at large which is more and more taking possession of the German people and is accompanied by political tendencies of a similar character."[78] The German church leaders thus practically admitted that such hopelessness led to the growth of extreme solutions.

Just as their practical economic analysis left German churchmen susceptible to fascist solutions, so also their theological debate reveals the mentality that would prepare the way for acceptance of the Nazi state. As Hans Wahl had stated, the growing German opposition to Life and Work was theological as well as political. In the early 1930s the German Life and Work constituency increasingly criticized the UCCLW's work as too economic and technical and insufficiently concerned with theology and social ethics. President Kapler of the *Kirchenausschuß* particularly voiced these views to the council and to other Germans.[79] One German criticized the UCCLW for having no confessional basis.[80] The *Sozialausschuß* nearly scrapped the Berlin meeting to prepare for the Basel conference, probably the highest point of economic analysis on the German side, because of concern that unemployment was too great a problem for the churches and should be left to political agencies.[81] Partly in response to this pressure from Germany, the concern of Life and Work shifted toward theology and social ethics after the Basel conference. The Theology Commission of the UCCLW sponsored a study conference in Geneva in August 1932 to discuss the social ethics of the different church traditions.[82] In March 1933 the larger Rengsdorf conference stressed a theological perspective.

In these discussions, German theology offered little hope or direction for the world crisis. For the German participants, God was still remote and human society still the community of sinners.[83] The Germans still viewed the Kingdom of God as eschatological, not earthly. The theology of the Kingdom still loomed large as a basis for German social ethics. The moderate Wilhelm Menn, who was active in the Evangelical Social Congress, wrote of his shock and disgust on reading the British article about Christ's conception of an earthly Kingdom in Percy Dearmer's *Christianity and the Crisis*.[84] At the Geneva study conference, Ernst Wolf, professor at Bonn, described Lutheran social ethics, while Martin Dibelius of Heidelberg discussed the social guidelines of the New Testament. Both these prominent German theologians emphasized the eschatological nature of the Kingdom. In the Lutheran view, Wolf argued, the only prefiguration of the Kingdom on earth was in the church. Lutherans built the Kingdom of God, Dibelius agreed, only when they won souls. The Germans applied activism only to matters of church life, not to society.[85]

So again, the German interpretation of the Kingdom of God precluded any expectation that society would be transformed by Christianity. At Geneva, Dibelius argued that both humanitarianism and utopianism were clearly unscriptural. Christ, he said, did not envision wide social intervention. He built no bridges between rich and poor. Nor did early Christians attempt social reform; they did not even free the slaves.[86] Johannes Herz, secretary of the Evangelical Social Congress, wrote that Jesus was indifferent to social questions in an age of sharp conflict. "Social" and "gospel" were contradictory concepts. The gospel had to do with God's relationship to man; the social concept concerned man's to man.[87] These are perhaps surprising words for the general secretary of the Evangelical Social Congress. But Kurt Nowak views Herz as responsible for pulling the Congress away from its leftish orientation and toward a moderate bourgeois position in the later 1920s.[88] For both Dibelius and Herz, the gospel encouraged Christians to speak out against selfishness and sin, inspiring moral thought, speech, and action. It was concerned primarily not with society but with the individual.

German theology allowed for some social criticism by the church, but it precluded the establishment of any concrete guidelines for society. In the preparations for Rengsdorf, churchmen such as Herz, Wolf, and Schoell argued that the church should examine and critique the social reality.[89] Even Kapler, in his address to the UCCLW executive meeting in 1932, declared that

Christians must proclaim to statesmen and politicians that the depression crisis signified disobedience to God's will.[90] But criticism must remain guarded. The German preparatory conference for Basel declared that because all political and economic decisions were compulsorily imposed (after Heinrich Brüning's invocation of Article 48 of the Weimar constitution, which gave the president virtually dictatorial powers), the church should maintain great reserve. Its statements would probably be misunderstood.[91]

The German position thus practically denied any normative role for the church. Criticism, remaining reserved, should only draw attention to the suffering and problems. All agreed that the church could not provide a static blueprint for a Christian social order. The Gospel did not say how to organize an economic system, Herz emphasized. The Lutheran tradition opposed such meddling, according to Ernst Wolf and Martin Dibelius. Luther himself had left the form of the state to the authorities; he had not searched for a right or just political system. The power of sin made it impossible for man to know God's will in such a matter.[92] Friedrich Brunstäd, who at Stockholm had lambasted the Enlightenment liberal tradition, gave an important presentation to the continental section of Life and Work in Geneva in August 1932, titled "Is a Social Ethic of the Church Possible?"[93] He argued that the church's task was not to improve the world but to live to God in the world. World improvement would be human power and self-righteousness—that was the error of Christian sociology. Brunstäd concluded: "There is no Christian society, no Christian economic order, no Christian state, also no Christian marriage and Christian culture. There can only be a struggle for a righteous social order, a true state, genuine marriage, genuine culture from the faith which points to the original state of creation." But for Brunstäd, this struggle was an existential and eschatological one. From the moment of creation to the end of deliverance, he continued, human beings are held by sin and death.[94]

In the German view, the church should provide no outline of the Christian society; the proper form would naturally be shaped by the demands of the situation. At Geneva, Dibelius even declared that no one Christian social ethic existed. Each individual, each group and nation, must find its own. Not the church, said Wolf, but specific societal conditions imposed the appropriate systems and forms.[95] Even more frighteningly, Ernst Wolf suggested that this "concretization," the development of the necessary forms, should be viewed as God working through history. It was man's calling, his vocation, Wolf said, to live in these complex conditions of creation and to obey.[96] Obedience to God meant obedience to his created forms. Rather than looking to the church for a Christian solution, these churchmen advised Germans to accept obediently the historically emerging solutions. By 1933 the solution emerging was fascism.

The great contradiction in the German position was the same one that had existed in the 1920s. The Germans declared that the church must endorse no system. They flaunted their political neutrality.[97] But they did not see it as inconsistent to condemn certain political, economic, or social systems such as socialism or liberalism. Consider the following statement proclaimed to Basel by the Berlin preparatory conference: "The Church, however, is not bound with any definite social or industrial or state system, and must therefore oppose all anarchy and all arbitrary experiment which might endanger the whole community."[98] The Germans apparently wrote this without any sense of the contradiction between the two clauses in the sentence: that is, that they could be politically neutral while opposing one system as an arbitrary experiment.

With this line of reasoning, the German churchmen could proceed at Berlin in February 1933 to condemn Marxism as a coerced economy (*"Marxismus = Zwangswirtschaft"*). Jacob Schoell, chairman of the *Sozialausschuß*, admonished that a planned economy must be refused from the Christian standpoint because it would destroy freedom. Bishop Simon Schöffel rejected the socialist ideal of an egalitarian society as inconsistent with God's order of creation. Also at Berlin a mining official from Saarbrücken, Werner Tessmar, condemned socialism for destroying personal responsibility and for being ethically false.[99] At Rengsdorf the next month, Professor Fritz Lieb of Bonn rejected Russian Communism as a this-worldly chiliasm, falsely trying to make the Kingdom of God into a Kingdom of men on earth. Communism, he added, made men the slaves of production.[100] Friedrich Karrenberg, a layman from the Rhineland, also lambasted liberalism at Berlin and Rengsdorf, calling it excessive individualism and anti-stateism. The liberal assumption that the unfettered pursuance of self-interest would restore social harmony, he said, had lost credence with the present crisis.[101] Finally, Herr Tessmar, who so vigorously rejected a planned economy, also rejected the current form of capitalist economy.[102]

The Germans had intellectually painted themselves into a corner with this theological debate over the depression crisis. They argued that no Christian political, social, or economic system or form existed. The contemporary situation would determine which forms were best or necessary. Conveniently, they ruled out socialism as an acceptable alternative. They offered no hope for contemporary capitalism or for Weimar liberalism; what alternative was left? Even more dangerously, they endowed situationally mandated forms with the aura of God's will working itself out in history. Finally, they demanded obedience to the will of God. It was with this social mentality that the German churchmen would make sense of the Nazi revolution, which began simultaneously with the Rengsdorf conference in early March 1933.

In 1932 the *Kirchliches Jahrbuch* reported that the social ethics of German Protestantism was being transformed. According to the journal, a new theory of the state was responding to the social crisis; theology must aid in this political movement: "The social question is a political one."[103] Indeed, the social question did become a political question. The German churches turned over to politics the guidance on social problems *before* Hitler took power. After 1933 the politicization of social issues would only accelerate for Life and Work, as the movement reacted to the rise of totalitarianism in Christian Europe.

5. THE SOCIAL MESSAGE AND THE NAZI STATE
1933-1937

THE horrifying progress of Nazism, and especially its relationship to the German church, dominated the attention of Life and Work from the spring of 1933 through 1937. Hitler's *Gleichschaltung* attempted to bring even the church under Nazi control, resulting in a splintering of different groups with varying responses to Hitler's church reforms. The ecumenical movement stayed in contact with all these groups, providing one of the few media through which they communicated with each other. With the *Kirchenkampf*, Life and Work leaders were no longer sitting on the sidelines discussing and pronouncing on events happening around them; they were now directly in the fray. It is no surprise that after 1933 the focus of Life and Work shifted from the economic problems of the depression to rising totalitarianism.

I shall not relate the dramatic and complex narrative of the German church struggle and the role of the ecumenical movement. It has been told admirably elsewhere.[1] Some background, however, is necessary to understand the German contributions to Life and Work in this period. The Rengsdorf ecumenical conference of 8-15 March 1933 convened at a moment of extreme tension in Germany. The Reichstag fire of 27 February had been followed by the mass arrest of Communists and the fateful emergency decree suspending civil liberties. In the elections of 5 March the Nazis had increased their number of seats in the Reichstag. But it was after Rengsdorf that the church was forced to confront the consequences of Hitler's regime. On 23 March the Enabling Act made Hitler a dictator and the Reichstag a sham. Legislation followed shortly thereafter purging Jews from universities and the civil service. In early April the Nazis organized a boycott of Jewish merchants. All this mobilized the ecumenical movement in April and May. The Anglican Bishop George Bell, new chairman of the UCCLW, wrote of his concern to the *Kirchenausschuß* president, Hermann Kapler. In mid-April the council sent General Secretary Louis Henriod and Hans Schönfeld to Berlin to observe the situation in Germany at firsthand.[2] In response, German church officials asked the Life and Work staff to reserve judgment.[3]

In late April, after meetings with Nazi officials, Kapler and the *Kirchenausschuß* agreed to draft a constitution for a new national church, the *Deutsche Evangelische Kirche* (DEK). This had been the goal of Nazi churchmen even before Hitler took power. The *Deutsche Christen,* a group of fanatically Nazi Protestants organized in 1931 to win support in Prussian church elections, had called continually for the twenty-eight provincial churches to become one German Evangelical Church. In May, while Kapler's committee was drafting a new constitution, the *Deutsche Christen* agitated for Ludwig Müller, Hitler's adviser in church matters, to receive the new post of *Reichsbischof.* Finally, at the meeting of the council of the German Church Federation in late May, the delegates from all the provincial churches approved the new constitution and elected Friedrich von Bodelschwingh, the Kapler committee's choice, as *Reichsbischof.* Through the summer Müller and the *Deutsche Christen* campaigned against Bodelschwingh, demanding that his election be revoked and that he be replaced by Müller. Hitler made public his support for Müller and refused to meet Bodelschwingh. Müller called Bodelschwingh, the leader of the Bethel social ministries, a man for deaconesses, not for the SA (brownshirts).

Kapler also came under attack from the *Deutsche Christen* for his support of Bodelschwingh. Fatigued by all the chicanery, he retired from his office in the Prussian church in June, citing health reasons. His retirement created a power vacuum in the Prussian church which the *Deutsche Christen* filled. Müller replaced him as head of the Prussian church, and *Deutsche Christen* replaced existing Prussian church officials in great numbers. Paralyzed by the Nazi elements within the new national church body, Bodelschwingh resigned in despair. Müller immediately proclaimed himself *Reichsbischof.* Hitler called for church elections to be held barely a week later, knowing that in such chaos the *Deutsche Christen,* with their organization and propaganda, would have the advantage. The elections of 23 July indeed brought the *Deutsche Christen* into control of most of the *Landeskirchen,* gaining them two-thirds of the seats in the new DEK assembly, which easily elected Müller as bishop.

Life and Work's annual executive meeting in early September came on the heels of this revolution in the German church. Adding to the crisis, just before the meeting convened in Novi Sad, Bulgaria, Müller's Prussian church passed the famous "Aryan paragraph," defrocking clergy of Jewish descent and even those married to non-Aryans. The new German church sent a large delegation to state its case officially to the ecumenical community. Bishop George Bell, who as president of Life and Work was obsessed with the German church struggle, presided at the meeting. At Novi Sad the UCCLW committee respectfully listened to the speeches by the Germans, who professed their intention to continue ecumenical cooperation.[4] However, on the last day of the meeting, a committee led by Bishop Bell expressed grave concern over restrictions placed on free thought and expression in Germany and resolved to aid "distressed Christians of Jewish descent."[5] From this point onward, Life and Work's ties to the German national church were tenuous and strained.

After the political machinations of the summer, the Aryan paragraph provoked a strong reaction in Germany. A group of Berlin pastors led by Martin Niemöller organized the Pastors' Emergency League (*Pfarrernotbund*), ostensibly to aid the clergy of Jewish descent.[6] The Emergency League was the beginning of organized Protestant opposition to Hitler's national church. Its membership swelled through the fall and winter as the *Deutsche Christen* grew more radical. At one frenzied rally in the Sports Palace in Berlin in November, the *Deutsche Christen* called for a purge of non-German elements from religious services and confessions, and even of Jewish elements of the Old Testament. With the *Deutsche Christen* challenging the theology as the well as the polity of the church, such excesses only bolstered the prestige of the opposition church movement. By late 1933 even Hitler was backing off from his support for Müller and the *Deutsche Christen.*

Throughout the winter and spring of 1934, Müller fired and transferred many *Notbund* pastors; others were subject to Gestapo searches or stints in jail. In April Müller deposed Bishop Theophil Wurm, head of the church in Württemburg, one of the few districts where the *Deutsche Christen* had failed in the church elections and the old church government had maintained itself. In May 1934 the opposition met at a synod in Barmen, where rebel pastors denounced Müller's church government, declaring themselves to be the true Evangelical Church of Germany. A group of theologians led by Karl Barth drew up the famous Barmen Confession, which rejected state control of the church as doctrinally false. After Barmen there were in fact two churches in Germany, the national church (*Deutsche Evangelische Kirche*), and the Confessing Church (*Bekennende Kirche*), as the Barmen associates called their group.

The organization of this rival Confessing Church created a dilemma for Life and Work. As president of the UCCLW, Bishop Bell had continually complained to Müller and Bishop Theodor Heckel, head of the *Kirchliches Außenamt* (the new church foreign office in charge of ecumenical affairs), about police action against dissenting clergy. When Bishops Theophil Wurm and Hans Meiser of Bavaria were arrested because of their support for the Confessing Church, Bell even talked to the German ambassador in London on their behalf.[7] Bell also sent a representative of Life and Work to the fall synod of the Confessing Church in Berlin-Dahlem.[8] Yet members of the Confessing Church were still technically a part of the national church, which had the legal power to choose its own delegation. When Bell had invited Confessing churchmen to the UCCLW meeting in Fanø, Denmark, as special guests, Bishop Heckel loudly complained.[9] The Confessing churchmen avoided confrontation by not attending.

The Fanø meeting of Life and Work in August 1934 came at a most tense moment in the relations between the ecumenical movement and the German church. As at Novi Sad, the national church sent a large official delegation, led by Bishop Heckel, who had been instructed to take a firm Nazi stance. Stating that they wanted no public discussion of the internal affairs of the German church, German church officials called press treatment one-sided and sensational. Dissatisfied by Heckel's stand, however, the German church authorities flew in a special delegate to speak on the last day of the conference.[10] It was to no avail. The UCCLW resolved "that autocratic Church rule, especially when imposed upon the conscience in solemn oath; the use of methods of force; and the suppression of free discussion are incompatible with the true nature of the Christian Church," and, moreover, the council declared its sympathy for the witness of the Confessing synod. Bishop Heckel protested against the resolution, especially against its support for Confessing Christians.[11]

The confrontation at Fanø nearly caused a break between the German church and the UCCLW. Shortly afterward, however, events in Germany defused some of the tension and antagonism. The house arrest of Bishops Wurm and Meiser was lifted later in the fall. In 1935, losing his faith in Müller and the *Deutsche Christen*, Hitler abandoned his plans for a closely controlled national church, bringing the *Gleichschaltung* to a temporary halt. In July 1935 he created a new Church Ministry under the former justice official Hans Kerrl. Although he refused to give up his office, Müller was stripped of his power. As Nazi control shifted from within the church to outside it, the distance between the national church and the Confessing Christians lessened. Though Hitler's anti-Christian views were as yet hidden, the *Kirchenkampf* was subtly shifting from an internal church conflict to a struggle between church and state.

Determined to restore order to the German church, *Reichsminister* Kerrl entrusted church government to a conciliatory committee headed by Wilhelm Zoellner, a respected elderly churchman identified with neither church faction. Zoellner also had close contacts with the troublesome ecumenical movement, having attended Stockholm in 1925 and several meetings thereafter. He wrote in 1936 to the Geneva office of Life and Work: "The Müller era is absolutely a thing of the past." The situation in church politics, he argued, had drastically changed since 1934.[12] Zoellner tried to bring the warring groups back together. What he succeeded in doing was fracturing the Confessing Church. The intact churches of Bavaria, Württemburg, and Hanover, those not taken over by *Deutsche Christen* in 1933, were inclined to cooperate with Zoellner's church government. The intact churches were more homogeneously Lutheran; the Confessing Church was becoming increasingly divided between Lutheran, Reformed, and United groups. The Lutherans formed their own council, which cooperated with Zoellner while remaining sympathetic to the Confessing Church. In the mid-1930s the Confessing Church was divided among three main groups: the intact churches, the Lutheran Council, and the more radical Dahlemite wing around Martin Niemöller and other leaders in Berlin's fashionable Dahlem suburb.

This somewhat relaxed position of the German church authorities after 1934 enabled Life and Work to maintain relations with all the groups, while busily preparing for the Oxford conference planned for 1937 on the subject "Church, Community, and State." In 1933 Hans Schönfeld, who remained in Geneva on behalf of the new German national church and became the UCCLW's director of research, had outlined a rather benign agenda focusing on economic ethics, vocations, and ecumenism. Bishop Bell, however, persuaded the administrative committee to opt for a more confrontational agenda, centering on the relationship of church and state.[13] Joseph H. Oldham, the secretary of the International Missionary Council, came into Life and Work at the Fanø meeting, where he was named leader of the preparations for Oxford.[14] After 1934 Oldham dominated the study and research work of Life and Work just as his compatriot Bishop Bell dominated its political and administrative affairs.

In the Oxford preparations Life and Work desired and achieved participation from both Confessing and national churches. In 1935 Bell traveled through Germany persuading leaders of the Confessing Church to be involved; he even talked to Joachim von Ribbentrop and Rudolf Hess to enable the rebel churchmen to participate. Though his term as president of Life and Work had expired, Bell remained the real link between the council and the German churches, the key British church leader informed and involved in the German church struggle to the end of the war.[15] At the 1936 UCCLW meeting at Chamby sur Montreaux, two leaders of the Confessing Church, Otto Dibelius and Karl Koch, met with Zoellner of the national church to discuss German representation at the Oxford conference. Zoellner had hoped to have a united German representation at Oxford with Confessing Christians included in the DEK delegation.[16] But the Confessing Christians refused, and the two sides reached a compromise whereby Zoellner's committee, the Confessing Church, and the Lutheran Council would each choose one-third of the delegates for Oxford.[17]

Although Oldham oversaw the entire preparations for Oxford, he left the actual work of coordinating German studies to the enigmatic Hans Schönfeld. This was perhaps a wise choice. While Bell and Henriod made no bones about their support of the Confessing Church, Schönfeld alone tried to maintain good relations with the national German Evangelical Church. Torn between loyalties to the German church and the ecumenical movement, Schönfeld throughout the depression crisis had refused to declare his views on social or economic issues. Similarly, in 1934-37 he tried to play off both sides in the German church struggle. He was close to officials in Heckel's church foreign office, which was responsible for ecumenical affairs, but he was also in touch with scholars loyal to the Confessing Church. Willem Visser't Hooft (later the first president of the World Council of Churches), even though he worked with Schönfeld daily in the Geneva office, recalls that he did not know where Schönfeld stood. "I am of the Confessing Church," Schönfeld would say, "but I am also of the national church." [18] Only later, during World War II, did he take a stand: he became involved with the German resistance, using his contacts in Germany and Geneva and his freedom of movement to carry information out of Germany. In 1941 and 1942 he even met secretly with Bishop Bell in Sweden to pass information to the British government concerning a planned assassination attempt against Hitler. [19] The years of conflicting loyalties, says Visser't Hooft, ultimately took their toll on Schönfeld. [20] He took his own life in 1954.

Schönfeld's lack of commitment to any side allowed him to elicit participation from all factions in the church conflict, providing a somewhat representative German contribution to the Oxford studies. [21] Actually, he had more influence over preparations by Confessing Christians than over those done on behalf of the national church. Bishop Heckel's *Kirchliches Außenamt* made its own plans for Oxford. Heckel's office named Heinz-Dietrich Wendland, a bright young theologian at Heidelberg, as coordinator for German preparations; he was instructed to limit his work to *Reichsdeutsche Theologen,* and to yield in naming coworkers to the oversight of church authorities. [22] Wendland organized study circles in several universities and involved a large group of prominent theologians—including Friedrich Brunstäd, Hermann Sasse, and Paul Althaus—in the Oxford work. However, his loyalty was in question by early 1936, and Bishop Heckel was ready to name Gerhard May, a right-wing German pastor in Yugoslavia, as coordinator.[23] In April 1936 Wendland was sent to provincial Kiel University, a definite demotion from prestigious Heidelberg, and later became involved with Confessing Church circles in Schleswig-Holstein.[24] After mid-1936 the *Kirchliches Außenamt,* particularly Heckel's assistants Friedrich Wilhelm Krummacher and Eugen Gerstenmaier, were the real coordinators of DEK Oxford preparations. Gerstenmaier edited the official volume of Oxford studies published in early 1937, *Kirche, Volk, und Staat,* which contained articles by Heckel, May, Althaus, Brunstäd, Wendland, and others. Under pressure from Alfred Rosenberg and Joseph Goebbels's Propaganda Ministry, Heckel's office even included in the volume an article by Ottmar von Verscheuer of Hitler's Race Hygiene Institute in Frankfurt am Main. However, at the last minute the Gestapo threatened to suppress the book, not because the content was offensive but because Rosenberg was against the whole Oxford conference by 1937.[25]

In October 1936 Heckel's office invited a few Confessing Christians to a DEK meeting to assist in the final Oxford preparations. Zoellner wanted to draw in Confessing Church participation so he could claim a united German preparation for Oxford. Confessing Christians Hanns Lilje, Otto Dibelius, and Friedrich Karrenberg politely declined the invitation. Only Walther Künneth attended from the rebel camp. Shortly thereafter came a letter from the executive committee, the Provisional Directory (*Vorläufige Leitung*), of the Confessing Church, which renounced any part in the Oxford work of Heckel's office.[26] Representatives of the Confessing Church simply sent their Oxford studies directly to Geneva, bypassing the DEK. The group's executive committee even composed its own set of official theses for Oxford.

All the scholarly preparations and plans for a German delegation were ultimately in vain. There would be no German presence at Oxford. By 1937 the National Socialist Party was becoming overtly anti-Christian. In 1933 Hitler had encouraged Nazis to join churches; in 1937 they began withdrawing in large numbers and boycotting religious services.[27] Under such conditions, Zoellner resigned as head of the church government in February 1937. German authorities stepped up their persecution of Confessing pastors. Minister for Church Affairs Hans Kerrl announced that there was a new authority to decide what Christ and Christianity really were—Adolf Hitler.[28] By May rumors were circulating throughout Life and Work that the Germans would not be allowed to attend Oxford in July. Shortly thereafter the Gestapo confiscated the passports of most of the Confessing delegation. In an act of solidarity protesting this action, the Lutheran Council announced its representatives also would not go. It did not matter. On 3 June, a month before Oxford convened, Hitler personally made the decision to allow no German delegation to attend the conference.[29]

British participation in Life and Work from 1934 to 1937 was largely in reaction to events in Germany. Bishop George Bell, chairman of the British section, kept the problems of the German church constantly in public view with his incessant lobbying and letters to the *Times*. But much of British participation was also in response to the opposing, and sometimes offensive, German views on state and church that came through the Oxford preparations.

In contrast to the German situation, one figure, Joseph Oldham, clearly dominated the British preparations for Oxford. Born in India in 1874, Oldham grew up in Scotland, where his father was a lay evangelist. At Trinity College, Oxford, he became active in the Student Christian movement. After three years in India as a missionary for the YMCA, he studied theology at Edinburgh University and later at Halle University in Germany, though he never became a parish pastor. He made his name as the executive secretary of the important Edinburgh conference on world missions in 1910, the first great international conference that charted the road toward ecumenism in the twentieth century. As secretary of the Edinburgh continuation committee, which became the International Missionary Council in 1921, Oldham remained at the center of the ecumenical movement in its early days.[30]

Oldham had had some connection with Life and Work before he took over the preparations for Oxford in 1934. For instance, he had planned to attend Stockholm in 1925 as the representative of the International Missionary Council. He even had his tickets and reservations when last-minute business kept him in London.[31] He did attend a few sessions of the Anglo-German theology conference in Canterbury in 1927. Until the early 1930s, however, his primary interests were foreign and especially African missions. The Jerusalem conference of the International Missionary Council in 1928 turned his mind toward the general problem of religion in a secular modern world.[32]

In the early 1930s Oldham became increasingly concerned that

Christianity was losing its influence on society. A main problem in the religious situation, he wrote in the early 1930s, was that the "loss of confidence, the sense of security has gone. Confidence in institutions and in the beliefs on which they have rested has vanished." Prophetically, he pointed to National Socialism as evidence that the church must look seriously at the problem of fanatical secularism. To save the world from such secularism, he wrote, the church must "recover the true balance between otherworldliness and this-worldliness." [33] In 1930 he organized an informal group in England, called the Moot, to discuss such problems. He gathered around him the most brilliant minds in the land, including theologians John Baillie and H.G. Wood, churchmen George Bell and William Temple, literary figures T.S. Eliot and John Middleton Murry, and even such secular thinkers Karl Mannheim and Bronislaw Malinowski.[34]

Until Life and Work turned its attention to the subject of church and state in 1934, Oldham had little interest in the movement. He attended the Life and Work conference in Paris in April 1934 as a representative of the Church of Scotland, mixing there with the likes of Emil Brunner, Karl Barth, and Heinz-Dietrich Wendland.[35] Greatly impressed with their work, he became committed to the concept of the Oxford conference, still in the discussion stage. Between April and the Fanø meeting in September, Oldham worked out a basic plan of research for Oxford. He presented his plan at Fanø and virtually volunteered to lead the work. The council obliged, and he became chairman of the International Commission on Research.[36]

Joseph Oldham *made* the Oxford conference. His ability was put to its best use in the Oxford preparations. Visser't Hooft called him "an engineer in the spiritual realm." His true talent was the ability to elicit great work from others and then to organize and synthesize it. Not an intellectual giant himself, he did possess a tremendous sensitivity for the critical issues of his time, as reflected in his work with the International Missionary Council, and he was keenly aware of the problems of imperialism and Christian missions. Through his leadership, these moral dilemmas were discussed at mission conferences and in his journal, the *International Review of Missions*. Only Oldham was able to attract such diverse scholars as those of the Moot and find a common ground for discussion and collaboration. His effect on the Oxford preparations was the same. Almost single-handedly, Oldham made the Oxford preparations the most thorough, intensive, and significant ecumenical study ever undertaken to that time. Visser't Hooft has said that without Oldham's efforts the World Council of Churches would never have come into being.[37]

Oldham influenced the entire course of Oxford preparations by setting agendas and general guidelines. Though he read German easily, he did not express himself comfortably in the language and left continental preparations to Schönfeld and national coordinators such as Wendland and Gerstenmaier in Germany. In Britain and America, however, he practically handpicked the hundreds of participants himself. He organized an Advisory Council in Britain for the conference, chaired by his friend at Oxford, Walter Moberly.[38] But the main work of drafting and criticizing papers came from three informal study circles that Oldham organized in the theological faculties at Oxford, Cambridge, and Edinburgh. Many of these theologians were among Oldham's contacts from the Moot; others were new acquaintances he made expressly to involve them in the Oxford preparations. Some even contacted him to volunteer their cooperation. The participants in the Oxford preparations included many of the leading figures in British theology in the 1930s. In general, however, the choice of contributors was very much influenced by his perception of things and his circle of friends. He made many of his contacts with these intellectuals at dinner parties and over lunch at his London club, the Athenaeum. Oldham's association with these scholars and theologians brought into Life and Work a British element that had been somewhat lacking before 1934.

Under Oldham's guidance, the Oxford preparations mobilized a diverse and representative group of British participants. Besides the three academic circles, he secured contributions ranging from the center to the fringe of British Protestant thought, from Archbishop Temple to R.H. Tawney who rarely attended church.[39] The Anglo-Catholics and the Christian Social Council, the mainstay of British involvement in Life and Work from 1930 to 1933, continued their participation. Most of the CSC leaders—Alfred Garvie, Ruth Kenyon, Malcolm Spencer, Maurice Reckitt, and of course V.A. Demant—contributed papers to the Oxford work. The CSC financially supported the research work of Oldham's commission.[40] But even though it remained the official organ for

Life and Work in Great Britain after 1933, the CSC no longer dominated the British side of the movement. Oldham's preference for the academic establishment in the Oxford preparations apparently did provoke some ill feelings within the CSC. Bishop Bell wrote, "They feel that Joe is too critical and almost contemptuous of them, though (poor things) they feel that they have done yeoman's work for twenty years in a field untrodden by others."[41] On several occasions Oldham preferred to send an Oxbridge theologian to represent Britain at an international conference rather than a CSC member.[42] However, influential churchmen such as Temple and Bell managed to maintain good relations with both the CSC and Oldham's circle, keeping the British group together. When nominating the delegates for the Oxford conference, the Anglican archbishops carefully chose figures representing all factions within the Church of England.[43]

Oldham's leadership in the Oxford preparations made the British material of 1934-37 much richer and more representative that it had ever been before. In the 1920s Ritschlian liberals such as Theodore Woods and Alfred Garvie had dominated the British participation with their calls for the establishment of the Kingdom of God on earth. From 1930 to 1933 the Anglo-Catholics of the CSC, most notably Demant, were dominant. The preparations for Oxford, however, were like a rich tapestry produced by Anglo-Catholics, Free Church liberals, and academic theologians with various confessional loyalties. In Oldham's words, the purpose of his work was "to be able to submit to the conference as a basis for its discussion as adequate an expression as possible of the present stage of Christian thought on the subject."[44] This goal he clearly accomplished.

For both British and German Protestantism, the Oxford preparations thus elicited a diverse range of participation. They also demonstrated a character that was lacking in earlier Life and Work endeavors. The Oxford preparations were more scholarly and intellectual than the work of the UCCLW had been before 1934. Although this was partly the result of Oldham's influence, it also indicated the changed religious and political climate of the 1930s. Since the Stockholm conference the Germans had criticized the movement for its false optimism and activism and for lacking a sound theological foundation.[45] As a condition of their continued participation they demanded an examination of the theological bases for social ethics. The theological discussions at Geneva in late 1932 and at Rengsdorf in early 1933 foreshadowed this preoccupation with theology in the last years of Life and Work. Moreover, in Germany after 1933 the church was no longer an autonomous institution in a pluralistic society. Any discussion of social ethics had first to sort out the relationship between the church and the totalitarian state. This necessitated a complex theoretical discussion on the nature of the state and the role of the church.

The shift toward abstract theology from the facile social statements of the 1920s also reflects the profound changes that took place within Protestant theology in the 1930s. Actually, the revolution had begun in the 1920s, although Life and Work remained immune to it. The real makers of Life and Work—Söderblom, Woods, Deissmann, Garvie, and the others—were a generation who had formed their theological presuppositions before World War I. Their belief in progress and their Ritschlian vocabulary established them clearly in the prewar theological world. In the 1920s a new generation of German-speaking theologians, shocked by the horrors of the Great War, reasserted the pessimistic themes of the Reformation. Karl Barth, the Swiss pastor who would soon be professor at Göttingen, charted the course of this neoorthodoxy in 1919 with his epochmaking commentary on Romans. Barth and his associates Emil Brunner and Friedrich Gogarten repudiated the liberal assumptions of a humanlike God and divine/human man. Like the reformers, Barth posited that "God is God," wholly other, majestic, distant, and mysterious. In contrast, man was nothing; he was totally corrupt. By the early 1930s, however, dialectic theology (as Barth's movement was called), had fragmented, as Friedrich Gogarten joined the *Deutsche Christen* and Barth became outspoken in his opposition to the Nazi heresy.

Also in the 1920s another group of theologians proclaimed a Luther renaissance and saw it as their mission to restore Lutheran orthodoxy against the wild young men of Barth's dialectical theology (after all, Barth was a Calvinist and had been a Christian socialist). Actually, their theology was more *völkisch* German than Lutheran. These theologians, among them Emanuel Hirsch, Paul Althaus, Werner Elert, and Wilhelm Stapel, articulated a nationalistic German theology that deified the state by making it a holy order given by God. They stood naturally opposed to the Weimar Republic as an abomination to the German nation. They discussed the strong ties between Christianity and the German *Volk* and thus made the renewal of the *Volk* appear to be a Christian cause. Viewed outside the context of interwar Germany, this *völkisch* theology seems curious indeed, but these theologians, like Barth, viewed themselves as reasserting the themes of the Reformation.[46] This neoconservativism growing in the 1920s and early 1930s, therefore, expressed itself in various ways. Its exponents agreed on little except their common repudiation of the liberal assumptions about man and the nature of creation.

In the 1920s the neoconservative theologians looked askance at the ecumenical movement as the epitome of liberal errors. Only Paul Althaus had attended the Anglo-German study conferences in 1927 and 1928, and he remained vocally opposed to the ecumenical movement in the early 1930s. Karl Barth was contemptuous of the Stockholm conference's optimistic speeches and its call for church-social activism. Not only did he distrust Stockholm as a whole; he also criticized the intransigent German nationalism displayed there.[47] Through the rest of the 1920s and early 1930s he wanted no part of the ecumenical movement. Barth's position changed only with Hitler's *Gleichschaltung* and Life and Work's support for the Confessing Church in Germany, for he was a leader of the Confessing Church who drafted its confession at Barmen in 1934. Out of gratitude to Life and Work for its support of the Confessing Christians, he lectured at the summer seminar in 1935 and joined the Theological Commission of the UCCLW.[48]

Barth's association with the ecumenical movement in the 1930s and his influence on the Confessing Church brought his thought into the Life and Work movement. Similarly the Nazi-supported state church turned to the *völkisch* theologians, particularly Althaus, to explain—and justify—recent events in German politics and church polity to the Christian community outside Germany. So the German church struggle in effect forced Life and Work to wrestle with the profound theological changes of the era.

The social question for the Germans in Life and Work hinged on their view of the state and its relationship to the church. The concept of orders of creation (*Schöpfungsordnungen*) provided the theological foundation for church-state teaching by those Germans writing on behalf of the *Deutsche Evangelische Kirche*. Paul Althaus, professor at Erlangen, was the foremost exponent in Germany of the theology of orders, and he became the chief spokesman for these views to Life and Work. A chaplain during World War I, Althaus had lost a son in the conflict and was naturally embittered by Germany's defeat. In several writings in the 1920s he had made known his opposition to socialism, weak liberalism, and Weimar democracy. In 1927 at the Königsberg *Kirchentag* he had given the stirring keynote address titled "Kirche und Volk," which in the opinion of Klaus Scholder laid the popular basis for a theological legitimation of the *völkisch* movement.[49] In the early 1930s Althaus became a *Deutsche Christen*, joining the *Christlich-Deutsch Bewegung*, a relatively moderate wing of the movement more in line with pre-1918 Prussian nationalism than with the neopaganism of radical *Deutsche Christen* groups. In 1932 he joined the more radical *Glaubensbewegung Deutsch Christen*.[50] He became opposed to the *Deutsche Christen* with Müller's election politics during the summer of 1933.[51] But later in 1933 Althaus and Werner Elert wrote the famous Erlangen response to the Aryan paragraph, in which they denied that such actions against Jews were contrary to the word of God.

Althaus's argument ran basically as follows. God had created man in union with Him and with his fellow man. Sinful man had rebelled against this call to community. Chaos and anarchy had resulted. God in his wisdom had therefore structured human existence through divinely appointed orders of creation. In this view, the state was a divine institution, a gift from God to protect humanity from the consequences of sin and conflict. Only through the state was community life possible as God intended. As Thomas Hobbes had said three hundred years earlier, the state was necessary to keep people from devouring each other. The state was then a primary order *for* order. Other orders existed—marriage and the family, the *Volk*,[52] the church—but the state took precedence in earthly matters, naturally coordinating all other social institutions. In Althaus's view, the state claimed authority over particular interest groups, even over the popular will if necessary, in order to carry out its appointed duty of maintaining order.[53]

Several of his associates agreed with Althaus and even took these ideas further. One said that the church must be subservient to the state: "Since Christians do not always love each other, the State cannot trust the Church and must legislate for the worst."[54] According to Bishop Heckel, sin made the authoritarian nature of the state self-evident and necessary. The error of liberalism and democracy was the assumption that the state existed to preserve the expression of individualism, to protect self-will. For Gerhard May, the strong Nazi supporter in Yugoslavia, liberalism was an anti-state ideology based on false assumptions about mankind and creation.[55] The errors of liberalism loosened the ties of national unity, said Paul Althaus, and required a totalitarian state to rescue a nation in danger. Gerhard May argued that the reason for the *totalität* of state was the *totalität* of sin.[56] In the view of these churchmen and theologians, people as sinners could not live without the state, whose authority came from God, reflecting His power and justice. The human instinct for obedience to authority was also God-given. It should be encouraged as a positive good.

To support their position on the divine authority of the state, several DEK spokesmen reasserted Luther's teachings on law. According to his *Lectures on Galatians* (1531), law possessed two functions: "One is the civic use. God has ordained civic laws, indeed all laws, to restrain transgressions. . . . The other use of the law is the theological or spiritual one . . . to reveal to man his sin, blindness, misery, wickedness, ignorance, hate and contempt for God, death, hell, judgment, and the well-deserved wrath of God."[57] For Luther, the first use of the law applied to all men; the second was known only to believers. The DEK theologians interpreted Luther to mean that God's law came to man in a general and original revelation (*Ur-offenbarung*) applying to all, both believers and nonbelievers. Friedrich Brunstäd, whose involvement in the Oxford preparations was ensured by his former students Gersten-maier and Wendland, explained that God's law was ordained in all reality. Creation contained it in its fullness, the common foundation of natural law perceptible to Christians and non-Christians alike.[58] Nazi supporter Rudolf Craemer, of Königsberg University, proclaimed that man had a moral faith not to be confused with Christian belief. Through recognition of natural law, the community was subjected to God's divine law. According to Craemer, Luther grounded political commands in "godly, natural law."[59] Heinz-Dietrich Wendland tried to make sure this emphasis on natural law did not taint German religion with the errors of humanism or Enlightenment rationalism. The *Naturrecht* to which Germans referred, he said, was not a rational or individual law, but an irrational law of blood, race, and nation.[60] In short, as Gerhard

May put it, "National law is also God's law." Disobedience to the law of the state is disobedience to God.[61]

In the context of this concept of law, these Germans asserted the Lutheran view of the relationship of law to gospel. They stressed the independence of both law and gospel. Gospel and law stood opposed to each other, they said, always in a state of tension. The gospel did not change or annul the content of the law but affirmed and fulfilled it. Christ's purpose was to forgive man of sin resulting from his failure to live up to the law, not to do away with the law. Karl Barth had proposed that this traditional Lutheran law/gospel formula be inverted to gospel/law. For Barth the law could be understood only in reference to the gospel: without the gospel's redemptive message, the law had no meaning.[62] Brunstäd and the DEK spokesmen rejected this concept: man did not understand the law in or through the gospel as the Barthians would have it; the law was understood independently.[63]

The church must preach both the gospel, which proclaimed freedom from sin, and the law, which still demanded obedience. Hermann Sasse, Althaus's colleague at Erlangen, argued that the gospel was only in the church; it dealt not with the world but with faith. Thus it was erroneous for Anglo-American activists to proclaim a social gospel that had nothing to do with the true gospel. Such a social gospel was really law, not gospel—the law of love, which could never be achieved. What liberalism had taught since the Enlightenment as gospel, he said, was really a natural, rational law that even non-Christians could perceive.[64] According to these spokesmen for the DEK, the law must always be preached independently of the gospel. The church could make no claims on the state or society in the name of the gospel. But the state could make claims on Christians in the name of the law.

Not all the national churchmen held this view of a natural law written in the hearts of all men by God. Others found God's revelation instead through history. The consequences, however, would be the same. The two key spokesmen for the latter view, Paul Althaus and Heinz-Dietrich Wendland, believed that their position mediated between *Deutsche Christen* natural-law theology and the Barthian rejection of natural law. Although Althaus originally was the chief exponent of the idea of an early and general revelation,[65] he came later to amend this view, arguing instead that there are no given, once-and-for-all norms, ethics, or truth that man could

perceive in his natural state. Such ethics and norms were historically relative, varying according to time and place. The state as an
order was divine and ultimate, he maintained, but the form it took
was historically relative. The same went for law. The purpose of law,
to prevent anarchy, had been ordained by God. But the content of
the law had been determined by historical needs and demands.[66]

This deprecation of natural law did not mean that man was left
without knowledge of God's will in earthly affairs. Althaus,
Wendland, and others taught that God still revealed himself, but
through history. Non-Christians, even animists, naturally perceived God in history. The God of history made known his will to
humanity through man's concrete existence, as in the *Volk* and
state. The events of the present had thus been ordained by God.[67]
The existing orders gave a clear indication of God's sovereign will
for humanity. As Martin Dibelius said: "God speaks ever afresh to
men by bringing them into new situations."[68] Of course, a complete knowledge of God was impossible. These Germans admitted
that history was not entirely holy; Satan also was at work there.
Ultimately, however, history belonged to God. It was full of his
work. The Christian saw history as incomprehensible but assumed
an underlying rationality of God's redemptive purpose at work.[69]

This postulation of God as the Lord of history necessarily
legitimized existing orders and powers. They existed; *ergo,* they
must have a divine mission. For Bishop Heckel, National Socialism
was the German destiny, a God-given mission that expressed itself
through history. For Gerhard May, the mission of the *Volk* was a
responsibility given by God, not chosen by the people.[70] The call to
the *Volk,* according to Althaus, came from God through a *Führer.*
Some states, he continued, had special, political, God-given
tasks.[71] Christians surrendered themselves to the claims of the
Volk, trusting that in the *Volk* they would meet the Lord of history.
The Nazi state was thus a special call from God.

This emphasis on history brought a renewed interest in es-
chatology. For Wendland and Althaus all history pointed toward
the end times, when the mysteries of history would be revealed and
the Kingdom of God established. The coming of the Kingdom was
not evolutionary; man could do nothing to bring it about.[72]
According to Martin Dibelius, the Christian knew that the present
orders were transitional; only God could set them right in the end
times. It was not man's business to question history. He could not

expect to change it according to any Christian norm, or even to inquire as to how long God wished to retain transitional yet divinely appointed orders.[73] In short, one simply accepted history as God's will and His call to holy obedience. As in the theology of orders, the key word in this eschatological view was obedience.

As a result of this kind of theology, the social message of the German church boiled down to political obedience. Morality and ethics were incorporated into an earthly manifestation through the orders of *Volk* and state. The responsibility for society belonged to the orders, not the church. The church was to be the church, proclaiming the gospel while the state took care of earthly matters. By the mid-1930s churchmen espousing these views no longer even encouraged old-fashioned private charity and individual ethics, the German solution of the 1920s. Such social problems as resolving the class struggle, Rudolf Craemer said, had now become political duties.[74] Constantin Frick, the leader of the Inner Mission through the Nazi years 1934-46, explained that the new Inner Mission was bound to the *Volk* through the *Führer's* conviction of life and community. Instead of private charity, the Inner Mission now did the work of the state.[75] Echoing Brunstäd's call of 1932, these Germans asserted continually that there could be no Christian social ethics, no Christian reform, no Christian society or state.[76] How, asked Hermann Sasse, could one call the caring for the poor and sick "Christian" when the state and even non-Christians did these things?[77] With this deemphasis of charity, all that remained in such a social ethic was obedience to the state.

For these DEK spokesmen such obedience did not imply passive neutrality. The church must not simply obey; it must also support the state in its work to preserve order. The church should not shy away from political preaching, they said. It had been too silent about Versailles.[78] It must be a national church like the one created by Hitler's *Gleichschaltung,* not an autonomous entity. The institutional form of the church must change, Bishop Heckel asserted, to fit the social life of the nation and framework of the state. The church must organize itself so as best to serve the *Volk.*[79] As Paul Althaus put it, God spoke to people in their nation and culture, through their own language. It followed that the church must be a *Volkskirche* working in and through the *Volk,* instructing the *Volk* in its calling and mission as a divine order, proclaiming obedience to God and state.[80] The Christian responsibility to serve the *Volk* even justified the eugenics movement and anti-Semitism. For Althaus the responsibility to preserve the *Volk* led to *Die Eugenik*. Craemer explained the Jewish question in terms of securing the purity and health of the *Volk* against destructive parasites.[81]

Were there limits to obedience and support for the state? The rhetoric of the national churchmen avoided this question as much as possible. Rudolf Craemer, the dogmatic Nazi supporter, went so far as to suggest that one could never ask whether the state was right or wrong. Any war for the fatherland became a Christian war. Any debate on anti-Semitism was purely a worldly debate. In other words, there could be Christian support of the state, but never Christian opposition.[82] Hermann Sasse rejected Calvinist views, expressed in some quarters of Life and Work, calling for resistance to the state. Instead he invoked Romans 13. God's law was clear, he said; it called for obedience even to un-Christian authorities. Gerhard May defined faith as hearing and obeying. Sin was disobedience to law and destiny.[83] Somewhat less submissive, Paul Althaus gave the church a responsibility to proclaim God's law as a measure for all national law. Since orders were transitional, he admitted, they could not be perfect. Similarly, Martin Dibelius acknowledged that the orders and indeed the historical process were ridden with sin.[84] But neither Althaus or Dibelius nor any of the DEK theologians articulated a basis for a Christian critique of the state, let alone for opposition to it. Although the church proclaimed God's law, Althaus specified that "the church has no right of supervision over the state. In fact it does not even claim to administer God's will." Dibelius declared that one must live with the imperfections in the orders, expecting them to be perfected only in the end times. One simply obeyed and waited.[85]

Some flexibility on this question was necessary, however, to fully legitimize the Nazi revolution. For these loyal German churchmen, the only valid basis for criticism of the state would be its failure to uphold its call and mission. When the Christian judged the state, Althaus observed, he must ask whether it was serving order and the *Volk*. Any state that did not—for instance, Weimar democracy—was not a divine order.[86] The only normative criterion for criticizing the state, then, was its success or failure in preserving order—and of course, the maintenance of order is something a totalitarian dictatorship does quite well. The authority of the state and its claim to obedience ended, explained Bishop Heckel of the church foreign office, when the state did not perform its established task.[87] Or, as Wendland wrote in the 1920s, the problem with the Weimar Republic was that it was not a state; it was a "struggle in the streets." The Weimar government, he continued, did not want to truly have the rule and obedience of a state.[88]

Once again the rhetoric coming from the national church amounted to an apology for Nazi authoritarianism. Freedom was a Christian notion only in a spiritual sense. The Christian understanding of freedom, according to Gerhard May, had nothing to do with political, social, or economic freedom. For support, he cited the New Testament position on slavery. Worldly freedom, Wendland argued, was the "satanic freedom of sinners," expressing itself against God and mankind to create that chaos which the orders must restrain. Christians were obligated to work against that kind of freedom.[89] This rhetoric rejected notions of secular freedom, but it also restrained freedom within the church. The argument for a *Volkskirche* legitimized the dictatorial measures within the German church since 1933. The church was free only in its spiritual functions of proclaiming the Word and administering the sacraments. Christian freedom of the individual was only before God, the freedom from sin and guilt. For Wendland true freedom was eschatological. Until the end times it meant obedience. Freedom from sin was not freedom from the law: "The slave becomes free in Christ, so also the free become the slaves of Christ."[90] Not only did this rhetoric display a susceptibility to authoritarianism; it reinforced such a system, once in place, with the continual message of obedience.

Participation in the Oxford preparations by representatives of the Confessing Church showed some significant departures from the positions of those representing the national church, yet in many ways the social message of the rebel churchmen echoed that of DEK spokesmen. Several of the Confessing Christians agreed wholeheartedly with the loyal Germans on the subjects of the orders and history. For example, Walter Künneth accepted the concept of orders of creation: "Each deviation from God's order leads to decay and chaos." The church, he said, must proclaim the orders as the will and law of God. The *Volk*, in particular, was God's order for mankind.[91] Hanns Lilje, a famous leader of the Confessing Church and secretary of the Lutheran Council, argued that all people were born into nations; the individual must therefore remain true to his national calling. For Lilje as for the DEK spokesmen, God dealt with humanity through the law: "According to the law of God, a nation is a people in whom God's natural ordinances are at work; God's will expressed in law is shown by the clear and inviolable ordinances which govern the life of nations." Lilje even accepted the idea of national missions, saying history testified to God's sovereignty over all the world and His call of some nations for special historic purposes.[92]

As students of the Lutheran Renaissance of the 1920s, Künneth and Lilje displayed the same intellectual heritage as did the other side in the church conflict. Their dissatisfaction with the DEK was a matter more of polity than of theology. In fact, Künneth was a disciple of Friedrich Brunstäd and was good friends with Bishop Heckel and his Nazi associate, F.W. Krummacher.[93] Both Künneth and Lilje had contributed to the *völkisch* theological literature of the early 1930s. These two figures represented the conservative wing of the Confessing Church, the Lutheran Council, which frequently bickered with others in the movement over confessional issues, particularly over what they viewed as excessive Barthian influence within the Confessing Church.[94]

Significantly different interpretations were advanced by Confessing Christians who came more under the influence of Karl Barth. Barth himself wrote an important article, "Revelation," for the Oxford conference after returning to his native Basel in 1935. Despite his exile, he remained a delegate of the Rhenish Church to the Confessional synods and was one of the Confessing Church's most active propagandists. Denying the view that revelation comes through the orders of creation or history, Barth wrote that revelation was in Christ alone: "Revelation means that God, without ceasing to be God, was made *man*, 'flesh.' 'Flesh' means man like us in all the finitude, infirmity and helplessness that characterizes our human life and results from our utter distance from God. Revelation means grace. Grace means condescension. Condescension means being made man. Being made man means being made flesh. Jesus Christ is all that. And that, and that alone, is revelation."[95] For Barth this recognition of Christ as the revelation, as the word made flesh, destroyed the concept of any indirect revelation in nature, history, or self-consciousness. Any other revelation than

Christ, be it Jewish, Stoic, Romantic, or Positivist, was certainly not a "Christian" revelation.[96]

Another Confessing Christian, Werner Wiesner, presented a more thoroughgoing critique of the *völkisch* views in several articles written for Oxford.[97] His views on the orders of creation differed greatly even from those of his Confessing associates Lilje and Künneth. Wiesner accepted the dark view of mankind, the dark view of the natural state of sin and anarchy, and the need for orders to protect human life. But he emphasized that the idea of orders was not scriptural. No certain institutions had been endowed for all time to fulfill God's will. Like Barth and the Barmen confession, Wiesner said the orders were not divine in themselves; only their task was divinely appointed. Instead of calling them archetypal orders of creation, he referred to them simply as orders of preservation. God as the preserver of humanity had given man a chance to check his self-destruction through law. But human laws or orders were not the actualization of divine will: "No human social organization is in accordance with the law of God."[98] Wiesner rejected the natural-law theology of the *Deutsche Christen* as based on rational conceptions and a false assumption about man. Any similarity between Christian morality and the Western concept of natural law came about because Christianity had so permeated the European ethos throughout history, not because any of these morals had been implanted by nature. Like Karl Barth, Wiesner argued that natural-law theology stemmed from Enlightenment rationalism. The *Deutsche Christen* heresy was thus the culmination rather than the antithesis of liberal theology.[99]

Wiesner also rejected the historical relativism of Wendland, Althaus, and Dibelius. The fact that an order or a law existed, he said, did not make it divinely appointed. History could not simply be accepted like the weather.[100] Friedrich Karrenberg, a Confessing Christian from the Rhineland, agreed with Wiesner. History was full of riddles, contradictions, and inconsistencies. To interpret the meaning of history in a categorical, unambiguous manner, as did the *Deutsche Christen* theologians, was erroneous. The Christian must acknowledge that God's will could not be recognized in history.[101] For these Confessing Christians, obviously influenced by Barth and the Barmen Confession, the only revelation of God to man was through his son Jesus Christ and the holy scriptures. They rejected emphatically the notion of revelation through natural law or history.[102] When natural law or history or any worldly ideal was conceived to be the content of divine will, then man was not subordinating himself to God. Law had become severed from the gospel. These Confessing churchmen were pointing to a different basis for judging the orders. The Christian, they said, must turn to Christ as the only standard of true righteousness by which to judge the law or any order.

This view meant a different conception of the limits of state authority. For the DEK spokesmen, the limit to obedience to the state came only when the state no longer maintained order. For these Confessing Christians, God's law determined such limits. Karrenberg said the church could not be indifferent to whether an order was good or bad, just or unjust. Speaking for the DEK, Paul Althaus also had proposed that God's law be a measure for national law. But he did not explain how to react should a discrepancy between the two standards of law occur, whereas to Werner Wiesner, if duty to state and duty to God should be in conflict, God's law—not man's—should be obeyed. A state lost its claim to obedience when it called on Christians to act contrary to the law of God.[103] Such situations would require "passive disobedience to the legal system," and Wiesner advised Christians to accept the consequences patiently: "He who transgresses the legal code, based upon the authority of the Divine purpose of preservation, has forfeited the preservation of his temporal life, according to the measure of his transgression to the penalty of death."[104] Revolutionary violence was never acceptable.

Wiesner's repudiation of violent resistance was not unique among Confessing churchmen. Similar ideas were expressed in a document drawn up by a subcommittee of the Provisional Directory that was formed to prepare for Oxford. The Provisional Directory was dominated by the more radical Dahlemite wing of the badly divided Confessing Church. Although the committee's theses explicitly called for obedience to the state in all earthly matters, they too maintained that God's law was above human law. In cases of conflict the Christian must obey God's law. In this conscientious disobedience the Christian was called not to violence but to suffering. Only the state could use compulsion and force as a part of its role as preserver of order, preventing anarchy by punishing the wicked and rewarding the good. Christ was the model for

Christians in refusing the sword, Christ, "who, when he was reviled, threatened not." [105]

The Christocentrism and the proclamation of God's law by the Barthian Confessing Christians entailed a stronger social message. But in some ways their social ethic was like that of their adversaries in the national church. The Provisional Directory's committee declared that no Christian order of any kind existed, nor any Christian principles of statecraft. The church's duty was not to establish or enforce law. Similarly, Wiesner refused to call anything Christian that did not directly relate to Christ. The error of English Christian sociology was to start from a false assumption that an objective ideal state of society could exist.[106] For Karl Barth, the visible church did not contain or hold God's truth and righteousness, just as the ordinances and the powers-that-be lacked revelation from God. The Christian, Barth said, cannot regard the moral beauty of Christian work or experience as identified with the righteousness or holiness of God. The Christian must "recognise without reserve the insignificance and the human frailty of all Christian experience and all Christian work. He will recognise without reserve that in them too sin triumphs." [107] Using this logic, therefore, the social work and criticism of the church, even the Confessing Church's critique of the opposition, could not claim to be the authoritative word of God. The quest for righteousness and obedience to the law constituted the only Christian challenge to the orders. When Germans on the opposing side called for obedience to God's law, it meant obedience to the created orders and the historically conditioned civic powers and laws. For the Confessing churchmen, obedience to God's law meant a call to actions of love, a revived social ethic.

These churchmen, however, had neither the goal nor the expectation that acts of love and obedience to God's law would change the world. The church's mission was not to reform society: "The sinful world cannot be improved by a progressive endeavor directed toward the ideal of love. . . . The sinful world can only be created anew by God himself." The committee report similarly had no expectations of success. No human order could overcome the power of sin. Christians must still and always struggle with this evil power.[108] Instead of believing in gradual progress and making the world better, Wiesner said, Christians believed in the end of the world and the coming Kingdom of God. Like the DEK spokesmen

Wendland and Dibelius, Wiesner argued that the world would be righted only in the end times. In their despair over this grim assessment, representatives of the national church advocated that Christians wait in obedience for the apocalypse. For Wiesner, Christians must seek after righteousness, act in love, and be a witness to the Kingdom that God would create in the end times. Acts of love were then eschatological signs. The church would always be at odds with the world, helping the sick, poor, and unwanted, caring for criminals and enemies. Such Christian activism tried, however, not to change the world but to cause people to think about the coming of Christ.[109] The social ethic of these Confessing Christians demanded action but offered no hope for any real effect on society.

German preparations for the Oxford conference even included the views of Confessing Christians to the left of the Provisional Directory. The more radical views of Dietrich Bonhoeffer's circle were represented through an article by Bonhoeffer's close associate Jürgen Winterhager. Bonhoeffer had attended the controversial Life and Work council meetings at Fanø in 1934 and Chamby in 1936 and was slated to be a Confessing Church delegate to the Oxford conference before Hitler disallowed German participation. Winterhager's article claimed to be a concise summary of the opinions and work of the former so-called Bonhoeffer circle of students in Berlin.[110] Many members of this circle would follow their mentor to Finkenwalde, Bonhoeffer's seminary on the Baltic, where he was teaching and writing in the summer of 1935.[111] Winterhager blatantly rejected the idea of a *Volkskirche*, unlike fellow Confessing Christians Lilje and Künneth (who embraced the concept) and Wiesner (who ignored it). Speaking for the Bonhoeffer circle, Winterhager emphasized that the message of the gospel was the same for all nations. He called *völkisch* theology a substitute medium (*Ersatzmittel*) that mangled the proclamation of God's word. In fact, the relationship in Germany between church and *Volk* had become so close that the continued existence of the church was measured solely by national, political, and historical— that is, human—standards.[112] Winterhager called for resistance to a German Christianity if its Germanness laid claim to the total value of individuals. In his protest, he compared himself to Luther, who protested against the medieval priesthood's totalitarian control over individual Christians.[113]

Beyond this explicit criticism of the conceptual foundations of Hitler's *Reichskirche,* Winterhager also provided a theological rationale for church criticism and social activism. He explained that the genuine church of God was not a *Volkskirche* but a minority that went beyond national boundaries; it was an ecumenical collection of true believers. Obviously referring to the Confessing Church, he declared that only this ecumenical minority of real believers knew the true will of God. This ecumenical church, either in a common synod of the minority or as a "supranational canonical lawcourt," he said, must direct the powers and orders of this world by clearly explaining what in this world is un-Christian and not in correspondence with God's will.[114] Besides suggesting that the Confessing Church spoke for God, Winterhager was obviously also making a strong plea for the world ecumenical movement to speak out more assertively about German affairs.

Winterhager's article displays the theological divisions between the Barth and Bonhoeffer circles within the Confessing Church. Barth, by limiting God's revelation to the person of Christ, denied that even the church possessed God's revelation to man. For Winterhager and Bonhoeffer, the genuine church did know God's will and must proclaim it or cease to be the church of Christ. Bonhoeffer's formula in his writings of the late 1920s had been "Christ existing as community."[115] His criticism of Barth's concept of revelation was that it neglected the church. With confidence that the church carried the plan of God, Bonhoeffer's deputy, Winterhager, made the interventionist assertions that were lacking in the contributions of other Confessing Church spokesmen. Going beyond talk about the church itself, Winterhager even concluded that "the human rights of individuals will be for the church in no way less important than the right of existence of the national community."[116]

Winterhager basically echoed statements made by his mentor, Bonhoeffer, who at the same time was completing his famous article "The Confessing Church and the Ecumenical Community." Bonhoeffer demanded that the ecumenical movement end its equivocal relationship with both the Confessing Church and the DEK by posing the troublesome question, is the ecumenical movement a church? Bonhoeffer astutely pointed out that the movement had always sought to avoid this question, presuming that the ecumenical cause would collapse if it claimed to be a church. Would the movement merely be a place for theological conversations, a movement proclaiming that unity came with diversity? Or would the ecumenical community realize, as Bonhoeffer hoped, that unity came only from truth; that when it sacrificed truth to achieve unity, it surrendered itself? [117] For Bonhoeffer, being the church of God meant confessing the truth of God. The church could not be neutral between Christ and the Antichrist.[118] The ecumenical community, he said, had taken a stand at Fanø; it had spoken the true word of the church, albeit with hesitation, when it spoke against the doctrines and practices of the *Deutsche Christen* and took sides with the Confessing Christians. According to Bonhoeffer, the ecumenical community became at Fanø a church confessing God's truth. So the real question he asked was whether it would continue to be a church and break ties with the Antichrist or surrender its confession of God's truth. He concluded, like Winterhager, by calling for this confession to go beyond ecclesiastical issues to social ones. He demanded that the ecumenical movement answer whether it would bear witness against the enemies of Christianity throughout the world, whether it would speak a word of judgment about war, race hatred, and social exploitation.[119]

The critique of the Nazi political philisophy and the call for Christian opposition to it came from the fringes of German Protestantism. Besides the Bonhoeffer circle, the only German voice of activism within the ecumenical movement was Paul Tillich's. Tillich was so far from the political mainstream that he had been removed from his chair of theology at Marburg in April 1933 with the Nazi crackdown on Jews and "undesirables" in the civil service and universities. He contributed to the Oxford preparations from exile at New York's Union Theological Seminary. He thus had more freedom of expression than did his compatriots in Germany.

Tillich blamed the lack of a Lutheran social ethic for the success of Nazi tyranny in the first place. In his Christian socialist critique of the 1920s he had consistently argued that the capitalist system had caused division and disintegration of Western Christian society. The German church, with its lack of concern for social questions, failed to provide a reintegrative principle. In the void, dictatorial forms of government rushed in to integrate the masses into one coherent whole. Not only did Tillich reject the traditional Lutheran dichotomy between private and public morality; he even suggested that Barth's neoorthodoxy reinforced German Lutheran tendencies to separate Christianity from the human sphere.

Tillich called for Christian action to change this world. For him history was the continual conflict between demonic forces and the Kingdom of God. The church should fight the battle. In Tillich's view, the greatest demon in his own day was the capitalist system. But the disintegration of Christian society that capitalism had caused meant the birth of the second demon, nationalism. Fanatical nationalism had by 1930 assumed a religious form that elevated race and nation to the rank of God. Tillich's recommendation to Christians was action. "Ecclesiastical politics" by church members, clergy, bishops, and synods was justified and necessary.[120]

Within German Protestantism there was clearly no real consensus on the question of the proper relationship between church and society, church and state. Within both the DEK and the Confessing Church there were many shades of opinion; moreover, the distance between some DEK and Confessing Christian spokesmen was quite minimal. Certain generalizations about Protestant social thought under Nazism are possible, however.

Generally, the DEK representatives turned responsibility for social matters over to the state. Their theological discussion of the orders of creation, natural law, and God's control over history made the church's social message one of subservience to the powers-that-be. The state's authority was tied to its efficacy in maintaining order. Similarly, many Confessing Christians continually preached obedience to the state in all earthly matters, limiting obedience only when the state interfered with the practice of religion. In 1936 Karl Barth called on the Confessing Church to challenge the Nazi state on issues other than simply church matters. Walther Künneth answered that this could not be done without disregarding the nature of the church.[121] Confessing Christians did not attack the concept of the totalitarian state or fascist ideology; they rejected only the state's interference within the life of the church. Even Werner Wiesner, the Confessing Church's chief spokesman to Life and Work, defended authoritarianism as necessary because all parts of life were ruined by sin and needed the state's maintaining hand.[122] The only form of resistance to the state recommended by the Confessing Christians, passive disobedience, was one that could never hope to change things in a totalitarian state. Likewise, the ethics and activism they preached promised results only in the end times. As Wiesner put it, the church would always remain a voice crying in the wilderness. Its concern was not about success or failure but about preaching the truth.[123] Even the more outspoken Confessing Christian circle around Bonhoeffer agreed that the community of true Christians would not be able to "restore this fallen and destroyed creation" but could only bear witness to the will of God.[124] Nor did Tillich's discussion of the Kingdom of God struggling with demonic forces hold out any promise of victory before the end times. The demonic might be subdued but never extirpated, he said. He admitted that he was no religious utopian. This feeble Protestant call to activism, then, was pessimistic and existential, offering no hope for the victory of a just society on this earth.

Such ideas from both parties, the DEK and the Confessing Church, may have contributed to the establishment of authoritarian Nazi control or to the paralysis of resistance to Hitler's regime. The ideas of the conservative Germans of the national church directly encouraged and legitimized totalitarian fascist rule, and most of the rebel Confessing Christians opposed totalitarianism only when total control extended to the church. Their critique and form of opposition could never be effective in a police state. Moreover, their social ethic directed Christians to unremitting acts of love but offered no hope for a fallen world. With the Confessing Christians teaching such a hopeless view of the future, indeed, Hitler's panacea may have appeared all the more attractive.

Unlike German social thought, its options limited to support, acquiescence, or passive disobedience, British religious rhetoric in the mid-1930s still called for a reformist, activist, and responsible social ethic. Yet it was no longer so idealistic as before. As on the continent, the social ideas expressed in preparation for the Oxford conference reflect the change in personnel within the Life and Work movement as well as the accelerating tension in world affairs. Consistent with the guidelines for the Oxford preparations, the subject of discussion shifted from the technical economic theory and details of the early 1930s to broader, more theological issues of church and state. This shift corresponded to the slow recovery from the depression after 1933 and the rising challenge of the totalitarian state.[125] Still, although Protestant social thought in Britain became more somber and realistic, it continued to claim a normative influence directing believers toward the ideal of the Christian society.

The guidelines for the Oxford preparations called for social ethics to be firmly grounded in theology. While German churchmen had found it difficult and almost artificial to ignore theology in the 1920s, the British found it nearly as awkward to introduce it in the 1930s. V.A. Demant, for example, admitted that Anglicans had never formulated the relationship between church and state on theological grounds; the relationship had been formed instead by historical events.[126] Oldham agreed that the English mind was neither theological nor theoretical: "Life rather than logic is its conviction." [127] Nevertheless, the British clearly articulated a coherent theology, which underlay their social ethics. In fact, despite the diversity of their backgrounds and denominational affiliations, the British participants in Life and Work shared remarkably consistent theological assumptions and subsequent social ethics.

As with the German churchmen, the roots of British ethics went back to their view of creation and the nature of man. Their earlier idealism and elevation of man were subdued in the rhetoric of 1934-37. By 1934, the British church leaders looked back to the past as an overly optimistic, somewhat naive age and now accepted evil and sin as realities of nature. Archbishop Temple, for example, questioned the optimism of modern rationalistic philosophy, which assumed nothing was wrong with human nature that education could not cure. Similarly, Oldham pointed out the inadequacy of modernism and liberal Protestantism with its "easy optimism, its too confident faith in human nature." The Enlightenment view, he argued, "is a childish fancy which has never faced reality or looked in to the abyss." [128] Oldham seemed to combine some neo-orthodox and Freudian pessimism, linking human depravity to the id: "The original stuff of human nature is seen to be a bundle of obscure impulses and subconscious instinctive desires. . . . To ignore these is to fail to understand the tragic nature of human existence—the incalculable risks of a life which hovers continually on the edge of the abyss." [129] But even though Oldham's view of man had become less optimistic, it did not encourage social quietism. Speaking rhetorically to continental pessimists, he said that if the only choice were between serving God in an "imperfect, faulty and all too human way or withdrawing from the dust and

heat of the conflict and allowing the forces of evil to go un-
challenged," he definitely would choose the former.[130]

Unlike Oldham, most British churchmen had not read deeply
in continental theology and were little affected by the revolution
taking place in Germany.[131] In fact, the British frequently discussed the remoteness of the new Barthian theology from the
British mind.[132] For the most part, the British maintained a relatively high view of humanity through the chaos of the 1930s. Said
Clement Webb of Oxford: "The image of God, in which man was
created, was not wholly lost in the fall; otherwise man would have
ceased to be man."[133] Thus he denied the doctrine of total depravity. Henry H. Farmer similarly stated: "I cannot help feeling
that much current teaching about the depravity of human nature
and demonic forces is without any satisfactory basis." Man was
just "a little lower than the angels," according to R.H. Tawney,
both fallen and elevated, both of heaven and of earth. Man was
indeed amphibious, Tawney said, acquiring his dignity from the
uniqueness of his position.[134]

Rejecting the continental theologians' pessimistic views of humanity, the British Life and Work thinkers posited a different
conception of the state of nature and creation. They held that God
created man in a world of order, not of chaos. For H.G. Wood, "the
Christian holds fast by the goodness of the creation"; as scripture
said, "God saw that it was good."[135] The fall of man and sin had
disrupted this natural harmony. While for the Germans the fall
meant that the state of nature was chaos, to the British the fall
signified a lack of perfection but not complete anarchy. The world
was not totally corrupted, Archbishop Temple explained; it still
bore the traces of its divine origin. H.G. Wood suggested that it was
an unfinished universe whose "possibilities are not exhausted."[136]

The British view of an incompletely corrupted creation meant a
different *raison d'être* for the orders of creation such as the state.
Marcus Knight, an Anglican representative at the Schloss Hemmen
conference in 1935, emphasized that "continental theologians lay
far more stress than we do on the Fall of man and on these orders as
due to sin." He continued: "We think that these orders are all part
of God's creative work. Not because of sin but because of God's
providence. He works in these orders, and whether man had
sinned or not, they would have been there as part of God's providence."[137] In the British view, the state did not exist to correct evil.

God had not ordained the state, as the Germans postulated, to protect humanity from the effects of sin. If that were the case, Demant argued, then the state would indeed need to be totalitarian because sin is infinite. The state was not negative but positive. Henry Farmer considered it a grievous mistake to argue that the cohesion of social groups rested on force and compulsion.[138] Temple, Demant, Garvie, and other British churchmen argued that God had created man as a social being. Sin perverted this nature but did not destroy it. The state therefore existed as the expression of man's social character and for cooperation in common goals and interests.[139] This was not a new argument; the British were paraphrasing both Aristotle and Aquinas. Since the British worked from assumptions so different from those of German theologians, Oldham was quite right in saying that the German theology of orders was unfamiliar and puzzling to British readers.[140]

The British view of humanity and creation gave human beings more control over their lives and environment. The state was not a gift from God that man should passively and gratefully accept. As Hobbes and Locke had maintained, it was an artificial creation of man.[141] The British churchmen emphasized the human will's autonomy and freedom. Man was no helpless creature at the mercy of creation. He could comprehend, apprehend, and control nature to make it less hostile; he could use it for his own advantage.[142] The British churchmen were prone to the heresy of Pelagius, the fifth-century British theologian condemned by the Council of Carthage. Pelagius rejected the doctrine of total depravity because it permitted an evasion of moral responsibility, arguing instead that man possessed free will and that divine grace merely helped a Christian to accomplish what was already within his power. Knight and Oldham admitted at Schloss Hemmen in 1935 that the British people were temperamentally Pelagian. Knight said: "We think that man is a fellow worker with God, much more than a subject of God." Oldham recalled a remark by Karl Barth while walking home after a dinner party in London: "Now I understand that Pelagius was an Englishman. They were all Pelagians."[143] This emphasis on the will was not just Anglican. It crossed confessional boundaries to be common among British Protestants in general. The well-known Scottish Reformed theologian John Baillie criticized the paper by the Swiss Reformed theologian Emil Brunner for disregarding the autonomy of the human will. Similarly, the high church Anglican theologian Austin Farrer of Oxford argued that the attainment of good must come from the exercise of personal choice.[144]

In the British view, the Christian will was instructed by divine guidance. As Marcus Knight argued, both reason and conscience were revelations from God. Although God revealed himself darkly in nature and history, Demant explained, he revealed himself clearly in redemption. Therefore, "redemption opens man's eyes to the real nature of things and their disorders."[145] William Temple believed that the will of God with regard to human conduct had been implanted by nature in the mind. The divine will was known to man in the concrete situation in which he lived.[146] Others argued that man must use his God-given reason as a guide for human will. John Baillie maintained that goodness was reasonable, saying a righteous will was a rational will. He criticized continental theology's "vilification of reason." Brunner had argued that sin came through the exercise of reason. Baillie responded that such an idea was heresy and that Luther had been guilty of the same when he called reason the devil's strumpet. To emphasize the remoteness of this view from British theology, Baillie quoted the Westminster Confession: "God created man, male and female, with reasonable and immortal souls, endued with knowledge, righteousness and true holiness, after his own image." Baillie emphasized that his intentions were to present not just his personal opinion but to speak for British theology in general. Others seconded Baillie's appraisal of Brunner's work. J.S. Boys-Smith, for example, denounced Brunner's "outrageous statements about what reason is" and his "denial of the worth of reason and moral insight."[147]

With this conception of the human will, the British view of history sharply contrasted with that of the German churchmen. The Germans put man at the mercy of history, which they interpreted either as God's will (the *Deutsche Christen* view) or as an eschatological mystery pointing men toward the end times (Wendland and the Barthians). The British theologians put human beings in charge of history through the exercise of free will. As Oldham said, the real stuff of history was the choices people made in their freedom and responsibility. Knight agreed: "History represents the working out and interest and values of men in the events of the choices which they make under the controlling hand of God. . . . He is not going to compel them in any particular direction."[148]

William Temple often compared history to a game of chess between God and mankind: God knew who the ultimate winner of the match would be but not the sequence of moves; these choices were left to the decision of man. Not all accepted this denial of God's foreknowledge of human history. But even for those who did not, such as Edwyn Bevan, history was still man's domain as much as God's. Bevan explained: "History is the total sequence of human lives on this planet with their experiences and their voluntary choices; the situation which each of us finds, when he comes as an individual into the world, is due to the innumerable voluntary choices made by men and women in the past, and we, by our voluntary choices each in our own measure, determine what the next moment in history will be." [149]

The British also allowed for the possibility of progress through human effort. Bevan argued that progress in history had been made by the exercise of the Christian conscience. Knight criticized continental theology for denying progress in morality. [150] Professor Wood of Birmingham stated that "progress is both possible and actual in history," particularly in Western civilization. Both Clement Webb and Alfred Garvie posited an evolutionary ascent of man, an improvement in morality and religion from barbarous to civilized stages in Western history. [151]

A British social ethic arose from this view of man, nature, and history which held Christians responsible for society and gave them hope that progress could be achieved. British churchmen taught that the Christian faith should be integrated into all areas of life. They flatly rejected the German dichotomy between church and society, between things spiritual and things temporal. J.S. Boys-Smith of Cambridge, a modernist Anglican theologian, blamed both Barthian and Nazi theologians for their moral irresponsibility. Maurice Reckitt similarly blamed the Germans, Barth included, for concerning themselves only with the soul and failing to make the gospel relevant to contemporary life. [152] Demant faulted Luther for making religion so purely internal that human relations and social life had no place in the scheme of redemption. [153] Instead of this false dualism, there must be integration of Christianity within society. Garvie stressed that since God is in all, through all, his sovereignty could not be confined to one realm: "Industry, culture and morality come within the range of the grace of Christ to be judged, cleansed and hallowed." Temple argued that the love of

God could not be a private affair between a man and his maker. The love of God was inseparable from the love of man. According to Edwyn Bevan, Christianity lost its secret strength when it became isolated from other spheres of life: "Most British thinkers would hold that while these spheres have a relative independence which must be recognised, they are at the same time continually subject to criticism from the Christian understanding of life."[154]

For these British spokesmen a Christian standard existed that could and indeed must judge all aspects of society. The church might judge institutions, Bevan explained, as to whether they serve good or evil. The standard for human personal relations, according to Henry Farmer, was Christ's divine love. The Christian had the mind of Christ in all his dealings with the world. Such Christian values, Farmer continued, made the Christian able to evaluate situations with more objective criteria than momentary impressions. Christianity gave meaning to reality. History might not be explained or accepted as God's will, but it acquired meanings of right and wrong.[155] Maurice Reckitt argued that the church must offer the world an interpretation of what was happening in it, a Christian sociology consonant with the needs of the age. Oldham agreed that the church must answer questions about the purpose and meaning of life, instructing man how to escape from the blind forces of reality.[156] This ability to establish purpose and meaning was religion's gift to society. Without it, disaster would result.

The British blamed the rise of totalitarianism on the failure of Christianity to perform these functions. Oldham came to this realization in the early 1930s, and it brought him into the Life and Work movement. Demant explained that when the church failed to proclaim the ends and purposes of life and society, secularization triumphed. He blamed humanism and liberalism for causing people to look at human life as an end in itself, at man as something absolute, sovereign in a world cut off from God.[157] Totalitarianism was a desperate attempt to correct this problem, to give direction and purpose to the functional orders of society. The totalitarian system, he said, at least perceived a truth that humanism did not, that humanity was not the law or ends of life. According to Demant, all the totalitarian regimes made their claims on society in the name of some purpose or goal that transcended the individual person, be it proletarian Communism or nation, blood, and race. The rise of totalitarianism simply meant that the church had not done its job in ordering man's life toward an absolute goal.[158] As Maurice Reckitt said: "The totalitarian states of to-day are the revenge of civilisation for the failure of skepticism to give man courage and the failure of the Faith to give him understanding," an indictment against the church "for failure to accept responsibility for the soul of civilisation." The German church, according to Reckitt and Demant, bore the most blame for its preoccupation with the spiritual state of man and not his whole being. Demant blamed Luther for this subjective, interior religion. Barth's preoccupation with transcendence had not helped, in Reckitt's view.[159] These were not just the ideas of the Anglo-Catholics. Oldham and Knight said virtually the same thing at the Paris and Schloss Hemmen conferences. The Scottish churchman John Baillie wished that Demant's paper expressing these views could be translated into German, because it so well illustrated British opinion on this subject.[160]

In order to perform its duties of interpreting reality and judging society according to Christian values, the church must be a free and independent entity. Garvie claimed that the church must have absolute independence from the state in order to exercise God's authority. The Church of England had asserted this autonomy only in the late nineteenth century, Demant argued. Before then the church had served the state. The Oxford movement had challenged this, lamenting that the supernatural authority of the church over the state had been forfeited since the Reformation. In the 1920s, argued Demant, with the General Strike and the Archbishops' Report on Industry, the church had begun to gain back this autonomy.[161] Archbishop Temple agreed. The church did not serve the state, but the state must serve God: "It is the duty of Westminster to obey God, and it is the duty of Lambeth to remind Westminster of that fact." John Baillie postulated a kinship between Christianity and democracy, for democracy was government by free discussion in which the church could make its contribution.[162]

Thus the British leaders gave churches the right and duty to criticize the state and to prescribe limits of obedience to political authority. Garvie explained that the Christian conscience could and should lead to remonstrance and even, at appropriate times, to resistance. The state should respect conscientious objection (though he handily disallowed such rights to Mormon polygamists or Hindu widow-burners whose practices "the accepted moral stan-

dards condemn").[163] Archbishop Temple wrote that national loyalty could not be absolute, because the state was not a pure
transmitter of the will of God. Only the Word and Christ deserved
such absolute obedience: "The Christian disciple and the Christian church, to whom that Word is entrusted, must therefore
appraise the action of his state in the light of his knowledge of the
will of God as disclosed in Christ"; the Christian is "under solemn
obligation to resist the state if, and so far as, he believes himself to
have a clear leading from God to do so." But this disobedience was
not to be merely passive disobedience, such as the Confessing
Christians advocated in Germany. For Temple, revolutionary action was sometimes necessary: "The stage may be reached in any
social development where the evil is so firmly fixed and so pervasive
that response to any kind of moral ideal is become impossible. . . .
In the body politic as in the physiological organism disease may go
so far that hope lies no longer in the physician's drug but only in the
surgeon's knife."[164] J.P.R. Maud, dean of University College, Oxford, agreed with Temple. The church, he said, must contribute
toward the improvement "and if necessary the revolutionizing of
the present economic and political system." Even the diplomatic
Oldham rejected passive disobedience as inadequate once evil had
infected the orders of society. Instead "war must be waged against it
there."[165]

The British social ethic meant changing the world, not accepting it and waiting for the end times. Again, this call for change was
not as idealistic as before. No one any longer proclaimed that the
Kingdom of God would soon be an earthly reality. Temple instructed Christians to pray for the coming of the Kingdom even
though they knew it could not be fulfilled on earth. Edwyn Bevan
also expected no progressive approximation of the Kingdom of
God; it lay in another world. Even Anglo-Catholics such as
Maurice Reckitt warned against confusing secular utopianism or
any social order with the Kingdom of God.[166] But that was no
cause for despair or quietism. Even though the Kingdom was not of
this world, Bevan argued, one should still work and hope that
things would get better. There were no assurances that conditions
would improve, but the affair was not doomed before the start. For
Archbishop Temple, the very fact of a fallen, sinful world was what
gave the church its social mission.[167]

Despite this somewhat jaded view of future possibilities, the

British considered Christian social action imperative. Even with the renewed emphasis on theology in the Oxford preparations, the British churchmen were almost antiintellectual in their call for action over dogma. To Oldham the Christian message of hope was unconvincing when the gulf between doctrine and life, between thought and action, was too large. The dogmatic meaning of the gospel was unknown unless action proclaimed it. Philosophers sought to understand the world; the business of Christians was to change it.[168] The British possessed an expectation that meaningful change could take place. The Germans had denied the possibility of a Christian society. Emil Brunner wrote in an Oxford paper that the very words "Christian" and "Civilisation" were paradoxical. J.S. Boys-Smith of Oxford wrote in contrast: "To me a *Christian Civilisation* is not a paradox or an impossibility, however remote it may be as an actuality." R.H. Tawney argued in favor of a distinctively Christian way of life to be brought about by examining, teaching, and applying Christian traditions.[169]

The church must proclaim these values and seek to change society accordingly. Of course, the British made the usual qualfications. They emphasized that the churches should attempt to pronounce not on technical matters but only on the broader goals. Thomas Jessop, professor of philosophy at University College, Hull, repeated a standard Ritschlian argument: religion dealt with questions of value, not fact; with the ends, not the means.[170] Oldham's friend Henry Clay of the Bank of England agreed. As a man of business, he welcomed church involvement in establishing and clarifying moral principles applicable to eonomic problems. But the church should leave it to the experts to devise the ways and means to meet those Christian goals. He used an analogy: "In the boxing ring it is possible for the rulers of the sport to rule out objectionable methods and practices . . . without taking upon themselves the responsibility of directing the parties to a match where they should place their blows or even how they should train."[171] Others stipulated that the church could identify with no political party or with any fixed political or social program.[172] But that did not mean absolute political neutrality. As H.G. Wood said, some political, economic, and social policies and forms were decidedly more Christian than others. Baillie glibly identified Christianity with democracy.[173] The Christian must "be prepared to take sides and participate in political action," advised J.P.R. Maud. The church should determine its attitudes to political parties based on the Christian view of the duties and rights of man.[174]

When the British finally got around to the subject of economics, this kind of reasoning led them again to denounce particular evils in the capitalist economy. They condemned as un-Christian the continued growth of monopolies, economic nationalism, and the growing insecurity brought about by industrial fluctuations and high unemployment.[175] Tawney explained that capitalist virtues were actually Christian vices—particularly the emphasis on material riches, the appeal to acquisitive appetites, the idealization of property, and the worship of power. Malcolm Spencer of the Christian Social Council continued the assault on monetary policy, underconsumption, and inadequate purchasing power that the council had begun earlier in the 1930s.[176] Others condemned class inequalities as un-Christian. For Tawney, human dignity and the Christian view of the brotherhood of mankind made class divisions intolerable. Social systems should discriminate among people on the basis of need rather than of such externals as class, sex, or income. J.P.R. Maud of Oxford and Ernest Barker, an Anglican political scientist at Cambridge, agreed that the inequalities of modern society were in conflict with the Christian life.[177]

The solutions offered to the problems of capitalism foreshadowed the coming welfare state. Indeed, they trespassed on the area of technical means and partisan politics. After insisting that the church could not describe the technical changes necessary for moral life, Ernest Barker called for legislation to regulate work and bring major industries and other large-scale business concerns under public control. Naturally, Tawney agreed, calling for higher taxation and inheritance duties and for state control of monopolies and large companies as the only way to end the shocking disparities of income, environment, health, and education in Great Britain.[178] Despite his statement that the church could not declare actual measures to be taken, Malcolm Spencer recommended redistributing purchasing power by raising pensions, restricting savings, developing public works, and expanding education. Moreover, the responsibility for monetary control should be moved from the hands of bankers to political authorities.[179]

By 1937 a significant number of British church leaders were advocating the partial socialism that would follow within a decade. Even Oldham said in 1934: "I do not feel sure . . . that a Christian, impelled by his own distinctive motive, might not under modern conditions be a socialist, though the motive would be radically different from that of most socialists." [180] These churchmen were, of course, far from Communism. Tawney still allowed for small properties to remain in private hands. Archbishop William Temple, who supported some collective ownership and state planning, believed that each citizen should own some property.[181] But their plans for social reform indicated that they were serious about the Christian's moral responsibility in society. Moreover, they were prophets of things to come.

Although by the mid-1930s the British had ceased to expect utopia, their social thought always pointed with hope toward the future. Their concepts of the state of nature and human will made mankind responsible for history, not at its mercy. Their view of Christian revelation through Christ, the Word, reason, and conscience gave humanity normative standards and goals toward which to work. In an age of economic uncertainty and growing political tension, their rhetoric still provided direction, purpose, and the confidence to keep going. Oldham said of the Christian witness: "In the midst of discouragement and despair, it is meant to shine forth as a beacon of hope." [182] Indeed it did for these British leaders.

6. CONCLUSION

IN an examination of the nature and dynamics of two very different social mentalities among Protestants, it probably comes as no surprise that British and German church leaders had different social outlooks. But what is startling perhaps is the extent to which they talked right past each other when confronted in the same arena with questions about human nature, society, and contemporary socioeconomic and political problems.

Geoff Eley, in his stimulating essay "The British Model and the German Road: Rethinking the Course of German History before 1914" (in Blackbourn and Eley, *The Peculiarities of German History*), argues that the ideas of liberal reformism were the British way to maintain social control, to preserve capitalism and middle-class hegemony before 1914. The German bourgeoisie, he says, simply took a different route, radical nationalism, to the same objective. My study could be used as some confirmation of Eley's interpretation. I would agree that when confronted with proletarian political and economic demands, the British bourgeoisie (here, the Protestants) tried to tame the beast, while their German counterparts wished to destroy him in head-to-head combat. On the other hand, my thesis is the very kind that Eley rejects. In his reductionist neo-Marxist analysis, Eley roots these two patterns of middle-class ideology in the structural conditions of production. I obviously take these ideas more seriously, as something more than mere epiphenomena. In any case, my study is less ambitious. I am not trying to explain with a theoretical model the origins of the different British and German social outlooks. I am not asking why there were differences so much as demonstrating how different mentalities operated to find meaning in the interwar situations and directed people toward appropriate social and political action.

With the socioeconomic problems of the 1920s and the depression of the early 1930s, these two interpretations and prescriptions corresponded to political developments in Britain and Germany. Theological differences were central to these varying perspectives. While the British viewed God as immanent and embodied in his human incarnation, Jesus, the Germans saw Him as otherworldly and incomprehensible. The British emphasized man as redeemed and therefore divine/human; the Germans saw man as hopelessly flawed and of a perverted nature. Where the British preferred to speak of man's ignorance, the Germans plainly spoke about sin. The British interpreted the Kingdom of God as belonging to this world; they hoped the divine and the temporal would be merged in a perfect synthesis. The Germans saw an irrevocable gulf between the spiritual and physical worlds, a historical dualism that expected the synthesis, the Kingdom of God, to come only in the end times.

These contrasting theologies encouraged very different social analyses and commentaries. The British did not hesitate to analyze the contemporary social, political, and economic situation from an explicitly Christian perspective. They described the immoral aspects of the capitalist economy, its accompanying social system, and the international political order, and, moreover, they made explicit suggestions for changes. They surrounded these specific analyses and recommendations with a host of optimistic platitudes calling for brotherhood, fellowship, and the Kingdom of God to come on earth. The German analysis remained narrowly theological. Sin was the root of all human problems. In the German view, no Christian analysis could go beyond this one; no Christian solution existed except conversion. The only real social policy the Germans offered was continued charity work to soothe the symptoms of social ills but not to attack the disease that caused them.

The British participation in Life and Work revealed a vivid and discomforting perception of division and polarity in modern society, but the rhetoric of their social gospel reconciled these oppositions. Probably most troublesome was the opposition of class, where rhetoric calling for a just redistribution mediated between the extremes of wealth and poverty. Similarly, the British deplored modern society's distinction between things secular and things sacred. Their rhetoric sacralized the profane by making all human activities a province of Christianity. It made the sacred less otherworldly by stressing a humanlike God and the Kingdom on earth.

John Mozley stated clearly at the Anglo-German meeting of 1927 that "the sharp distinction between 'this-worldly' and 'other-worldly' cannot be maintained. This is the truth latent in the old 'liberal' Protestant position which interpreted the Kingdom as an immanent ethic."[1] Within Christianity, the British reports for Stockholm warned against both religious escapism and perverted apocalyptism, finding salvation on this earth.[2] In politics and economics the choice seemed to be between modern mass movements such as Bolshevism and nineteenth-century-style capitalist individualism. The reconciliation was the call for collective responsibility with respect for the integrity of the human personality. During the depression years of the early 1930s, the British churchmen increasingly pointed toward a Keynesian planned economy, in many ways a merger of capitalism and socialism; the hoped-for result would be a controlled capitalism safe for property and individuals but cleansed of flagrant abuses against human dignity.

The rhetoric and its extensive use of symbols functioned to deny the perceived oppositions.[3] The concepts of family and the Kingdom of God and terms such as brotherhood and responsibility all served continually to deny the reality of social inequality and class conflict and to inspire people with hope for a better world. The British church leaders passed through the 1920s and early 1930s without despair or intellectual withdrawal into what they called "false otherworldliness," a veiled reference to Barthianism. By defining the problems of society, explaining them, and proclaiming solutions for them, the British managed to preserve their optimism. Their activist rhetoric may have produced little action, few tangible results for the working classes, but it undoubtedly served as an effective placebo for those who absorbed these views. It is historically important that British leaders *thought* they had solutions for the problems, whether these solutions were realistic or not. A sense of a moderate solution was precisely what the Germans seemed to lack. This British confidence would discourage any radical solution and point toward the gradual reform with which the nation limped through the difficult interwar years.

The German churchmen, though keenly aware of social and political difficulties, particularly the estrangement of the classes and the outcome of the postwar settlement, offered little hope for the resolution of these problems. Instead of denying oppositions with the rhetoric and symbolism of the social gospel, the Germans perpetuated an opposition with their Lutheran dualism of the two kingdoms. They offered no hope in this world but only in an afterlife. Unlike the British, who blamed the system for the problems of society, the Germans blamed the nature of man. A system can be repaired, but what can be done about human nature? While the British disclaimed the immutability of natural laws of society and economics in the views of Adam Smith or Thomas Malthus, the Germans emphasized that the temporal realm followed its own laws with which the church must not tamper. After their denial of the legitimacy of socialism or Weimar liberalism, their delegation of society's problems to the state, to historical forces, only meant a green light for emerging fascist solutions.

Like the British, the Germans were aware of the problems, but they had no sense of a religious solution. German churchmen, apart from a small group of liberals, faced the problems of modern society without a mythic or symbolic system to defuse the alarming oppositions of middle class versus proletariat, of Christianity versus atheism, of capitalism versus communism. For the British, Christian brotherhood denied the opposition of class; the Germans looked to the nation, the *Volk,* to do so. German Protestantism did not attempt to resolve the problems of a chaotic world.

Consequently, while British Protestants remained complacent and confident, German churchmen were left suspicious, fearful, and somewhat desperate when faced with social conflict and economic crisis. The contrast between the two attitudes was evident in a survey carried out by the Social Institute of Life and Work in 1928-29. In 1928 Adolf Keller distributed a questionnaire concerning social attitudes to informants (mostly clergy) in the Protestant churches of Europe and America. The survey revealed that while the British Protestants of the late 1920s were optimistic about class relations, German Protestants were fearful and upset with the social milieu in which they lived. In Germany, Keller concluded, "Marxism has become the religion of the working classes, and its famous book, *Das Kapital,* takes the place of the Bible." In Britain the response was different:

> There is no hostility in this country between Church and Labour; of course, there are all kinds of criticism, but not that antagonism or that hostility which is characteristic of the organized Socialist-Labour on the Continent. Whilst Continental organized Labour has a strong

interest in the philosophy and theory of the movement, such as Karl
Marx has given it, British Labour is much nearer to the realities of life
than to philosophical or social theories. It does not believe to the
same extent in class struggle, or in class war, but is ready to discuss the
possibilities of co-operation with Capital. It has not lost contact with
religion or with the Church to the same extent as Continental Labour.[4]

Of course, these profoundly different perceptions were partly
rooted in historical fact. Although the British Labour Party had no
explicit religious policy, it was not anti-Christian. Historically, it
had close ties with Nonconformists; many party leaders such as
Ramsay MacDonald were practicing Christians. The German SPD,
on the other hand, did express anti-Christian tendencies and maintained a vaguely Marxist orientation throughout the 1920s. The
differences between the Labour Party and the SPD were real and
significant. However, the results of the questionnaire revealed basic,
important differences in the way British and German Protestants
perceived the working classes in the late 1920s. German fear and
distrust contrasted sharply with British optimism, even though this
optimism was perhaps naive.

When the Great Depression arrived, British Protestant leaders
were in a position to throw into gear their liberal social gospel,
explaining the crisis in Christian terms and prescribing specific
remedies to alleviate social and economic distress. Malcolm Muggeridge said of Britain in the 1930s, "Denunciations of slums from
the pulpit have been more common than denunciations of sins."[5]
German Protestant leaders had no such explanation or solution to
offer. Despairing, they were intellectually prepared only to turn
over the matter to secular politics, with the disastrous consequences that are so well known to all students of history.

After Hitler's accession to power in 1933, the social messages
of German and British churchmen remained on different wave-
lengths. The British continued their rhetoric of social activism,
responsibility, and reform; although their idealism was somewhat
subdued and their calls for reform no longer so utopian, they still
saw moral progress in society as possible. To establish a Christian
society, British spokesmen outlined broad socioeconomic goals
and specific changes needed to achieve them, all of which encouraged reform and a greater state role in the economic recovery after

1933. In many ways their plans foreshadowed the coming welfare state. Perhaps they lent some moral legitimacy to socialist policies. The social message for German churchmen representing the DEK, on the other hand, became one of virtual obedience to the state. In their view of Luther's two kingdoms and the theology of the orders, it was right and natural that the state, not the church, be responsible for such matters. Social ethics thus meant supporting the state as it fulfilled its divinely given duty.

In fact, the German and British formulas for the relationship of church to state were exactly opposite. The British called for the state (and the economy and society) to obey God's commands. The church was not bound to obey the state. For the German DEK spokesmen, the church must obey the state. The state was not bound by Christian concepts but operated according to its own rules. The British claimed that the church knows the will of God and reminds the state of God's commands. The state by no means transmitted the will of God. For the Germans, it was again the other way around. The state as an order of God and product of God's revelation in history was the transmitter of God's will. Two key terms used frequently in the rhetoric of the mid-1930s rightly show these different conceptions. The British leaders called for a "Christian civilization" in which Christianity would guide, influence, and provide norms and values for society and the nation.[6] The German churchmen, including some Confessing Christians such as Hanns Lilje and Walter Künneth, spoke constantly of a *Volkskirche* in which the church, instead of guiding the state toward Christian goals, expresses the will of the *Volk* and works for the good of the nation.

The Germans and British naturally differed, then, on the question of obedience. For the British leaders, Christian disobedience could be right and necessary. Even revolution might be necessary if political, economic, or social evils were so pervasive that reform became impossible. Spokesmen for the German national church did not even broach the subject of disobedience, assuming that the ideals of state and *Volkskirche* were the same. But even most Confessing Christians, who faced daily the conflict between the commands of the Nazi state and their own Christian consciences, allowed only passive disobedience as the proper Christian response. Such a tactic might work in British India or the United States, but it could hardly be effective in a totalitarian land with its Dachaus and

Buchenwalds. One might not expect German Protestants to proclaim a radical call for rebellion against Nazi rule. Questions of
physical survival were involved, as the fate of Dietrich Bonhoeffer
reminds us.[7] But statements by Wendland, Althaus, Dibelius,
Heckel, and the others presenting the DEK view were by no means
forced apologies given in the face of death. These theologians had
been saying the same thing before Hitler took power. None of those
who wrote articles for the Oxford conference were forced to participate. Had they disagreed with the official policy they could have
said nothing. Instead, they preached a message of support and
obedience, with Confessing Christians confining their passive disobedience to occasions of state interference in church affairs. Of all
those writing on behalf of the Confessing Church, only Bonhoeffer's deputy Jürgen Winterhager articulated a foundation for Christian resistance, though he made no explicit call for such action.
One other German, Paul Tillich, preached church resistance to
political forces, but he did so from his chair at New York's Union
Theological Seminary, the bastion of Anglo-Saxon liberalism on
the safe side of the Atlantic.

   One of the more original conclusions of this study is the finding
of similar theological mentalities and assumptions of both the DEK
churchmen and the Confessing Christians represented in the Life
and Work sample. The extensive literature on the *Kirchenkampf*
presents just the other picture. The standard portrayal of two
adversarial groups, heroes and villains, probably reflects the tremendous literary productivity of those involved in the struggle and
the domination by former Confessing Christians in the church
administration and theological faculties of postwar Germany. Only
recently have historians taken a more skeptical look at the history
of the Confessing Church.[8] The personalities in my study of German ideas in the 1930s did not fit neatly into the categories posited
by the literature on the church struggle. Those Confessing Christians and DEK representatives involved in the Life and Work movement were neither so heroic nor so villainous but they actually had
much in common.

   Both Confessing Christians and national church spokesmen
had been preaching the same message before 1933, a nationalistic,
antisocialistic, antiliberal message that was conducive to the victory of Nazism regardless of the dissent some would later display.
The Confessing Christian Friedrich Karrenberg had helped shape

this conservative German view as it emerged in depression-era meetings of Life and Work. It was Ernst Wolf, who later lost his university chair because of his activity in the Confessing Church, who in the early 1930s presented the view of God's will operating in history and man's call to obey the historically emerging forms. The two most famous Confessing Church leaders, Martin Niemöller and Otto Dibelius, were well known for their nationalistic, *völkisch* sympathies. Dibelius, who had condemned the Stockholm conference for its easy liberalism, in a radio broadcast in April 1933 defended the Jewish boycott as necessary to curtail Jewish influence on public life in Germany.[9] Martin Niemöller voted National Socialist in the 1933 election and, when the war began in 1939, volunteered for service from his Dachau cell. Niemöller's Emergency League, which really began the organized Protestant resistance to Hitler's church policy, only proposed to aid "Christians" of Jewish descent who fell victim to Nazi anti-Semitism. Walter Künneth summed up Protestant views in his famous essay in 1933, "The Jewish Problem and the Church," in which he argued that the state should distinguish between Christian Jews and those who remained a culturally alien body within the Christian German nation. For Künneth, the only Jewish "problem" was the treatment of Christian Jews. He did not concern himself with the Jews "in their exclusive world of the synagogues." [10]

On the other hand, many of the church officials who so vociferously presented the nationalistic anti-Versailles rhetoric of the 1920s ended up as victims of the *Gleichschaltung* of 1933. Hermann Kapler was all but forced out of office when Nazi *Deutsche Christen* made his job impossible in the summer of 1933. The Munich banker Baron Wilhelm von Pechmann, who was president of the *Kirchentag* from 1921 to 1930 and leader of the group who authored the chauvinistic *Vaterländische Kundgebung* of 1927, led the debate in the *Kirchenausschuß* against Nazi interference in church affairs and spoke against Hitler's anti-Semitic policies. He even resigned from the *Kirchenausschuß* and withdrew his membership from the new DEK in protest.[11] Even if German church leaders such as Kapler and von Pechmann shared many of Hitler's goals before 1933, that did not mean they automatically became good Nazis, irrevocably loyal to Hitler. Nonetheless, as influential molders of public opinion, they had done their part to encourage the success of radical nationalism.

Like these victims and opponents of Hitler's church policies, those on the side of the national church displayed a certain ambivalence toward the new regime. They shared the nationalistic mentality that would see Hitler's foreign, economic, and social policies as national renewal. But several DEK spokesmen too had second thoughts about Nazi church policies. In the summer of 1933 Friedrich Brunstäd, Heinz-Dietrich Wendland, and even Theodor Heckel cooperated with future Confessing Church leaders Martin Niemöller, Hanns Lilje, and Walther Künneth, to form the Young Reformation Movement, a group opposed to the politicking of Nazi *Deutsche Christen* in the church elections. Some historians see the Young Reformation Movement as the precursor to the Confessing Church.[12] Several Germans who wrote on behalf of the DEK had some association with the Confessing Church. Hermann Sasse, for example, was on the theology commission that helped Karl Barth draft the famous Barmen Confession before he, as a strict Lutheran confessionalist, grew disenchanted with the movement because of its United and Reformed tendencies. Paul Althaus, the former *Deutsche Christen* member and a chief proponent of the *völkisch* theology of the orders, attended the Confessing Church synod at Berlin-Dahlem in October 1934 out of support for his bishop, Bishop Hans Meiser of Bavaria, who was under house arrest because of Confessing Church activities. Heinz-Dietrich Wendland, the coordinator of DEK preparations for Oxford, became involved with the Confessing Church in 1936 and later in the 1930s was denounced by three of his Kiel University colleagues for "upsetting the ideological unity of the faculty."[13] Interestingly, of all those Germans directly involved in the Life and Work movement, the two who were later active in the German resistance were not Confessing Christians but employees of the DEK. Hans Schönfeld in Geneva and Eugen Gerstenmaier, Bishop Heckel's assistant in Berlin, were involved with the Kreisau circle of conspirators in Berlin. Gerstenmaier was instrumental in involving Lt. Col. Klaus von Stauffenberg in the plot against Hitler, which very nearly succeeded in July 1944, and he was one of the few in the inner circle of conspirators who did not lose his life following the plot's failure.[14]

Therefore, most German participants in the Life and Work movement, both Confessing Church and DEK, shared anti-Communist and antiliberal views, a theological pessimism, and a willingness to turn over responsibility for society to the state which only encouraged a Nazi solution. After 1933 they preached that the state should be obeyed in worldly matters. They differed mainly on the degree to which they opposed Hitler's intervention in church affairs.

Yes, there were theological differences between the DEK and the Confessing Christians. Even the Confessing Church was divided theologically. The conservative wing with Lilje and Künneth's Lutheran Council shared the theological outlook of the national church. But even the Barthian Confessing Christians shared with their opposition a grim assessment of man and the possibilities for human society. Like Nazism, Barthian theology was, above all, a revolution against liberalism, humanism, and the post-Enlightenment world view. The British, remember, were reluctant to identify with the Confessing Church because they could not stomach its Barthian theology. One British theologian, J.S. Boys-Smith, called Barthianism "theological fascism." The same original impetus was behind both sides in the German church struggle: a violent rejection of liberalism. For those who did not like Nazi policies, Barthianism was a theological alternative, but both shared similar conceptions of life, man, and God. Boys-Smith said of both the totalitarian state and its theological opposition: "I find the ground of my dislike substantially the *same* in each case. In both I seem to find a neglect, sometimes a contempt, of moral personality and the best aspect of human civilisation, human freedom, the worth of the individual, moral responsibility, reason seem to have little value for either . . . whether it is the state or God that wields this power and crushes these fine flowers of Christian humanity seems to me to make little difference; the spirit is the same." [15] There is a tendency to read the later Barth, with his increasingly vocal call for Christian political activism, into the earlier Barth who was still waging battle against the liberal social gospel. Despite the fact that Barthian theology became the theology of opposition after 1933, it was consonant with the cultural mentality that encouraged the acceptance of Nazism in the first place.

In *Theologians under Hitler*, Robert P. Ericksen studies three German theologians, Gerhard Kittel, Paul Althaus, and Emanuel Hirsch, who lent their support publicly to the Nazi regime. He argues that Christians in Germany looked to Hitler to end the destructive influences of modernism—secularism, moral ambiguity, pluralism—and to restore a traditional Christian, German sense of community. He explains how well-meaning, intelligent, educated Protestants could put their hopes in Hitler and the Nazi party to achieve a victory for "Christian" ideals. There is much truth in Ericksen's findings. An intellectual and cultural crisis was at hand in interwar Germany. Even many intellectuals who later dissented from Nazi policies such as Karl Barth and Paul Tillich, contributed to the culture of crisis.

Ericksen, however, concludes pessimistically that reason and Christianity are no protection against making disastrous political mistakes. He critiques the Western Christian and intellectual heritage for leading good men like Kittel, Althaus and Hirsch astray. After this devastating argument, Ericksen leaves the reader with only one guiding truth or moral: one must not depend on Christian theology, on reason, or on a knowledge of history as a guide to what is morally right. My conclusions are less pessimistic. Ericksen equates the German views of the 1920s and 1930s with "Christianity." He assumes that the "Christian" view is the interwar German view he describes: that is, that cultural, moral, and intellectual unity is necessary for the Christian community to exist. In other words the implication is that Christianity is inherently opposed to diversity, pluralism, and ultimately democracy. I argue that we should look at this German theology as a distinctive, historically conditioned pattern of Christian social thought. The British example and even Bonhoeffer in Germany, with his concept of "religionless Christianity," indicate that Christians did not inevitably wage war on the modern world. There could be other Christian ways to deal with change in the twentieth century. I do not presume to identify the "correct" Christian theology, to single out the German view as wrong and elevate the British view as right. My purpose is not to condemn or to applaud but to understand.

The German and British church leaders involved in the Life and Work movement, 1925-37, were part of the intellectual struggle in the twentieth century to find meaning and resolution for the painful conditions of contemporary society. British and German church leaders resolved the problems of this world in strikingly different ways. The British social gospel, like a placebo, maintained hope and confidence that the sickness could be healed. The German solution was a much more bitter pill. In this case the cure was worse than the pain.

NOTES

1. Introduction

1. See Colin Cross, *The Fascists in Britain* (London: Barrie and Rockliff, 1961); Robert Skidelsky, *Oswald Mosley* (New York: Holt, Rinehart and Winston, 1975); and Gerald D. Anderson, *Fascists, Communists and the National Government: Civil Liberties in Great Britain 1931-1937* (Columbia: University of Missouri Press, 1983).

2. See Barrington Moore, *Social Origins of Dictatorship and Democracy: Lord and Peasant in the Making of the Modern World* (Boston: Beacon Press, 1966), pp. 433-452; and Moore, *Injustice: The Social Bases of Obedience and Revolt* (White Plains, N.Y.: M.E. Sharpe, 1978), pp. 398-433.

3. David Blackbourn and Geoff Eley, *The Peculiarities of German History* (New York: Oxford University Press, 1984). This edition is a revised and expanded version of the authors' *Mythen deutscher Geschichtsschreibung: Die gescheiterte bürgerliche Revolution von 1848* (Frankfurt/M: Ullstein, 1980), which prompted a wide debate among historians and in the German press.

4. Charles S. Maier has demonstrated how the capitalist political economy was recast in the early Weimar Republic in a way that established economic power even more in private hands than before. He believes that the birth of a "new Europe" in 1918 is an overdrawn picture. See his *Recasting Bourgeois Europe: Stabilization in France, Germany and Italy in the Decade after World War I* (Princeton, N.J.: Princeton University Press, 1975).

5. For a full comparison see W.A. Lewis, *Economic Survey 1919-1937* (London: George Allen and Unwin, 1949).

6. Ibid., p. 44; and see Peter Kingsford, *The Hunger Marchers in Britain 1920-1939* (London: Lawrence and Wishart, 1982).

7. Some useful references for the history of interwar Britain and Germany include Charles Loch Mowat, *Britain between the Wars 1918-1940* (Chicago: University of Chicago Press, 1955); A.J.P. Taylor, *English History, 1914-1945* (Oxford: Oxford University Press, 1965); and Gordon Craig, *Germany 1866-1945* (New York: Oxford University Press, 1978).

8. The literature supporting this generalization is overwhelming. For just a sample see Owen Chadwick, *The Secularization of the European Mind*

in the Nineteenth Century (Cambridge: Cambridge University Press, 1975); K.S. Inglis, *Churches and the Working Classes in Victorian England* (London: Routledge and Kegan Paul, 1963); Jeffrey Cox, *The English Churches in a Secular Society: Lambeth 1870-1930* (New York: Oxford University Press, 1982), pp. 69-70; and Hugh McCleod, "The De-Christianization of the Working Class in Western Europe 1850-1900," *Social Compass* 27 (1980): 191-214.

9. See Richard F. Hamilton, *Who Voted for Hitler?* (Princeton, N.J.: Princeton University Press, 1982); Michael H. Kater, *The Nazi Party: A Social Profile of Members and Leaders 1919-1945* (Cambridge, Mass.: Harvard University Press, 1983); and Thomas Childers, *The Nazi Voter: The Social Foundations of Fascism in Germany, 1919-1933* (Chapel Hill: University of North Carolina Press, 1983).

10. See Clifford Geertz, *The Interpretation of Cultures* (New York: Basic Books, 1973); and Peter L. Berger, *The Sacred Canopy: Elements of a Sociological Theory of Religion* (New York: Doubleday, 1969).

11. Geertz, *Interpretation of Cultures*, pp. 142-169.

12. See Max Weber, *The Sociology of Religion* (Boston: Beacon Press, 1963); and Johannes Faber, *Jamaa: A Charismatic Movement in Katanga* (Evanston, Ill.: Northwestern University Press, 1971.)

13. It is not my purpose to write a history of the Life and Work movement. For a fuller treatment of its institutional development see the relevant sections in David Gaines, *The World Council of Churches* (Peterborough, N.H.: Richard R. Smith, 1966); Charles MacFarland, *Steps toward the World Council: Origins of the Ecumenical Movement as Expressed in the Universal Christian Council for Life and Work* (New York: Fleming H. Revell, 1938); and Ruth Rouse and Stephen Neill, eds., *A History of the Ecumenical Movement 1517-1948*, vol. 1, 2d ed. (Philadelphia: Westminster Press, 1967).

2. The British and German Traditions

1. For an exhaustive presentation of the social conservatism of the Anglican Church see Richard Allen Soloway, *Prelates and People: Ecclesiastical Social Thought in England 1783-1852* (London: Routledge and Kegan Paul, 1969). Soloway's argument is not unique: see also Inglis, *Churches and the Working Classes;* and Alan Gilbert, *Religion and Society in Industrial England: Church, Chapel, and Social Change 1740-1914* (London: Longman, 1976).

2. Ford K. Brown lists hundreds of charitable and reform organizations in early nineteenth-century London; see his *Fathers of the Victorians* (Cambridge: Cambridge University Press, 1961), pp. 329-340. For an amusing caricature of the Evangelical conscience see Charles Dickens, *Bleak House*.

3. Inglis, *Churches and the Working Classes*, pp. 13, 80; Soloway, *Prelates and People*, pp. 435-438; and Malcolm Thomis, *The Town Labourer and the Industrial Revolution* (London: B.T. Batsford, 1974), pp. 170-171.

4. Donald O. Wagner, *The Church of England and Social Reform since 1854* (New York: Columbia University Press, 1930), p. 99; and Edward R. Norman, *Church and Society in England 1770-1970: A Historical Study* (Oxford: Clarendon Press, 1976), p. 131.

5. See Gareth Stedman Jones's penetrating study of philanthropy in *Outcast London: A Study in the Relationship between the Classes in Victorian Society* (Harmondsworth: Penguin Books, 1971), pp. 244-258.

6. Norman, *Church and Society*, p. 164; and Robert F. Wearmouth, *Methodism and the Struggle of the Working Classes 1850-1900* (Leicester: Edgar Backus, 1954), pp. 152-153.

7. In *Outcast London*, his insightful study of class relations in Victorian England, Gareth Stedman Jones argues that this strong humanitarian impulse was common to the middle and upper classes in general in the late nineteenth century in their attempt to ensure social stability and the maintenance of the existing order.

8. See Wearmouth, *Methodism*, p. 215; Norman, *Church and Society*, p. 127; and Peter d'A. Jones, *The Christian Socialist Revival 1877-1914: Religion, Class and Social Conscience in Late-Victorian England* (Princeton, N.J.: Princeton University Press, 1968), p. 6.

9. For a full account of this early Christian socialism see Jones, *Christian Socialist Revival;* and Maurice Reckitt, *From Maurice to Temple: A Century of the Social Movement in the Church of England* (London: Faber and Faber, 1947).

10. G. Kitson Clark also sees a threefold transition in Christian social attitudes in the nineteenth century, from the traditional attitudes of the *ancien régime* to laissez-faire charity to incipient collectivism. But he puts the transition points in 1832 and 1867, with the passage of the two reform bills. I see these changes as coming some twenty years later in each case. See his *Churchmen and the Condition of England 1832-1885: A Study in the Development of Social Ideas and Practice from the Old Regime to the Modern State* (London: Methuen, 1973).

11. For a discussion of British theology in the late nineteenth and early twentieth centuries see Thomas A. Langford, *In Search of Foundations: English Theology 1900-1920* (Nashville, Tenn.: Abingdon Press, 1969); and Arthur Michael Ramsay, *An Era in Anglican Theology from Gore to Temple: The Development of Anglican Theology between "Lux Mundi" and the Second World War 1889-1939* (New York: Scribner, 1960).

12. Ritschl's major interpreter to the English-speaking world was Alfred Garvie, a future leader of Life and Work in Great Britain. See Garvie, *The Ritschlian Theology: Critical and Constructive* (Edinburgh: T. and T. Clark, 1899).

13. Langford, *In Search of Foundations*, p. 219.

14. Ramsay, *Anglican Theology*, p. vii.

15. Norman, *Church and Society*, pp. 221-222, and Jones, *Christian Socialist Revival*, p. 217, make this argument in their perceptive studies. Roger Lloyd disagrees in *The Church of England in the Twentieth Century*, 2

vols. (London: Longmans, Green, 1946, 1950), 1:100. Lloyd's work, however, is more a polemic against modernism than a work of history.

16. Randall T. Davidson, ed., *The Five Lambeth Conferences 1867, 1878, 1888, 1897, and 1908* (London: S.P.C.K., 1920), pp. 140, 268-269.

17. Ibid., p. 140.

18. Ibid., p. 185.

19. *The Lambeth Conferences 1867-1948: The Reports of the 1920, 1930, and 1948 Conferences with Selected Resolutions from the Conferences of 1867, 1878, 1888, 1897 and 1908* (London: S.P.C.K., 1948), pp. 65, 70-71.

20. Langford, *In Search of Foundations*, p. 230.

21. See John Harvey, William Temple, et al., *Competition: A Study in Human Motive* (London: Macmillan, 1917).

22. Norman, *Church and Society*, pp. 231, 240, 255. The best biography of Temple is F.A. Iremonger, *William Temple, Archbishop of Canterbury: His Life and Letters* (London: Oxford University Press, 1948).

23. Stephen Koss, *Nonconformity in Modern British Politics* (Hamden, Conn.: Archon Books, 1975), pp. 8-10.

24. Cox, *The English Churches in a Secular Society*, pp. 129-176, 244-262. See also David W. Bebbington, *The Nonconformist Conscience: Chapel and Politics 1870-1914* (London: George Allen and Unwin, 1982).

25. See Michael Bentley's description in *The Liberal Mind 1914-1929* (Cambridge: Cambridge University Press, 1977), p. 2. The Schlegel sisters in E.M. Forster's *Howard's End* are a memorable fictional portrait of the fashionable liberal elites of Edwardian Britain. See also Peter Clarke's discussion of the "new" liberalism of the early twentieth century in *Liberals and Social Democrats* (Cambridge: Cambridge University Press, 1978).

26. Roger Lloyd and S.W. Sykes argue that the heyday of Christian liberalism in Britain was during the Asquith years preceding World War I. See Lloyd, *Church of England*, 2:29; and Sykes, "Theology," in C.B. Cox and A.E. Dyson, eds., *The Twentieth Century Mind: History, Ideas, and Literature in Britain*, 3 vols. (London: Oxford University Press, 1972), 2:146-147. David Bebbington puts an end to the liberal conscience among Nonconformists in 1910; see *The Nonconformist Conscience*, p. 160.

27. A similar revival in liberalism and the social gospel occurred in America after the war. See Robert Moats Miller, *American Protestantism and Social Issues 1919-1934* (Chapel Hill: University of North Carolina Press, 1958); and Paul H. Carter, *The Decline and Revival of the Social Gospel: Social and Political Liberalism in American Protestant Churches* (Ithaca, N.Y.: Cornell University Press, 1954).

28. Alec Vidler, *The Church in an Age of Revolution: 1789 to the Present Day* (Harmondsworth: Penguin Books, 1961), p. 200; and Bentley, *The Liberal Mind*, p. 165.

29. G.K.A. Bell, *Randall Davidson, Archbishop of Canterbury*, 2 vols. (New York: Oxford University Press, 1935), 2:951.

30. United Kingdom, *Parliamentary Debates* (Lords), 5th ser., vol. 64 (1926): 49-50; and Bell, *Randall Davidson*, 2:1306-1311.

31. John Oliver, *The Church and the Social Order* (London: A.R. Mobray, 1969), pp. 84-92.

32. For Tawney's life and background, see Ross Terrill, *R.H. Tawney and His Times: Socialism as Fellowship* (Cambridge, Mass.: Harvard University Press, 1973).

33. R.H. Tawney, *The Acquisitive Society* (New York: Harcourt, Brace, 1920); and Tawney, *Religion and the Rise of Capitalism* (1926; Harmondsworth: Penguin Books, 1975).

34. Gerald Studdert-Kennedy, *Dog-Collar Democracy: The Industrial Christian Fellowship 1919-1929* (London: Macmillan, 1982), pp. 136, 144.

35. Ibid., pp. 40, 75, 140, 165-166.

36. See G.D.H. Cole, *Guild Socialism: A Plan for Economic Democracy* (New York: Frederick A. Stokes, 1920).

37. See Oliver, *The Church and the Social Order*, pp. 118-126; and Norman, *Church and Society*, pp. 319-321.

38. Norman, *Church and Society*, pp. 290, 306-307.

39. See his biography, Owen Chadwick, *Hensley Henson: A Study in the Friction between Church and State* (Oxford: Oxford University Press, 1983), pp. 163-164; and Oliver, *The Church and the Social Order*, p. 74.

40. Norman, *Church and Society*, pp. 290-292; and Oliver, *The Church and the Social Order*, pp. 66-74. The *Times* (London) had a special correspondent at Copec whose favorable daily reports were published 7-14 April 1924.

41. Two classic works on Lutheran social teachings are H. Richard Niebuhr, *Christ and Culture* (New York: Harper and Row, 1951); and Ernst Troeltsch, *The Social Teachings of the Christian Churches*, 2 vols., trans. Olive Wyon (London: George Allen and Unwin, 1931). For additional background on Lutheran social theology, see William O. Shanahan, *German Protestants Face the Social Question: The Conservative Phase 1815-1871* (South Bend, Ind., Notre Dame University Press, 1954); and Paul Althaus, *The Ethics of Martin Luther*, trans. Robert C. Schultz (Philadelphia: Fortress Press, 1972).

42. For an explanation of the territorialism of the German churches see Henry Drummond, *German Protestantism since Luther* (London: Epworth Press, 1951), pp. 173-183. The few exceptions to this general pattern were a few Calvinist enclaves and the more autonomous churches of Baden and Württemburg.

43. See the manifesto of the Inner Mission in Johann Wichern, ed., *Die Mission der deutschen evangelischen Kirche: Eine Denkschrift an die deutsche Nation des Central-Ausschuss für die Innere Mission*, 3d ed. (Hamburg: Agentur des Rauhen Hauses, 1889), pp. 1-30. For an account of Wichern's anti-Communism see Günter Brakelmann, *Kirche und Sozialismus im 19. Jahrhundert: Die Analyse des Sozialismus und Kommunismus bei Johann Hinrich Wichern und bei Rudolf Todt* (Witten: Luther-Verlag, 1966), pp. 40-54; Hans-Volker Herntrich, *Im Feuer der Kritik: Johann Hinrich Wichern und der Sozialismus* (Hamburg: Agentur des Rauhen Hauses,

1969), pp. 79-97; and Karl Kupisch, *Das Jahrhundert des Sozialismus und die Kirche* (Berlin: Kathe Vogt Verlag, 1958), pp. 89-92.

44. Shanahan, *German Protestants Face the Social Question*, pp. 70-94, 236, 249; and John Groh, *Nineteenth-Century German Protestantism: The Church as Social Model* (Washington, D.C.: University Press of America, 1982), pp. 246-248, 266-269, 310-331.

45. Groh, *Nineteenth-Century German Protestantism*, p. 401.

46. Quoted in W.R. Ward, *Theology, Sociology and Politics: The German Protestant Social Conscience 1890-1933* (Bern: Peter Lang, 1979), p. 26. For a full account of Wichern's life and the Inner Mission see Richard Grunow, *Wichern-Ruf und Antwort* (Gütersloh: Rufer-Verlag, 1958); and Martin Gerhardt, *Ein Jahrhundert Innere Mission: Die Geschichte des Central-Ausschusses für die Innere Mission der Deutschen Evangelischen Kirche*, 2 vols. (Gütersloh: C. Bertelsmann, 1948).

47. See Margaret Bradfield, *City of Mercy: The Story of Bethel* (Bethel/Bielefeld: Verlagshandlung der Anstalt Bethel, 1964).

48. Shanahan, *German Protestants Face the Social Question*, pp. 170-176, 186-191, 220-221.

49. There are no satisfactory biographies of Stöcker in English. See Karl Kupisch, *Adolf Stöcker: Hofprediger und Volkstribun* (Berlin: Haude and Spenersche, 1970); Walter Frank, *Hofprediger Adolf Stoecker und die christlichsoziale Bewegung*, 2d ed. (Hamburg: Hanseatische Verlagsanstalt, 1935); Rudolf Todt, *Der radicale deutsche Sozialismus und die christliche Gesellschaft* (Wittenberg: E. Rust, 1877).

50. Johannes Rathje, *Die Welt des freien Protestantismus: Ein Beitrag zur deutsch-evangelischen Geistesgeschichte Dargestellt an Leben und Werk von Martin Rade* (Stuttgart: Ehrenfried Klotz Verlag, 1952), pp. 517-518.

51. Ward, *Theology, Sociology, and Politics*, p. 33.

52. See Agnes von Zahn-Harnack, *Adolf von Harnack* (Berlin: Hans Bott Verlag, 1936), pp. 156-172.

53. Note particularly his speech on the opening of the Reichstag in 1890, printed in Günter Brakelmann, ed., *Kirche, soziale Frage und Sozialismus: Kirchenleitungen und Synoden über soziale Frage und Sozialismus 1871-1914* (Gütersloh: Gerd Mohn, 1977), pp. 254-255.

54. The letter is printed in Brakelmann, *Kirche, soziale Frage und Sozialismus*, pp. 86-90.

55. For the history of the Evangelical Social Congress see Gottfried Kretschmar, *Der Evangelisch-Soziale Kongress: Der deutsche Protestantismus und die soziale Frage* (Stuttgart: Evangelisches Verlagswerke, 1972); and Ward, *Theology, Sociology, and Politics*, pp. 55-77.

56. Ward, *Theology, Sociology, and Politics*, p. 60.

57. For an account of the coalescence of the new German right at the end of the century see Geoff Eley, *Reshaping the German Right: Radical Nationalism and Political Change after Bismarck* (New Haven. Conn.: Yale University Press, 1980).

58. The text of the decree is printed in Karl Kupisch, ed., *Quellen zur Geschichtidees deutschen Protestantismus 1871-1945* (Göttingen: Mus-

terschmidt, 1960), pp. 85-88; for minutes of the debate on the *Oberkirch-enrat's* decree in the General Synod see Brakelmann, *Kirche, soziale Frage und Sozialismus,* pp. 193-216.

59. Kaiser Wilhelm, quoted in Groh, *Nineteenth-Century German Protestantism,* p. 507.

60. Kupisch, *Das Jahrhundert des Sozialismus und die Kirche,* p. 120; and Ward, *Theology, Sociology, and Politics,* p. 82. See also E.I. Kouri, *Der deutsche Protestantismus und die soziale Frage 1870-1919: Zur Sozialpolitik im Bildungsbürgertum* (New York: Walter de Gruyter, 1984), p. 170.

61. The best biography of Naumann is Theodor Heuss, *Friedrich Naumann: Der Mann, das Werk, die Zeit,* 3d ed. (Munich: Siebenstern, 1968). For his Christian social ideas see Karl Kupisch, "Friedrich Naumann und die evangelisch-soziale Bewegung" (Ph.D. diss., Friedrich Wilhelms University, Berlin, 1937).

62. The best general work on the fortunes of theological liberalism in Germany is Johannes Rathje's study of Martin Rade and his circle, *Die Welt des freien Protestantismus.*

63. Peter Gay argues persuasively that in culture—music, art, literature, theater and cinema, philosophy—the wild men of prewar Germany were the new establishment of the Weimar Republic. See his *Weimar Culture: Outsider as Insider* (New York: Harper and Row, 1968).

64. Ernst Christian Helmreich, *Religious Education in German Schools: An Historical Approach* (Cambridge, Mass.: Harvard University Press, 1959), pp. 105-106. See also Theo M. Breitsohl, "Die Kirchen- und Schulpolitik der Weimarer Parteien 1918-1919" (Ph.D. diss., Tübingen University, 1978).

65. J.R.C. Wright, *"Above Parties": The Political Attitudes of the German Protestant Church Leadership 1918-1933* (London: Oxford University Press, 1974), pp. 17-18.

66. See the excellent discussion of the constitutional changes concerning the church in Ernst Christian Helmreich, *The German Churches under Hitler: Background, Struggle, and Epilogue* (Detroit: Wayne State University Press, 1979), pp. 61-73; and Wright, *Above Parties,* pp. 17-28.

67. Wright, *Above Parties,* p. vi; other literature confirming this view includes Karl Kupisch, "Stromungen der Evangelischen Kirche in der Weimarer Republic," *Archiv für Sozialgeschichte* 11 (1971): 373-415; Karl Wilhelm Dahm, "German Protestantism and Politics," *Journal of Contemporary History* 3 (January 1968): 29-49; and E. Bramsted, "The Position of the Protestant Church in Germany 1871-1933, Part II: The Church during the Weimar Republic," *Journal of Religious History* 3 (1964): 61-79.

68. His speech is printed in Kupisch, *Quellen zur Geschichtides deutschen Protestantismus 1871-1945,* pp. 143-144.

69. Quoted in Wright, *Above Parties,* p. 51.

70. Dahm, "German Protestantism and Politics," p. 32.

71. *Allgemeine Evangelisch-Lutherische Kirchenzeitung* 58 (1925): 315.

72. For an account of Naumann's relationship to the DDP see Lothar Albertin, *Liberalismus und Demokratie am Anfang der Weimarer Republik: Eine vergleichende Analyse der Deutschen Demokratischen Partei und der Deutschen Volkspartei* (Düsseldorf: Droste Verlag, 1972), pp. 100-104, 243-248, 297-301.

73. S. William Halperin, *Germany Tried Democracy: A Political History of the Reich from 1918 to 1933* (Hamden, Conn.: Archon Books, 1946), p. 128; see also Lewis Hertzman, *DNVP: Right-Wing Opposition in the Weimar Republic 1918-1924* (Lincoln: University of Nebraska Press, 1963).

74. Daniel R. Borg, *The Old-Prussian Church and the Weimar Republic: A Study in Political Adjustment* (Hanover, N.H.: University Press of New England, 1984), pp. 79-80. The literature agrees that the *DNVP* was the party of the Protestant Churches. See Wright, *Above Parties*, pp. 49, 57; Dahm, "German Protestantism and Politics," p. 38; Kurt Nowak, *Evangelische Kirche und Weimarer Republik: Zum politischen Weg des deutschen Protestantismus zwischen 1918 und 1932* (Göttingen: Vandenhoeck und Ruprecht, 1981), pp. 101-105; Hertzman, *DNVP*, p. 45; and Gottfried Mehnert, *Evangelische Kirche und Politik 1917-1919: Die politischen Stromungen in deutschen Protestantism von der Julikrise 1917 bis zum Herbst 1919 (Düsseldorf: Droste Verlag, 1959)*, pp. 139-149.

75. Karl Wilhelm Dahm, *Pfarrer und Politik: Soziale Position und politische Mentalität des deutschen evangelischen Pfarrerstandes zwischen 1918 und 1933* (Cologne: Westdeutschen Verlag, 1965), p. 104.

76. Wright, *Above Parties*, pp. 32-50.

77. The literature about the German churches in the Weimar years does not agree on the extent to which the church accommodated the republic. While Nowak and Borg emphasize the anti-republicanism of the church leadership throughout the Weimar years, Wright and Motschmann argue that the church did accept the republic. See Claus Motschmann, *Evangelische Kirche und preussischer Staat in den Anfängen der Weimarer Republik: Möglichkeit und Grenzen ihrer Zusammenarbeit* (Lübeck: Matthiesen Verlag, 1969).

78. See Charles Edward Bailey, "Gott Mit Uns: Germany's Protestant Theologians in the First World War" (Ph.D. diss., University of Virginia, 1978); and Karl Hammer, *Deutsche Kriegstheologie 1870-1918* (Munich: Koesel-Verlag, 1971).

79. Wright, *Above Parties*, pp. 67, 70; and *Kirchliches Jahrbuch 50* (1923): 177. On the continuing discussion in the 1920s about the war and Versailles see Reinhard Gaede, "Kirche, Christen, Krieg und Frieden: Diskussion im deutschen Protestantismus während der Weimarer Zeit" Ph.D diss., University of Münster, 1972.

80. Theodor Strohm, *Kirche und demokratischen Sozialismus: Studien zur Theorie und Praxis politischer Kommunikation* (Munich: CHR Kaiser Verlag, 1968), pp. 55-56.

81. See Renate Breipohl, *Religioser Sozialismus und burgerliches Geschichtsbusstsein zur Zeit der Weimarer Republik* (Zurich: Theologischer

Verlag, 1971); and the frequent scathing editorials in the *Allgemeine Evangelisch-Lutherische Kirchenzeitung*.

82. See particularly *Mary Barton* and *North and South* by Elizabeth Gaskell; *Hard Times* by Charles Dickens; and Charles Kingsley's *Alton Locke*.

83. See Ferdinand Laun, *Soziales Christentum in England: Geschichte und Gedankenwelt der Copecbewegung* (Berlin: Furche Verlag, 1926).

84. Karl Kupisch, "Stromungen der Evangelischen Kirche," p. 376.

3. Protestant Social Thought, 1925-1929

1. "Minutes of the Meeting of the International Executive Committee, April 24, 1924 at Berlin," p. 3, Randall Davidson Papers, Subjects: Life and Work, Lambeth Palace Library, London. The eleven British reports prepared for the Stockholm conference are titled *The Nature of God and His Purpose for the World; Education; The Home; The Relation of the Sexes; Leisure; The Treatment of Crime; International Relations; Christianity and War; Industry and Property; Politics and Citizenship;* and *The Social Function of the Church.* Pamphlet File: Life and Work, World Council of Churches Library, Geneva, hereafter cited as WCC; each report is cited hereafter by title. The Life and Work archives in this library are hereafter cited as LW.

2. Davidson to Söderblom, 9 May 1924, Davidson Papers.

3. G.K.A. Bell, ed., *The Stockholm Conference 1925: The Official Report of the Universal Christian Conference on Life and Work held in Stockholm, 19-30 August 1925* (London: Oxford University Press, 1926), pp. 25-27.

4. Edward S. Woods and Frederick B. MacNutt, *Theodore, Bishop of Winchester, Pastor, Prophet, Pilgrim: A Memoir of Frank Theodore Woods 1874-1932* (London: S.P.C.K., 1933), pp. 88, 90, 112, 118-120.

5. See Garvie's autobiographical sketch in Eric Stange, ed., *Die Religionswissenschaft der Gegenwart in Selbstdarstellungen* (Leipzig: Meiner, 1928), pp. 62-113; and Garvie's memoirs, *Memories and Meanings of my Life* (London: George Allen and Unwin, 1938).

6. *Life and Work: Bulletin of the International Christian Social Institute* (Eng. ed.) no. 7 (April/May 1929): 15-16.

7. The correspondence of Söderblom and Siegmund-Schultze has been published in Friedrich Siegmund-Schultze, ed., *Nathan Söderblom: Briefe und Botschaften an einen deutschen Mitarbeiter* (Marburg: Oekumenischer Verlag Edel, 1966).

8. For an account of Siegmund-Schultze's career and involvement in pacifist causes see Adam Weyer, *Kirche im Arbeiterviertel* (Gütersloh: Gerd Mohn, 1971).

9. See *Die Eiche* 7 (December 1919): 238-243; 9 (January 1921): 106; and 11 (January/April 1923): 40.

10. See Horst Gründer, *Walter Simons, die Okumene und der Evan-*

gelisch-Soziale Kongress: Ein Beitrag zur Geschichte des politischen Protes-tantismus im 20. Jahrhundert (Soest: Mocker und Jahn, 1974), p. 144.

11. *Die Eiche* 9 (January 1921): 106; and *Kirchliches Jahrbuch* 53 (1926): 11.

12. Before April 1924, Söderblom traveled to Berlin to convince Hermann Kapler, vice-president of the *Kirchenausschuß*, of the need for official German participation. The Crown Prince of Sweden and Söderblom invited Kapler and Siegmund-Schultze to dine at the Swedish embassy. After dinner, while Siegmund-Schultze entertained the ladies and the ambassador, Söderblom took Kapler into another room, where he won him over to the cause. See Siegmund-Schultze, *Nathan Söderblom*, p. 78.

13. Wright, *Above Parties*, p. 69.

14. As vice-president of the *Kirchenausschuß*, Herman Kapler was in charge of ecumenical relations; he oversaw the production of the studies. Early drafts of these preparatory studies are located in Akten 17 of the Kirchliches Außenamt Papers in the Evangelisches Zentralarchiv, West Berlin. The four volumes printed as *Gutachten der deutschen Gruppe* (hereafter cited as *Gutachten*), in Pamphlet File: Life and Work, WWC.

15. *Die Eiche* 13 (1925): 66-67; and Siegmund-Schultze to President Moeller, 30 June 1925, Akten 18, Kirchliches Außenamt Papers.

16. Bengt Sundkler, *Nathan Söderblom: His Life and Work* (London: Lutterworth Press, 1968), p. 346.

17. *Die Eiche* 13 (1925): 350, 370.

18. Rathje, *Die Welt des freien Protestantismus*, p. 325.

19. Kapler to Söderblom, 11 July 1925, in Correspondence: Hermann Kapler, Söderblom Archives, University of Uppsala Library, Uppsala, Sweden. See also several letters from Kapler to delegates in early July, Akten 18, Kirchliches Außenamt Papers.

20. Letter from Auswärtiges Amt to Kirchenausschuß, 24 July 1925, Akten 19, Kirchliches Außenamt Papers; and Wright, *Above Parties*, p. 69.

21. *Church Times*, 4 September 1925, in Extracts de Journaux Anglais, Eugène Choisy Papers, Box 2, WCC; See also Henri Monnier, *Vers l'union des églises: La conférence universelle de Stockholm* (Paris: Librarie Fischbacher, 1926), p. 23.

22. *Die Eiche* 13 (1925): 364, 367, 370-372.

23. Siegmund-Schultze, a stubborn individualist, remained at odds with the German church establishment into the 1930s. He was on the Nazis' black list in 1933. When Hitler suppressed his journal, *Die Eiche*, that year, Siegmund-Schultze left Germany and resumed publication from Zurich. See Hermann Maas, "Friedrich Siegmund-Schultze und der Weltbund für Freundschaftsarbeit der Kirchen," in *Lebendige Ökumene: Festschrift für Friedrich Siegmund-Schultze zum 80. Geburtstag* (Witten: Luther-Verlag, 1965), pp. 39-40.

24. Sundkler, *Nathan Söderblom*, p. 340; and "Minutes of the Meeting of the Continuation Committee, September 2-5, 1928, Prague, Czecho-Slovakia," p. 22, in Pamphlet File, WCC.

25. See "Auszug aus der Verhandlungsniederschrift des Deutschen

Evangelischen Kirchenausschuß vom 24-25 Juni in Eisenach," pp. 4-5, Akten 20, Kirchliches Außenamt Papers.

26. Hans Schönfeld's doctoral thesis had been published in Germany: *Kritische Studien zum wirtschaftlichen Problem des Zwei und Dreischicten- systems in Hochofenbetrieben* (Jena: Gustav Fischer, 1926); see also Hans Lokies, "Hans Schönfeld: Erst Direktor der Studienabteilung," in Günter Gloede, ed., *Ökumenische Profile: Brückenbauer der Einer Kirche*, 2 vols. (Stuttgart: Evang. Missionsverlag, 1963), 2:369, 375.

27. *Kirchliches Jahrbuch* 53 (1926): 413.

28. Quoted in Nils Karlström, "Movements for International Friendship and Life and Work 1920-1925," in Rouse and Neill, *History of the Ec- umenical Movement*, p. 540.

29. It is remarkable that such a diverse commission could produce a common theological document. The commission included Quakers, Meth- odists, Welsh Presbyterians, a Jesuit priest, the Bishop of Oxford, the noted Cambridge theologian John Oman, and Evelyn Underhill, a famous mystic author. See Conference on Christian Politics, Economics, and Citizenship, *The Nature of God and His Purpose for the World* (London: Longmans, Green, 1924), pp. ix-xi.

30. *The Nature of God and His Purpose for the World*, p. 3. (This is the abridged report for Stockholm. Later citations to *The Nature of God* refer to this edition unless otherwise indicated).

31. Ibid., p. 9.

32. John Martin Creed, "Recent Tendencies in English Christology"; and A.E.J. Rawlinson, "Corpus Christi," both in G.K.A. Bell and Adolf Deissmann, eds., *Mysterium Christi: Christological Studies by British and German Theologians* (London: Longmans, Green, 1930), pp. 129, 225-244. For further Anglican views on the incarnation see Michael Ramsay, *Anglican Theology*, pp. 16-43.

33. *The Nature of God*, p. 3.

34. Edwyn Hoskins, "Jesus the Messiah," in Bell and Deissmann, *Mys- terium Christi*, pp. 69-71.

35. See *The Nature of God*, pp. 6-8.

36. Ibid., p. 8.

37. English liberals of the *Lux Mundi* school were more willing to apply the tools of historical criticism to the Old Testament than to the gospels of the New Testament. Charles Gore, the preeminent social theologian of his day, welcomed historical criticism but took his stand on the historical accuracy of the New Testament. See his *Doctrine of the Infallible Book* (New York: George H. Doran, 1925). English theologians who, like Albert Schweitzer, challenged the historical accuracy of the New Testament picture of Christ were not those involved in the church-social movement. For a discussion of historical criticism in British theology, see Michael Ramsay, *Anglican The- ology*, pp. 171-174; and Vidler, *The Church in an Age of Revolution*, pp. 190-200.

38. *Education* p. 4.

39. Bell, *Stockholm Conference*, p. 87.

40. *The Nature of God,* pp. 8, 11; and *Education,* p. 9.

41. *The Nature of God,* pp. 12, 14.

42. Edwyn G. Hoskins, "The Other-Worldly Kingdom of God in the New Testament," *Theology* 14 (1927): 251.

43. Bell, *Stockholm Conference,* pp. 123-129, 463-470; see also the speech by the Bishop of Plymouth, pp. 592-596, and *The Nature of God,* p. 5.

44. Conference of Christian Politics, Economics, and Citizenship, *The Nature of God and His Purpose for the World,* p. 24.

45. William Temple's quarterly review, the *Pilgrim,* devoted its entire October 1923 issue to the Kingdom and its implications for the world.

46. *Stockholm: International Review for the Social Activities of the Churches* 1 (1928): 2.

47. *The Nature of God,* p. 6.

48. See the speeches of W. Moore Ede and William Ashley in Bell, *Stockholm Conference,* pp. 123-129, 156-161.

49. Ibid., pp. 40-41.

50. *Stockholm* 1 (1928): 1.

51. *Theology* 14 (1927): 258-260.

52. Ibid., pp. 264-266.

53. Bell, *Stockholm Conference,* p. 226.

54. See the speech by J.A. Kempthorne, Bishop of Lichfield, in Bell, *Stockholm Conference,* pp. 415-418; and E.G. Selwyn, "The Kingdom of God and the Church," *Theology* 14 (May 1927): 286-288.

55. *Stockholm* 1 (1928): 354. Lidgett founded Bermondsey Settlement in London in 1891 and lived there until 1949. He was president of the National Council of Free Churches in 1906 and became the first president of the new United Methodist Church of Great Britain in 1932.

56. *The Nature of God,* p. 5.

57. Besides Tawney, the thirty-one-member commission included executives of steel and canning companies, a Yorkshire textile union leader, the warden of Oxford House settlement in London, an M.P. from Leeds, and various clergy and professors. See Conference on Christian Politics, Economics, and Citizenship, *Industry and Property* (London: Longmans, Green, 1924), pp. ix-xi.

58. *Industry and Property* (see note 1, this chapter; unless otherwise stated all citations are to the edition in WCC), p. 16.

59. Bell, *Stockholm Conference,* p. 124; and Alfred Garvie, "The Contrast of the Golden Rule and the Competitive Industrial System," *Stockholm* 2 (1929): 221-234.

60. Samuel E. Keeble, "Social Literature since the War 1918-1927," *Stockholm* 1 (1928): 289-294; and Garvie, "The Contrast," p. 227.

61. *Industry and Property,* p. 8.

62. Bell, *Stockholm Conference,* p. 127; *The Home,* p. 13; *The Treatment of Crime,* p. 6; and *Leisure,* p. 16.

63. *Industry and Property,* pp. 7-11.

64. Bell, *Stockholm Conference,* pp. 127, 160. In 1924 Ashley had served on the important parliamentary commission on industry and trade.

65. Garvie, "The Contrast," p. 234.

66. *Industry and Property*, p. 16.

67. *The Home*, p. 12; and *Leisure*, p. 6.

68. *Industry and Property*, p. 15.

69. Bell, *Stockholm Conference*, p. 87.

70. *The Social Function of the Church*, pp. 12-13.

71. A.J. Carlyle, "Social Progress in Great Britain during the Last Fifty Years," *Stockholm* 1 (1928): 266-272. Carlyle was a former member of the Christian Social Union and friend of Sidney and Beatrice Webb. His life's work was a six-volume *History of Medaieval Political Theory in the West* (Edinburgh: W. Blackwood, 1903-1936).

72. *Industry and Property*, pp. 9, 14; and *Leisure*, p. 14.

73. Garvie, "The Contrast," p. 233; and F.S. Livie-Noble, "Youth in Britain," *Stockholm* 2 (1929): 170-174.

74. Bell, *Stockholm Conference*, p. 235; and *The Home*, pp. 11-14.

75. *Politics and Citizenship*, p. 3.

76. *The Social Function of the Church*, p. 10; and *The Home*, p. 12.

77. Bell, *Stockholm Conference*, p. 416.

78. *Politics and Citizenship*, p. 9; and Ashley speech in Bell, *Stockholm Conference*, p. 157.

79. See *International Relations*, pp. 6-7; and speech by Harold Buxton in Bell, *Stockholm Conference*, p. 532.

80. *International Relations*, pp. 7-8.

81. Bell, *Stockholm Conference*, pp. 417-419, 466-467.

82. Ibid., pp. 532, 582-586, 592-596; and *International Relations*, p. 12.

83. George Thélin to Elie Gounelle, 24 May 1927, Box 3, Gounelle Papers, WWC.

84. *International Relations*, p. 13.

85. Willem Visser't Hooft, the youngest delegate to Stockholm, remembers this in his *Memoirs* (Philadelphia: Westminster Press, 1973), p. 26.

86. Heinrich Frick, "The Hidden Glory of Christ and its Coming Revelation"; and Gerhard Kittel, "The Jesus of History," both in *Mysterium Christi*, pp. 247, 49. For a further look at Kittel's theology and his relationship to the Nazi movement see Robert P. Ericksen, *Theologians under Hitler: Gerhard Kittel, Paul Althaus, and Emanuel Hirsch* (New Haven, Conn.: Yale University Press, 1985).

87. Jacob Schoell, "Der evangelische Berufsgedanke und das Arbeitsleben der Gegenwart," *Gutachten*, 2:36; and Magdelene von Tiling, "Die Beziehung der Geschlechter," *Gutachten*, 3:11, 13 (individual *Gutachten* articles, after initial citation, are cited by author).

88. Just, "Verbrechen und Strafe," *Gutachten*, 3:36.

89. Bell, *Stockholm Conference*, pp. 54, 72-73.

90. Ibid., pp. 54, 76, 186; Brunstäd was influential in the DNVP and worked closely with the Christian Social League, a descendant of Adolf Stöcker's social conservative party, which rivaled the Evangelical Social Congress. See Ward, *Theology, Sociology, and Politics*, pp. 226-228; and Eugen

Gerstenmaier's essay about Brunstäd in Friedrich Brunstäd, *Gesammelte Aufsätze und kleinere Schriften,* ed. Eugen Gerstenmaier and Carl G. Schweitzer (Berlin: Lutherisches Verlagshaus, 1957), pp. 7-14.

91. Schoell, *Gutachten,* 2:44; and "Soziale Botschaft der evangelischen Kirche," *Gutachten,* 2:4.

92. Schoell, *Gutachten,* 2:35, 44; Ludwig Ihmels, "Bericht zur sozialen Kundgebund," *Gutachten,* 2:11; and Wilhelm Schneemelcher, "Der Evangelisch-soziale Kongress und seine Gedankenwelt," *Gutachten,* 1:23.

93. Schoell, *Gutachten,* 2:35; and Bell, *Stockholm Conference,* p. 78.

94. Wilhelm Stählin, "The Kingdom of God and the State," *Theology* 14 (1927): 293; and Bell, *Stockholm Conference,* 136-137, 215, 638.

95. Ihmels, *Gutachten,* 2:10-11.

96. Bell, *Stockholm Conference,* p. 78, 186. In a pamphlet written the same year as the Stockholm conference, Brunstäd continued his attack on the Enlightenment tradition. See "Evangelium und öffentliches Leben," in Brünstad, *Gesammelte Aufsätze,* pp. 211-216.

97. Heinrich Frick, "The Idea of the Kingdom of God from Luther to the Present Day," *Theology* 14 (1927): 282-283.

98. Jacob Schoell (*Gutachten,* 2:35) wrote, "Gewiss ist Gottes Reich nicht von dieser Welt" (God's Kingdom is certainly not of this world).

99. Johannes Steinweg, *Inneres Mission und Gemeindienst in meinem Leben* (Berlin: Wichern Verlag, 1959), p. 108.

100. Bell, *Stockholm Conference,* pp. 74-75.

101. Ibid., pp. 136-137, 186, 215, 451.

102. See Edward Shillito, *Life and Work* (London: Longmans, Green, 1926), pp. 68, 103; Alfred Garvie, "The Challenge of the Social Gospel," *Review of the Churches* 3 (1926): 516-523; and accounts of the conference printed in *Christian World,* 3 September 1925, and *Church Times,* 4 September 1925, both in Extracts de Journaux Anglais, Choisy Papers.

103. Nathan Söderblom and Adolf Keller, "Echoes of Stockholm," *Review of the Churches* 3 (1926): 360; Gerhard Füllkrug, *Die Weltkonferenz für praktisches Christentum von 19. bis 30 August 1925* (Berlin: Wichern Verlag, 1925), p. 27; and Erich Stange, *Vom Weltprotestantismus der Gegenwart* (Hamburg: Agentur des Rauhen Hauses, 1925), pp. 33-40.

104. Wilhelm von Pechmann quoted in Garvie, "The Challenge," p. 519; Adolf Deissmann, "The Present Position of Ecumenical Christianity," *Review of the Churches* 3 (1926): 393-397; and Adolf Deissmann, *Stockholmer Bewegung: Die Weltkirchenkonferenz zu Stockholm 1925 und Bern 1926 von innen betrachtet* (Berlin: Furche Verlag, 1927), pp. 86-92. For other accounts of the Kingdom controversy see Max Pribilla, *Um Kirchliche Einheit, Stockholm Conference, Lausanne, Rome: Geschichtlich- Theologische Darstellung der Neueren Einigungsbestrebungen* (Freiburg: Herder, 1929), pp. 74-90; Friedrich Mahling, *Die Weltkonferenz für praktisches Christentum in Stockholm 19-30 August 1925: Bericht über ihren Verlauf und ihre Ergebnisse* (Gütersloh: C. Bertelsmann, n.d.), pp. 8-9; Friedrich Heiler, *Evangelische Katholizität Gesammelte Aufsätze und Vorträge* (Munich: Ernst Reinhardt, 1926), pp. 142-143; Charles Journet,

L'union des églises et le christianisme pratique (Paris: Bernard Grasset, 1927), pp. 139-148; Monnier, *Vers l'union des églises*, pp. 29-30; and Karl Krczmar, *Einheit der Kirche in Leben und Wirken: Die Stockholmer Weltkirchenkonferenz für Praktisches Christentum vom Jahre 1925* (Vienna: Reinhold Verlag, 1930), pp. 38-46.

105. Karl Ludwig Schmidt, "The Other Worldly Kingdom of God in our Lord's Teaching," *Theology* 14 (1927): 156-157; and "A Brief Report of a Conference between German and English Theologians at the Deanery, Canterbury April 4-9, 1927," pp. 3, 6, George Bell Papers, vol. 62, Lambeth Palace Library, London.

106. Gerhard Kittel, "The This-Worldly Kingdom of God in our Lord's Teaching," *Theology* 14 (1927): 260-262; "A Brief Report," p. 7 (Bell Papers); and Stählin, "The Kingdom of God and the State," pp. 292-295. Stählin recalled the conferences years later in his memoirs, *Via Vitae: Lebenserinnerungen von Wilhelm Stählin* (Kassel: Stauda, 1968), pp. 243-44. Stählin, a theologian of great stature after World War II, was known in the 1920s for *völkisch* and anti-Semitic remarks. See Richard Gutteridge, *Open Thy Mouth for the Dumb! The German Evangelical Church and the Jews 1874-1950* (Oxford: Basil Blackwell, 1976), pp. 39-40.

107. H. Frick, "The Idea of the Kingdom of God, p. 282; see also Frick, *Das Reich Gottes in americanischer und in deutscher Theologie der Gegenwart* (Giessen: Alfred Töpelmann, 1926); and "A Brief Report," pp. 3, 26, 33-34 (Bell Papers).

108. Bell, *Stockholm Conference*, pp. 78, 638; "Soziale Botschaft," *Gutachten*, 2:5; and Ihmels, *Gutachten*, 2:7, 10.

109. Friedrich Mahling, "Die evangelische Kirche und die sozialen Probleme," *Gutachten*, 1:18; and Schoell, *Gutachten*, 2:42.

110. "A Brief Report," pp. 34-35 (Bell Papers); and Bell, *Stockholm Conference*, pp. 77-78.

111. Ihmels, *Gutachten*, 2:8; Alfred Tilemann, "Der Gebrauch der Musse," *Gutachten*, 3:40; "Soziale Botschaft," *Gutachten*, 2:5-6; Ihmels, *Gutachten*, 2:7.

112. Bell, *Stockholm Conference*, p. 78; "Soziale Botschaft," *Gutachten*, 2:5-6; and Ihmels, *Gutachten*, 2:13.

113. Wilhelm Kahler in Bell, *Stockholm Conference*, pp. 129-131; Mahling, *Gutachten*, 1:7-19; and D. Ulrich, "Die soziale Arbeit der evangelischen Kirche und Inneren Mission in Berlin," Stockholm 1 (1928): 272-281.

114. Johannes Steinweg, "Die Neuregelung der öffentlichen Wohlfahrtspflege und die Evangelische Kirche," *Gutachten*, 4:4-5, 27-35. For Steinweg's work in the Inner Mission see his memoirs, *Inneres Mission und Gemeindienst in meinem Leben.*

115. Schoell, *Gutachten*, 2:39, 42; and Mahling, *Gutachten*, 1:17.

116. Arthur Titius, "Evangelisches Ehe- und Familienleben und seine Bedeutung in der Gegenwart," *Gutachten*, 2:15-27; and Springer speech in Bell, *Stockholm Conference*, p. 215.

117. C.A. Burberg, "Reform und Weiterentwicklung der Ford-Methoden," *Stockholm* 2 (1929): 34-46; and W. de Leporte, "Das Wohnungse

lend in Deutschland und die Abwehrbetrebungen christlicher Kreise," *Stockholm* 1 (1928): 260-266. See also F. Baltrusch's article calling for public works to counteract seasonal unemployment, pp. 232-238 (1928), and Friedrich Zahn's article suggesting tax breaks for families, pp. 244-253 (1928).

118. A major thesis of Daniel Borg's important book *Old-Prussian Church* is that the revolution inspired a conservative, *völkisch* activism among German churchmen who wished to defend traditional values in the godless republic.

119. Schneemelcher, *Gutachten*, 1:22-23; and Mahling, *Gutachten*, 1:11.

120. Shillito, *Life and Work*, p. 34. Mumm was influential in the DNVP. For his political opinions, see his *Was jeder Christ von den heutigen Parteien wissen muß* (Hamburg: Agentur des Rauhen Hauses, 1924).

121. Schoell, *Gutachten*, 2:32; "Soziale Botschaft," *Gutachten*, 2:6; and Ihmels, *Gutachten*, 2:11.

122. "Soziale Botschaft," *Gutachten*, 2:5; Ihmels, *Gutachten*, 2:15; and Schoell, *Gutachten*, 2:40.

123. Bell, *Stockholm Conference*, p. 272; and Tilemann, *Gutachten*, 3:40.

124. Sundkler, *Nathan Söderblom*, p. 347; and Kapler to Söderblom, 11 July 1925, in Correspondence: Hermann Kapler, Söderblom Archives.

125. Bell, *Stockholm Conference*, p. 452. Klingemann was well known in Germany as an ultraconservative war theologian. See his war pamphlets *Wo für kämpfen wir?* (Witten: Evangelischen Preßbüro, 1915); and *Glaube und Vaterlandsliebe* (Essen: G.D. Baedeker, 1915). See also Nowak, *Evangelische Kirche und Weimarer Republik*, p. 197.

126. Bell, *Stockholm Conference*, pp. 451-452, 536-537. Wolff, like Klingemann, had been a propagandist for the German cause in the Great War. See his *Alles, alles für unser Vaterland* (Berlin: Verlag des Evangelischen Bund, 1917).

127. Bell, *Stockholm Conference*, pp. 480-482; and *Deutsche Volkstum*, September 1925, quoted in Friedrich Gaertner, "Deutsche und ausländische Stimmen über Stockholm," *Die Eiche* 14 (1926): 70.

128. Bell, *Stockholm Conference*, p. 510; and Sundkler, *Nathan Söderblom*, p. 373.

129. Negative reviews of the conference appeared in *Neuwerk*, *Hamburger Nachrichten*, *Evangelischen Allianzblattes*, and *Deutsche Volkstum*. See Gaertner, "Deutsche und ausländische Stimmen über Stockholm," pp. 51-70.

130. Journals and newspapers that printed articles of this persuasion included *Neuen Preussischen Zeitung*, *Tagliche Rundschau*, *Inneren Mission*, *Aus Gottes Garten*, and *Protestantenblattes* (ibid., pp. 51-61).

131. Ibid., pp. 52-67.

132. The text of the letter is in Davidson Papers.

133. "Auszug aus der Verhandlungsniederschrift des Deutschen Evangelischen Kirchenausschuß 8-9 Dezember 1926 in Berlin," Akten 29, Kirch-

liches Außenamt Papers; and "Minutes of the Meeting of the Continuation Committee, August 26-30th, 1926, Berne, Switzerland," pp. 21-23, in Pamphlet File, WCC. See also Bell's notes sent to Archbishop Davidson, in Davidson Papers. Gerhard Besier's excellent study, *Krieg, Frieden, Abrüstung: Die Haltung der europäischen und amerikanischen Kirchen zur Frage der deutschen Kriegsschuld 1914-1933* (Göttingen: Vandenhoeck und Ruprecht, 1982) gives a detailed account of the ecumenical discussion of the war-guilt question; see particularly chap. 10, "Von Stockholm nach Bern 1925-26," pp. 206-233.

134. *Life and Work* no. 1 (May 1927): 4; Sundkler, *Nathan Söderblom,* pp. 395-397; Georges Thélin to Elie Gounelle, 24 May 1927, Box 3, Gounelle Papers; Winchester 1927, p. 74; and Adolf Keller, *The International Christian Social Institute, Geneva 1927-1928* (Geneva: International Christian Social Institute, 1928), p. 1.

135. "Seine Aufgabe wird inbesondere sein, zu sorgen, daß das Sozialwissenschaftliche Institut der christlichen Kirchen in einer für Deutschland befriedigenden Weise eine gegenüber dem International Arbeitsamt selbstandige Linie zur Geltung bringt." *Kirchliches Jahrbuch* 53 (1926): 413.

136. "Minutes of the Meeting of the Continuation Committee, September 2-5, 1928, Prague, Czecho-Slovakia," p. 40 (WCC); and "Protokol der Institutskommission vom 31. August 1929 im Hotel Furstenhof in Eisenach," Box 3, Gounelle Papers, WCC.

137. *Stockholm* 2 (1929): 214-215. See also the discussion about the proclamation in Besier, *Krieg, Frieden, Abrüstung,* pp. 253-269.

138. *Verhandlung des zweiten Deutschen Evangelischen Kirchentages in Königsberg, 1927* (Berlin: Evangelischen Preßverband, 1927), pp. 338-340.

139. See Nowak, *Evangelische Kirche und Weimarer Republik,* pp. 173-179; Borg, *Old-Prussian Church,* pp. 177-178; and Bramsted, "Position of the Protestant Church," pp. 68-69.

4. Response to the Economic Crisis, 1930-1933

1. The Church of England filled fifteen of its thirty seats with representatives from the standing social and industrial committee of the National Assembly and the other half with representatives of the Industrial Christian Fellowship. Six seats also went to representatives of the Baptist, Congregationalist, and Wesleyan Methodist churches and three seats each to Presbyterians, Primitive Methodists, Unitarians, and the Society of Friends. See "Report of the Work of the British Section of the Universal Christian Council for Life and Work," presented by P.T.R. Kirk to the executive committee meeting at Ridley Hall, Cambridge, 1931 (in LW, D24, Box 1: Minutes).

2. Schönfeld to Demant, 12 September 1930, and Demant to Schönfeld, 19 September 1930, in WCC, General Secretariat Correspondence: Demant.

3. Some of these reports presented to Life and Work were printed

leaflets; others were mimeographed. After initial citation, each is referred to by short title.

4. "Minutes of the Meeting of the Research Committee, September 21, 1933," p. 2, LW, 0.2 Christian Social Council, folder: Earlier Papers.

5. See Dahm, *Pfarrer und Politik*, p. 152; and Biographical Sketches of German Delegates for Stockholm, Box 3, Choisy Papers. For information on the party see Günter Opitz, *Der Christlich-Soziale Volksdienst: Versuch einer protestantischen Partei in der Weimarer Republik* (Düsseldorf: Droste, 1969).

6. See the correspondence of Schönfeld to Schoell in LW, Schönfeld's Correspondence with Germany.

7. For example, Schönfeld wanted Siegmund-Schultze to attend the Geneva study week in 1932, yet he invited Ernst Faber, a well-known Nazi, to write for *Stockholm*. See Schönfeld to Dibelius, 29 July 1932, General Secretariat Correspondence: M. Dibelius; and Schönfeld to Faber, 7 July 1931, General Secretariat Correspondence: Schönfeld.

8. See Georg Wobberin, *Arthur Titius: Ökumenische Theologie zur Befriedung der Kirche* (Berlin: Arthur Collignon, 1937), pp. 6-12.

9. LW, D57/I, folder: *Stockholm*.

10. Wahl to Schönfeld, 31 January 1931, LW, R8/A, folder: Kirchenausschuß, 1930-1931.

11. Schoell to Kirchenausschuß, 14 September 1931, Akten 36, Kirchliches Außenamt Papers.

12. Memorandum from the Evangelischen Preßdienst, 17 August 1932, Akten 37, Kirchliches Außenamt Papers.

13. See Kirchenausschuß correspondence in Akten 35-36, Kirchliches Außenamt Papers.

14. Wright, *Above Parties*, p. 71; and Menn to Schönfeld, 25 January 1932, LW, Schönfeld's Correspondence with Germany. For a detailed look at political tension between the German church and the ecumenical movement, 1930-1932, see Besier, *Krieg, Frieden, Abrüstung*, pp. 279-319.

15. Schönfeld to Schoell, 15 October 1931, LW, Schönfeld's Correspondence with Germany; and Kirchenausschuß to Social Institute, 9 January 1932, and H. Kapler to A. Titius, 13 August 1932, General Secretariat Correspondence: Hosemann.

16. "For the Unemployed: A Ministry of Christian Friendship," p. 5, LW, D 57/II, folder: Expertenkonferenz, London 1930.

17. "Draft Report on Unemployment," LW, D59/II, folder: Nacharbeit, Basel, 1932; and E.J. Hagan, "L'éthique sociale du Calvinisme écossais," in *Une enquête sur l'éthique sociale des églises* (Geneva: UCCLW, 1935), p. 50.

18. V.A. Demant, "The Doctrine of Creation," LW, D24 Box 1, Item 14; Demant, "Christian Sociology and the Economic Paradox," p. 1, LW, International Christian Social Institute, Meetings and Conferences, 1929-1932, Item 30; and Bishop of Woolwich, "The Application of Christian Principles to Social and Industrial Problems," *Stockholm* 4 (1931): 143.

19. Demant, "Christian Sociology," p. 2 (LW); Bishop of Lichfield, "Secularism," *Stockholm* 3 (1930): 10-11; and Demant, "Our Present Prob-

lems in Christian Sociology," p. 3, LW, D24 Box 2, Theological Study Conference.

20. Lichfield, "Secularism," p. 11; Demant, "Doctrine of Creation," p. 4; and Demant, "Present Problems," p. 3.

21. Ruth Kenyon, "Les enseignements sociaux de l'Eglise d'Angleterre," in *Une enquête sur l'éthique sociale des églises*, p. 57.

22. See in particular Woolwich, "Application of Christian Principles," p. 194; and B.C. Plowright, "Prolegomena to a Christian Economics," *Stockholm* 4 (1931): 106.

23. Percy Dearmer, ed., *Christianity and the Crisis* (London: Victor Gollancz, 1933), pp. 11, 31, 120, 590.

24. Oliver makes this assessment of the book in his *Social Thought in the Church of England 1918-1939*, p. 184.

25. "For the Unemployed;" also "Draft Report on Unemployment," pp. JD42-JD43, recommended the same type of remedies to the Church of Scotland.

26. "For the Unemployed," p. 5; Ruth Kenyon, "Unemployment," p. 5, LW, R.2, folder: Arbeitslosigkeit 1930-1933, 1935; and Kirk, "Christian Faith and the Economic Depression: The Second Conference of Clergy, February 20-24, 1933," p. 3, LW, Ehrenström Papers Box 2, folder: The Churches and Unemployment Efforts in 1932.

27. Demant, "Christian Sociology," p. 2; Demant, "A Map of Christian Sociology," p. 1, LW, O.2 Christian Social Council, folder: Earlier Papers; and "Unemployment: A Message to the Churches from the Christian Social Council," p. 1, LW, R/2, folder: Not der Arbeitslosen 1930-1933, 1935.

28. Demant, "What Is Christian Sociology," p. 1, LW, D24 Box 1, Rengsdorf 1933; and William Watson, "The Church and Unemployment: An Address at the first Conference of Clergy, October 1932," p. 8, LW, Ehrenström Papers Box 2, folder: The Churches and Unemployment Efforts in 1932. William Watson had been procurator for the Church of Scotland, 1918-22, and M.P. for South Lanarkshire, 1913-18. From 1929 to 1948 he was a judge, Lord of Appeal in Ordinary.

29. Alfred E. Garvie, Editorial, *Stockholm* 3 (1930): 207; and Kirk, "Starving in a World of Plenty," LW, R.2, folder: Arbeitslosigkeit, 1930-1933, 1935.

30. "The Christian Mind and the Social Crisis," p. 1, LW, O.2 Christian Social Council, folder: Earlier Papers; Garvie, "Christian Sociology and Natural Law," *Stockholm* 4 (1931): 6; and Demant, "Present Problems," pp. 1-2.

31. Kenyon, "Unemployment," p. 2; "The Churches and the Unemployed," p. 1, LW, D59/II, folder: Unemployment Conference Basel, 1932; and "The Christian Mind and the Social Crisis," p. 4.

32. "Unemployment: A Message," p. 2; See also "Statement from the Christian Social Council to Basel Conference," p. 2, LW, Unemployment, folder: Heidenheim Conference October 1932, Unemployment; "Christianity and the Problems of Unemployment and Rationalisation," *The Churches and Present-Day Economic Problems: Conference of Christian Social Work-*

ers, London, July 12th to 17th, 1930 (Geneva: UCCLW, 1930), p. 64; and Council of Christian Ministers on Social Questions, "The Present Economic Distress," p. 1, LW, Unemployment, folder: Heidenheim Conference October 1932, Unemployment.

33. Kirk, "Starving in a World of Plenty," p. 7; "Draft Report on Unemployment," p. JD42; Watson, "The Churches and Unemployment," p. 7; and Woolwich, "Application of Christian Principles," p. 194.

34. Demant, "Unemployment and Rationalisation," in *The Churches and Present-Day Economic Problems: Conference of Christian Social Workers, London, July 12th to 17th, 1930* (Geneva: UCCLW, 1930), p. 55; and Demant, "Christianity and the Problems of Unemployment and Rationalisation," p. 64.

35. Kirk, "This Economic Chaos," p. 9, LW, R/2, Folder: Arbeitslosigkeit, 1930-1933, 1935; and Demant, "Christianity and the Problems of Unemployment and Rationalisation," p. 64.

36. Demant, "Unemployment and Rationalisation," pp. 55-56; and "Unemployment: A Message," pp. 3-4.

37. Demant, "Christianity and the Problems of Unemployment and Rationalisation," p. 66; and Demant, "Unemployment and Rationalisation," p. 57.

38. See Malcolm Spencer, "The Modern Equivalent of the Just Price," *Stockholm* 2 (1929): 367-376.

39. "Unemployment: A Message," p. 2; and "The Churches and the Unemployed," p. 8.

40. "Religion and the Social Crisis," September 1933, LW, D.2, Christian Social Council, folder: Earlier Papers, p. 2; Kirk, "This Economic Chaos," p. 10; and Kirk, "Starving in a World of Plenty," pp. 5-6.

41. "The Churches and the Unemployed," p. 3; "Religion and the Social Crisis," p. 3; "Statement on Unemployment for Basel Conference," LW, Box: Unemployment, folder: Heidenheim Conference, 1932, p. 1; and Kirk, "This Economic Chaos," p. 12.

42. Demant, "Christianity and the Problems of Unemployment and Rationalisation," p. 65; Demant, "Unemployment and Rationalisation," p. 57; "The Churches and the Unemployed," p. 4 (LW); and "Unemployment: A Message," p. 3.

43. "Statement on Unemployment for Basel Conference," p. 2; and Kirk, "This Economic Chaos," p. 12.

44. Kirk, "This Economic Chaos," p. 14; and Kenyon, "Unemployment," p. 7.

45. J.E. Turke, "Unemployment," *Stockholm* 4 (1931): 41.

46. Kirk, "This Economic Chaos," p. 10; "The Churches and the Unemployed," p. 8; Kenyon, "Unemployment," pp. 5-6; and "Draft Report on Unemployment," p. JD43.

47. Watson, "The Church and Unemployment," p. 12; and "The Christian Mind and the Social Crisis," p. 9.

48. "The Present Economic Distress"; "The Churches and the Unemployed," p. 9 (LW); and "Draft Report on Unemployment," p. JD42.

49. See John Maynard Keynes, *The End of Laissez-Faire* (London: L. and V. Woolf, 1926); and Keynes, *Collected Works*, vol. 20, *Activities* (London: Macmillan, 1981).

50. "Minutes of the Meeting of the Research Committee, May 18, 1931," LW, D.2, Christian Social Council, folder: Earlier Papers.

51. Kirk to Henry Atkinson, 24 September 1931, WCC General Secretariat Correspondence; Demant, "Christianity and the Problems of Unemployment and Rationalisation," p. 67; and Kirk, "This Economic Chaos," p. 12.

52. "Draft Report on Unemployment," p. JD43; and Fred Hughes, "Unemployment," *Stockholm* 4 (1931): 48.

53. Demant, "Christianity and Property," *Stockholm* 3 (1930): 19-20, 25-26.

54. "Religion and the Social Crisis," p. 2; and "Unemployment: A Message," p. 2.

55. See W.A. Brown to Malcolm Spencer, 1 November 1933, General Secretariat Correspondence: Spencer; Tissington Tatlow to George Bell, 24 January 1933, vol. 18, pt. 2, Bell Papers; and Ehrenström to Schönfeld, 30 January 1931, LW, General Correspondence 1931-1935.

56. Quoted in Norman, *Church and Society*, pp. 326-327.

57. "The Present Economic Distress," p. 1; and Kirk, "Christian Faith and the Economic Depression," p. 1.

58. Kirk, "Christian Faith and the Economic Depression," p. 1; and "Draft Report on Unemployment," p. JD41.

59. "The Churches and the Unemployed," p. 10; and "The Christian Mind and the Social Crisis," p. 10.

60. Hosemann to Graf (of the Reich Finance Office), 5 April 1932, Akten 92, Kirchliches Außenamt Papers.

61. "Report of the German Study Conference," VI, p. 1, LW, International Christian Social Institute Geneva: Meetings and Conferences 1929-1932, item 37. The UCCLW translated the German report into English for use at Basel. The English heading "The War as a Disturbing Element" was considerably weakened in translation from the German original, "Der Krieg als Ursache" (the war as the cause).

62. "Urgebnisse eines Fragebogens über die Arbeitslosigkeit in Hannover," II, Der Krieg, LW, R.2, folder: Not der Arbeitslosen, 1930-1933, 1935; and "Protokoll der Pfingsttagung 1931 am 27.u.28. Mai in Hannover," p. 7, LW, The Churches and the World Economic Crisis, Box 1, folder: Basel, 1932.

63. "Report of the German Study Conference," VI, pp. 1-2.

64. Ibid., V, pp. 1-4; and Hans Schönfeld, "The Churches and Unemployment," in *The Churches and Present-Day Economic Problems*, pp. 30, 35.

65. See General Secretariat Correspondence: Schönfeld, and LW, Schönfeld's Correspondence with Germany.

66. Kuno Renatus, *The Twelfth Hour of Capitalism*, trans. E.W. Dickes (New York: Knopf, 1932), pp. 242-246. Schönfeld presented a summary of Renatus's theses to the Basel conference.

67. Menn to Schönfeld, 25 January 1932, LW, Schönfeld's Correspondence with Germany; see also Schönfeld to Menn, 25 January 1932, and Menn to Schönfeld, 24 October 1930, LW, R.3, International Christian Social Institute Geneva, folder: Correspondence about *Newsletter* 1930-1933.

68. Schönfeld, "The Churches and Unemployment," pp. 30, 33-34; and Karl Rupp to Schönfeld, 6 November 1930, LW, Schönfeld's Correspondence with Germany.

69. "Urgebnisse eines Fragebogens über die Arbeitslosigkeit in Hannover," II, Bedrohung der Existenz der Betriebe durch Lohnerhöhungen u. öff. Lasten.

70. Friedrich Ulrich, "Die Mitwirkung der Kirche und Inneren Mission bei der Bekämpfung der Arbeitslosigkeit in Deutschland," *Stockholm* 4 (1931): 140-144; and UCCLW *Newsletter* no. 7 (8 July 1932): 6.

71. Schönfeld, "The Churches and Unemployment," p. 33; and "Report of the German Study Conference," VII, p. 1.

72. See Max Schleuker, "Rationalisierung und Arbeitslosigkeit," *Stockholm* 4 (1931): 211-216.

73. Schönfeld, "The Churches and Unemployment," p. 31; and Wilhelm Menn, "The Problem of Rationalisation," in *The Churches and Present-Day Economic Problems,* pp. 45, 49. For a survey and evaluation of rationalization in German industry, see Robert A. Brady, *The Rationalization Movement in German Industry: A Study in the Evolution of Economic Planning* (Berkeley: University of California Press, 1933).

74. "Report of the German Study Conference," VII, pp. 2-3.

75. "The Message of Basel," in UCCLW *Newsletter* no. 7 (8 July 1932): 3.

76. *Kirchliches Jahrbuch* (1932): 415.

77. Bell to Schönfeld, 18 May 1932, Bell Papers, vol. 1.

78. "Report of the German Study Conference," VII, p. 2.

79. Kapler to Schönfeld, 27 April 1931, LW, Research Work, 1930-1933, folder: Correspondence about Non-Industrial Child Labour, 1931-1932; and Menn to Wahl, 27 February 1931, LW, Schönfeld's Correspondence with Germany.

80. A. Keller to Amelink, 13 June 1930, LW, Research Work 1930-1933, folder: Evang. Arbeitnehmer.

81. Schoell to Kirchenausschuß, 26 March 1931, LW, The Churches and the World Economic Crisis, folder: Schönfeld's Correspondence.

82. The reports of this conference were published in 1935 as *Une enquête sur l'éthique sociale des églises.*

83. Simon Schöffel said at Berlin, "God is remote, unavailable," manifest only in Christ. "Protokoll der deutschen Studienkonferenz, 24/25 Februar, Berlin," p. 2, LW, D24 Box 1, Rengsdorf 1933, item 1; Martin Dibelius, "Les directives sociales dans le Nouveau Testament," in *Une enquête sur l'éthique sociale des églises,* p. 15.

84. "Aus einem Schreiben von Lic. W. Menn, Dezember 1933," WCC, Germany, Church Struggle, RW.1933-1936.

85. Dibelius, "Les directives sociales dans le Nouveau Testament," p. 4; "Theologische Studientag: Die verschiedenen Auffassungen einer christlichen Sozialethik in der Geschichte der Kirche, Genf, 15-18 August 1932," LW, D 36/11, Research Work, 1930-1934, pp. 4, 8, 37-38; and Ernst Wolf, "De l'éthique sociale du Luthéranisme," in *Une enquête sur l'éthique sociale des églises,* p. 33. Dibelius's presentation was basically a restatement of ideas he had discussed in his *Evangelium und Welt* (Göttingen: Vandenhoeck und Ruprecht, 1929).

86. Dibelius, "Les directives sociales dans le Nouveau Testament," pp. 4-5. See also his *Evangelium und Welt,* pp. 164-165.

87. Johannes Herz, "Recht und Wesen des evangelisch-sozialen Gedankens," *Stockholm* 3 (1930): 131-133.

88. Nowak, *Evangelische Kirche und Weimarer Republik,* p. 101.

89. "Protokoll der deutschen Studienkonferenz," pp. 4, 7; see also Schönfeld, "The Churches and Unemployment," p. 32.

90. A French translation of his speech is printed in Wilfred Monod, ed., *A la croisée des chemins (organisations de la paix): Discours prononcés durant la session du conseil oecuménique du christianisme pratique* (Geneva: UCCLW, 1932), pp. 8-9.

91. "Report of the German Study Conference," I, p. 3.

92. Herz, "Recht und Wesen des evangelisch-sozialen Gedankens," pp. 131-132; "Protokoll der deutschen Studienkonferenz," pp. 1-4; and "Theologische Studientag Genf," p. 34.

93. German authorities were passing copies of Brunstäd's speech around to everyone in 1932 and 1933. See Akten 63-64, Kirchliches Außenamt Papers.

94. Brunstäd, "Ist eine Sozialethik der Kirche möglich?" in his *Gesammelte Aufsätze,* p. 283.

95. Dibelius, "Les directives sociales dans le Nouveau Testament," p. 24; and Wolf, "De l'éthique sociale du Luthéranisme," p. 34.

96. Wolf, "De l'éthique sociale du Luthéranisme," p. 34; and "Theologische Studientag Genf," p. 51.

97. See Herz, "Recht und Wesen des evangelisch-sozialen Gedankens," p. 135; and Schoell to Kirchenausschuß, 26 March 1931, LW, The Churches and the World Economic Crisis, folder: Schönfeld's Correspondence.

98. "Report of the German Study Conference," I, p. 2.

99. "Protokoll der deutschen Studienkonferenz," p. 6; and Minutes, "25 Februar 1933," pp. 3-4, LW, Ehrenström Papers, Box 3, folder: Die Kirche und der Problem der Gesellschaftlichen Ordnung, Berlin, Februar 1933. Schöffel had recently published, with Adolf Köberle, *Luthertum und die soziale Frage* (Leipzig: Dörffling und Franke, 1931), in which he pointed out the inadequacies of both socialism and capitalist individualism. After the Nazi revolution and the new church order of 1933, he was installed as Bishop of Hamburg. See Hans Kressel, *Simon Schöffel: Magnalia und Miniaturen aus dem Leben eines Lutherischen Bischofs* (Schweinfurt: Historischen Verein und Stadtarchiv, 1964), p. 35. Tessmar was invited as an economic expert who, living in the Saar region, was naturally well informed on postwar

economic problems. He also came recommended as deeply committed to the social work of the church. See D. Stoltenhoff to Hosemann, 5 April 1932; and Schönfeld to Kapler, 15 March 1932, Akten 92, Kirchliches Außenamt Papers.

100. Fritz Lieb, "Das Geistige Gesicht des Bolshevismus," p. 11, LW, D24 Box 1 Rengsdorf, item 26. Lieb's career had many parallels to Karl Barth's. Both men were Swiss scholars teaching at Bonn University, expelled in 1934 and 1935 by the Nazis. Afterward Lieb worked in Paris, where he continued his opposition to the Nazi regime. See the biographical sketch by Eugene Porret in Fritz Lieb, *Sophia und Historie: Aufsätze zur östlichen und westlichen Geistes- und Theologiegeschichte*, ed. Martin Robkrümer (Zurich: EVZ, 1962), pp. 3-12.

101. M.F. Karrenberg, "Theses on Liberalism," LW, D24 Box 1 Rengsdorf, item 22. Karrenberg, an industrialist and active church member, had studied sociology in Frankfurt. His dissertation was published in 1932, *Christentum, Kapitalismus und Sozialismus* (Berlin: Junker und Dünnhaupt, 1932).

102. Minutes, "25 Februar 1933," p. 4.

103. *Kirchliches Jahrbuch* 59 (1932): 396-397. Hermann Sasse was editor of the yearbook in 1932. He had attended the Anglo-German meetings of 1927 and 1928 and was a German delegate to Rengsdorf. For a discussion of the politics within the German church and the *Kirchenausschuß* and their relations with growing National Socialism in 1930-33, see Wright, *Above Parties*, pp. 48-142.

5. The Social Message and the Nazi State, 1933-1937

Portions of this chapter appeared, in earlier versions, in the *Journal of Church and State* 31 (Winter 1989): 101-14, and *Zeitschrift für Religions-und Geistesgeschichte* 40 (Heft 2): 151-69; they are reprinted by permission of the publishers.

1. The literature on the German church struggle (*Kirchenkampf*) is voluminous. For the best surveys in English, see Helmreich, *The German Churches under Hitler;* Klaus Scholder, *The Churches and the Third Reich,* trans. John Bowden, 2 vols. (Minneapolis: Augsburg-Fortress, 1987-88); and J.S. Conway, *The Nazi Persecution of the Churches 1933-1945* (New York: Basic Books, 1968). For a thorough examination of the role of the ecumenical movement see Armin Boyens, *Kirchenkampf und Ökumene 1933-1939: Darstellung und Dokumentation* (Munich: Chr. Kaiser, 1969); and Ronald C.D. Jasper, *George Bell, Bishop of Chichester* (London: Oxford University Press, 1967), pp. 100-120, 201-223.

2. "Minutes of the Meeting of the Executive Committee, Novi Sad, Bulgaria, September 9-12, 1933," Pamphlet File, WCC, p. 5.

3. Boyens, *Kirchenkampf und Ökumene*, pp. 39, 51; and *Churches in Action* no. 2 (June 1933): 1. *Churches in Action* was the new newsletter published cooperatively by Life and Work and the World Alliance.

4. Boyens, *Kirchenkampf und Ökumene*, p. 61.

5. "Minutes of the Meeting of the Executive Committee, Novi Sad," pp. 37, 64.

6. Actually there were only thirty-seven Jewish Protestant pastors out of eighteen thousand clergy in 1933 in Germany (Helmreich, *The German Churches under Hitler*, p. 148).

7. "Minutes of the Administrative Committee, Chichester, October 25-26, 1934," LW, D24 Box 1, Minutes.

8. Alphons Koechlin of Basel attended the Dahlem synod at Bell's request and became Bell's informant on German church affairs throughout the Nazi era. Bell and Koechlin's correspondence is published in German translation; see Andreas Lindt, ed., *George Bell, Alphons Koechlin: Briefwechsel 1933-1954* (Zurich: EVZ, 1969).

9. The German Foreign Office had complained to Heckel about the invitation to the Confessing Christians. See Roediger of the *Auswärtiges Amt* to Heckel, 6 August 1934, Akten 39, Kirchliches Außenamt Papers.

10. "Minutes of the Meeting of the Council, Fanø, August 24-30th, 1934," Pamphlet File, WCC, pp. 37, 42.

11. Ibid., pp. 51-52.

12. Zoellner to Henry Henriod, 12 June 1936, Akten 42, Kirchliches Außenamt Papers.

13. Boyens, *Kirchenkampf und Ökumene*, p. 88.

14. "Minutes of the Meeting of the Council, Fanø," p. 59.

15. Boyens, *Kirchenkampf und Ökumene*, p. 134; and Jasper, *George Bell*, pp. 207-208; see also Gordon Rupp, *"I Seek My Brethren": Bishop George Bell and the German Churches* (London: Epworth Press, 1975).

16. Zoellner to Henriod, 12 June 1936, Akten 42, Kirchliches Außenamt Papers.

17. Jasper, *George Bell*, p. 214.

18. Willem Visser't Hooft, interview, 26 June 1981, Geneva, Switzerland.

19. Peter Hoffmann, *The History of the German Resistance 1933-1945*, trans. Richard Barry (Cambridge, Mass.: MIT Press, 1977), pp. 216-224.

20. Visser't Hooft, interview.

21. The true extent of the UCCLW's relationship to the Confessing Church is not revealed in the Life and Work papers. Fearing a Nazi invasion of Switzerland in World War II, the cautious Schönfeld removed and burned many papers that might have compromised churchmen in Geneva and Germany. Letter from Willem Visser't Hooft to the author, 5 August 1981.

22. Krummacher to Wendland, 5 April, Akten 96, Kirchliches Außenamt Papers.

23. May relocated to Berlin to begin the work but mysteriously thereafter returned to Yugoslavia. See Akten 3523, Gerhard May Files, Kirchliches Außenamt Papers.

24. See Heinz-Dietrich Wendland's autobiography, *Weg und Umwege: 50 Jahre erlebter Theologie 1919-1970* (Gütersloh: Gerd Mohn, 1977), pp. 149-150.

25. Eugen Gerstenmaier, *Streit und Friede hat seine Zeit: Ein Lebensbericht* (Frankfurt/M: Propyläen, 1981), pp. 81-82. Karl Barth called the Gerstenmaier edition a "theological prop for the Third Reich . . . the achievements of a bunch of snake artists" (quoted in Boyens, *Kirchenkampf und Ökumene*, p. 138).

26. See the correspondence of October 1936 in Akten 21, Kirchliches Außenamt Papers; and Hans Böhm to Reichskirchenausschuß, 13 November 1936, Akten 21, Kirchliches Außenamt Papers.

27. See Helmreich, *The German Churches under Hitler*, p. 204.

28. Jasper, *George Bell*, p. 220.

29. The drama leading to Hitler's decision is described in Boyens, *Kirchenkampf und Ökumene*, pp. 144-156. Actually, a few Germans already outside the country did manage to attend Oxford, as did a representative each from the Methodist and Baptist churches of Germany.

30. A good biography of Oldham is needed. For his life and background, see J.W.C. Dougall, "J.H. Oldham," *International Review of Missions* 59 (January 1970): 8-22; and John W. Cell's editor's introduction to *By Kenya Possessed: The Correspondence of Norman Leys and J.H. Oldham 1918-1926* (Chicago: University of Chicago Press, 1976). For Oldham's social ethics see Hans-Joachim Kosmahl, *Ethik in Ökumene und Mission: Das Problem der "Mittleren Axiome" bei J.H. Oldham und in der christlichen Sozialethik* (Göttingen: Vandenhoeck und Ruprecht, 1970).

31. Oldham letter, 27 July 1925, LW, Box 01, folder 1.

32. Such nonmission specialists as R.H. Tawney and William Temple were on the program. See Darril Hudson, *The Ecumenical Movement and World Affairs: The Church as an International Pressure Group* (Washington, D.C.: National Press, 1969), p. 93.

33. "Notes by Joseph Oldham," LW, Oldham Files, 1930-1933, folder: Scottish Group; and Willem Visser't Hooft, interview.

34. Oldham correspondence, 1930-1932, LW, Oldham Files, 1930-1933; and Visser't Hooft, interview.

35. Schönfeld to Brunner, 2 March 1934, LW, Study Conference, Paris 1934, Correspondence.

36. "Minutes of the Meeting of the Council, Fanø," p. 59.

37. See Visser't Hooft's eulogy of Oldham in *Ecumenical Review* 21 (July 1969): 261-265.

38. Besides Oldham and Moberly, the Advisory Council included the Bishops of Chichester, Manchester, Southwark, and Winchester, the Dean of St. Paul's and Archdeacon of Oakham, H.G. Judd, M.E. Aubrey, Ernest Barker, S.M. Berry, Hutchison Cockburn, T.S. Eliot, H.W. Fox, A.E. Garvie, Eleonora Iredale, Thomas Jones, Scott Lidgett, J.H. Rushbrooke, E.K. Talbot, R.H. Tawney, J.P.R. Maud, and the Marquess of Lothian. See Oldham to Schönfeld, 21 November 1935, General Secretariat Correspondence: Oldham.

39. Oldham said of Tawney, "He does not mix easily with ecclesiastics of any kind and finds them rather uncongeneal [*sic*]." See Oldham to Schönfeld, 6 October 1936, LW, 0.4, folder: Fenn-Schönfeld Correspondence.

40. Minutes of Meeting of 27 February 1935, LW, O.2 Christian Social Council, folder: 1935-1939.

41. Bell to Eric Fenn, 24 November 1936, LW, 0.3, folder: Bishop of Chichester.

42. Oldham to Schönfeld, 6 March 1936, General Secretariat Correspondence: Oldham.

43. William Temple to Cosmo Lang, August 1936; Lang to Temple, 6 August 1936; and Lang to Bell, 3 September 1936, all in Cosmo Lang Papers, vol. 76, Lambeth Palace Library, London.

44. Oldham to W.H. Drummond, 17 June 1935, LW, 0.5, folder: Oxford Correspondents, 1934-1935.

45. For example, see Hermann Sasse's criticism in *Kirchliches Jahrbuch* 59 (1932): 529.

46. See the excellent discussion of this group in Wolfgang Tilgner, *Volksnomostheologie und Schöpfungsglaube* (Göttingen: Vandenhoeck und Ruprecht, 1966); and Hans Tiefel, "The German Lutheran Church and the Rise of National Socialism," *Church History* 41 (1972): 326-336.

47. See *Revolutionary Theology in the Making: Barth-Thurneysen Correspondence 1919-1925*, trans. James D. Smart (Richmond, Va.: John Knox Press, 1964), pp. 242, 247; and Willem Visser't Hooft, "Karl Barth and the Ecumenical Movement," *Ecumenical Review* 32 (April 1980): 130-131.

48. When dismissed from his university post and forced to leave Germany in 1935, Barth was offered a position as permanent lecturer at the ecumenical seminar in Geneva. He accepted instead a call to the University of Basel in his home town. Despite his collaboration with ecumenical leaders, especially regarding the German church struggle, he did not endorse the aims of the ecumenical movement and was not truly at home there in the 1930s. He fully made his peace with the movement only after 1948. See Visser't Hooft, "Karl Barth," p. 132; and Henriod to Deissmann, 14 January 1936, General Secretariat Correspondence: Deissmann.

49. Klaus Scholder, *Die Kirchen und das Dritte Reich*, 2 vols. (Frankfurt/M: Propyläen, 1977), 1:142.

50. James Zabel, *Nazism and the Pastors: A Study of the Ideas of Three "Deutsche Christen" Groups* (Missoula, Mont.: Scholars Press, 1976), p. 223. For a discussion of Althaus see Ericksen, *Theologians under Hitler*, pp. 79-119; and Tilgner, *Volksnomostheologie und Schöpfungsglaube*, pp. 179-201. Ericksen makes Althaus out to be a moderate; he makes no mention of his membership in the *Deutsche Christen*.

51. Scholder, *The Churches and the Third Reich*, 1:347.

52. The German word *Volk* has no full equivalent in English. It is broad enough to include the concepts of nation, people, and race.

53. This is the general argument of Althaus's theses presented to the Paris Conference, 1934, "L'église et l'état," LW, 24/I; and his contribution, "Kirche, Volk, und Staat," in the volume of German preparations for Oxford edited by Eugen Gerstenmaier, *Kirche, Volk, und Staat: Stimmen aus der Deutschen Evangelischen Kirche* (Berlin: Furche Verlag, 1937), pp. 17-35. Althaus had published his ideas on the orders in *Theologie der Ordnungen*

(Gütersloh: C. Bertelsmann, 1935); and Althaus, *Kirche und Staat nach Lutherischer Lehre* (Leipzig: U. Deichertsche, 1935).

54. Quoted from a German participant at the UCCLW's Youth Conference at Gland, Switzerland, in 1933, in *Churches in Action* no. 3 (October 1933): 10.

55. See Theodor Heckel, "Le problème de l'état et l'église du Christ," Paris, 1934, LW, 24/I; and Gerhard May, "Der Totalitätsanspruch des heutigen Staates und das christliche Freiheitsverständnis," in *Totaler Staat und Christliche Freiheit* (Geneva: UCCLW, 1937), p. 118. May had contributed to the growing body of *völkisch* Christian literature with his *Die volksdeutsche Sendung der Kirche* (Göttingen: Vandenhoeck und Ruprecht, 1934). Before the end of the war he would be named Bishop of the Protestant Church of Austria, a post he held until 1968.

56. Paul Althaus, "L'église et l'état," p. 2; May, "Der Totalitätsanspruch des heutigen Staates," p. 117; see also Heinz-Dietrich Wendland, "'Christliche' Freiheit, kreatürliche Freiheit und totaler Staat," in *Totaler Staat und Christliche Freiheit*, p. 166.

57. *Luther's Works*, American ed., vol. 26 (St. Louis: Concordia, 1963), pp. 308-309.

58. Friedrich Brunstäd, "Gesetz und Evangelium," in Gerstenmaier, *Kirche, Volk, und Staat*, pp. 38, 41.

59. Rudolf Craemer, "Volk, Staat, und Kirche," pp. 2, 9, December 1936, LW, 12/II. Craemer's participation was solicited by Friedrich Wilhelm Krummacher, the only Nazi party member in the *Kirchliches Außenamt*. See Krummacher to Wendland, 5 April 1935, Akten 96, Kirchliches Außenamt Papers. Craemer was a close friend of Wendland and had worked with him in Brunstäd's Evangelical Social School in Berlin-Spandau in the late 1920s. See Wendland, *Weg und Umwege*, p. 44. Life and Work authorities knew the Königsberg professor would present the Nazi position and elicit much discussion among Anglo-Saxon circles. See Schönfeld to Craemer, 27 February 1936, General Secretariat Correspondence: Craemer, Rudolf; and Schönfeld to Oldham, 20 October 1936, LW, 04, folder: Fenn/Schönfeld Correspondence.

60. Wendland, "'Christliche' Freiheit," p. 167.

61. May, "Zur evangelischen Lehre von Volk," p. 2, September 1935, LW, 13/II, folder 4. This German view of natural law was greatly influenced by Althaus's colleague at Erlangen, Werner Elert; see his *Morphologie des Luthertums*, 2 vols. (Munich: C.H. Becksche, 1931-32), 2:336-342.

62. Barth wrote in a letter to French Protestants in 1939 that Luther's error on the relationship of law to gospel created a heritage that has confirmed and idealized the natural paganism of Germany instead of limiting and restraining it. Hitler had then been "Christianized" in a Lutheran form. The letter is printed in Karl Barth, *This Christian Cause: A Letter to Great Britain from Switzerland* (New York: Macmillan, 1941).

63. Brunstäd, "Gesetz und Evangelium," pp. 37-40.

64. Hermann Sasse, "Gesetz und Evangelium," pp. 3-8, December 1936, and "Kirche und Welt," p. 8, July 1936, LW, Box 8. Sasse had attended

the first synod of the Confessing Church at Barmen and was on the commission, with Karl Barth, that drew up the famous confession. However, he was the only commission member who dissented from the message. A strict Lutheran confessionalist, he opposed the confession and the Confessing Church for really "confessing" nothing, because the doctrinal differences between Lutheran and Reformed elements had been ignored. He later became a bitter opponent of the Confessing Church, calling it the worst sect in German history. His criticisms were used effectively by the national church. See Arthur C. Cochrane, *The Church's Confession under Hitler* (Pittsburgh: Pickwick Press, 1976), pp. 135-136, 153, 193-196.

65. See Althaus's comments in Minutes of Paris Conference, 5-7 April 1934, p. 5, LW, D2415 Box 1, folder 1; see also Althaus, "Ur-Offenbarung," *Luthertum* 46 (1935):8.

66. Althaus, "Kirche, Volk, und Staat," p. 29; Althaus, "L'église et l'état," p. 1 (LW). See also May, "Zur evangelischen Lehre von Volk," p. 3; Wendland, "The Relations between the Kingdom of God and History," p. 2, January 1935, LW, D242 Box 14, folder 1; and Martin Dibelius, "The Message of the New Testament and the Orders of Society," in Conference on Church, Community, and State, *Christian Faith and the Common Life* (Chicago: Willett and Clark, 1938), pp. 28, 35.

67. Dibelius, "The Message of the New Testament," p. 24; and Wendland, "The Relations between the Kingdom of God and History," pp. 1-2, 5 (LW).

68. Dibelius, "The Message of the New Testament," p. 27. Dibelius worked closely with the inner circle of the national church around Heckel, Gerstenmaier, and Wendland. See Krummacher to Schönfeld, 5 April 1935, General Secretariat Correspondence: Krummacher.

69. Althaus, "Kirche und Volk," p. 3; and Wendland, "The Relations between the Kingdom of God and History," p. 7.

70. Heckel, "Le problème de l'état et l'église du Christ," pp. 2-3; and May, "Zur evangelischen Lehre von Volk," p. 2.

71. Althaus, "Kirche und Volk," September 1935, LW, 12/I, p. 5.

72. Wendland, "The Kingdom of God and History," pp. 1-3, LW, Study Conference, Paris, 8-14 April 1934; and Althaus, "Reich Gottes und Geschichtswelt," p. 1, presented at Paris Conference, December 1934, LW, 24/I.

73. Dibelius, "The Message of the New Testament" p. 39.

74. Craemer, "Volk, Staat, und Kirche," p. 14.

75. Constantin Frick, "Dienende Kirche: Ein Bericht aus der deutschen Inneren Mission," in Gerstenmaier, *Kirche, Volk, und Staat*, pp. 309-310.

76. See particularly Brunstäd, "Gesetz und Evangelium," p. 53; Dibelius, "The Message of the New Testament," p. 21; and "Volk und Kirche," Report of the Hannover Study Group, September 1935, LW, 12/I.

77. Sasse, "Gesetz und Evangelium," p. 4.

78. See Paul Althaus, *Die deutsche Stunde der Kirche*, 3d ed. (Göttingen: Vandenhoeck und Ruprecht, 1934), p. 15.

79. Heckel, "Le problème de l'état et l'église du Christ," p. 4; May, "Der

Totalitätsanspruch des heutigen Staates," p. 114; and "Volk und Kirche," p. 6.

80. Althaus, "Kirche und Volk," pp. 2-3, 5.

81. Althaus, "Kirche, Volk, und Staat," p. 20; and Craemer, "Volk, Staat, und Kirche," p. 10.

82. Craemer, "Volk, Staat, und Kirche," pp. 10, 13. In earlier publications Craemer grounded this *völkisch* obedience in German Christian tradition going back from Bismarck, the model Christian statesman, to Luther. See his *Evangelische Reformation als politische Macht* (Göttingen: Vandenhoeck und Ruprecht, 1933), and *Der Kampf um die Volksordnung von der preuß-ischen Sozialpolitik zum deutschen Sozialismus* (Hamburg: Hanseatische Verlagsanstalt, 1933).

83. Sasse, "Kirche und Welt," p. 8; and May, "Zur evangelischen Lehre von Volk," pp. 3-4.

84. Althaus, "Kirche und Volk," p. 4; and Dibelius, "The Message of the New Testament," p. 39.

85. Althaus, "Kirche, Volk, und Staat," p. 31; and Dibelius, "The Message of the New Testament," p. 39.

86. Althaus, "L'église et l'état," pp. 1-2.

87. Heckel, "Le problème de l'état et l'église," p. 3.

88. Quoted in Nowak, *Evangelische Kirche und Weimarer Republik*, pp. 242-243.

89. May, "Der Totalitätsanspruch des heutigen Staates," p. 110; and Wendland, "'Christliche' Freiheit," p. 152.

90. Wendland, "'Christliche' Freiheit," pp. 152-164; and Wendland, "Die neutestamentliche Verkündigung der Freiheit," p. 1, presented at Schloss Hemmen, Holland, April 1935, LW, 25/II.

91. Walther Künneth, "Leitsätze über Naturrecht und Ordnungen," pp. 1-6, LW, 9/I; and Künneth, "Leitsätze zu dem Thema 'Volk als Ordnung,'" pp. 3-6, presented at Sigtuna, Sweden, August 1935, LW, 13/II, folder 3.

92. Hanns Lilje, "Church and Nation," in Conference on Church, Community, and State, *Church and Community* (Chicago: Willett and Clark, 1938), pp. 103, 108-111. Lilje had written earlier about God's revelation through history in his *Luthers Geschichtsanschauung* (Berlin: Furche Verlag, 1932), pp. 103-123. Lilje would eventually spend the last year of the war imprisoned in Nuremburg for his opposition to Hitler. He was sentenced to death and saved only by the American occupation of the city.

93. Schönfeld to Künneth, 31 May 1935, General Secretariat Correspondence: Künneth.

94. See Künneth's autobiography, *Lebensführungen: Der Wahrheit verpflichtet* (Wuppertal: Brockhaus, 1979), pp. 103-134.

95. Karl Barth, "The Christian Apprehension of Revelation," LW, 23/II, p. 4.

96. Ibid., pp. 1, 3.

97. Wiesner was a Confessing Christian who in 1936 was denied permission to teach in a German university. Schönfeld presumed the reason was his activity for the Confessing Church. In 1937 he was headmaster of a Protestant

preparatory school for future theology students at Halle. See Schönfeld to Oldham, 25 September 1936, General Secretariat Correspondence: Oldham; and Conference on Church, Community, and State, *Christian Faith and the Common Life*, p. xi.

98. Werner Wiesner, "The Law of Nature and the Orders," pp. 12-13, 19, November 1936, LW, 11; and Wiesner, "The Law of Nature and Social Institutions," pp. 13-14, March 1937, LW, 10.

99. Wiesner, "The Law of Nature and the Orders," p. 6; and Wiesner, "The Law of Nature and Social Institutions," p. 2. Even though the *Kirchliches Außenamt* had no control over the Oxford preparations by the Confessing Church, Eugen Gerstenmaier still tried to use his influence with his friend Hans Schönfeld to keep Wiesner's work from being printed in the Oxford materials. Shortly before the conference he telegraphed Schönfeld asking that Wiesner's work be withdrawn and the next day explained his reasons: Wiesner had criticized the Lutheran teachings of the orders as "the transferring of idealistic Greek cosmology into theology." Gerstenmaier wanted no criticism of the DEK preparations which, he emphasized, had proceeded as "unpolemically as possible" (quoted in Boyens, *Kirchenkampf und Ökumene*, p. 138).

100. Wiesner, "The Law of Nature and the Orders," pp. 7-8.

101. Friedrich Karrenberg, "Church, State and Economic Life," p. 1, June 1937, LW, 15/II. Karrenberg was a Rhineland industrialist who had attended several Life and Work meetings in the early 1930s. He became an active lay member of the Confessing Church and in its behalf wrote on economic issues on several occasions. See his biography by Hans Meyer in the Festschrift that honored him: Joachim Beckmann and Gerhard Weissler, eds., *Gemeinde und Gesellschaftswandel* (Stuttgart: Kreuz Verlag, 1964), pp. 344-347.

102. See also Karrenberg, "Church, State and Economic Life," p. 6; and Wiesner, "The Law of Nature and the Orders," p. 8.

103. Karrenberg, "Church, State and Economic Life," p. 1; and Wiesner, "The Law of Nature and the Orders," pp. 16-17.

104. Wiesner, "The Law of Nature and the Orders," p. 17.

105. "Kirche, Volk und Staat: Bericht des Oekumenischen Ausschusses der vorläufigen Leitung der Deutschen Evangelischen Kirche," pp. 3-5, April 1937, LW, 26/I.

106. Ibid.; Wiesner, "The Law of Nature and the Orders," p. 16; Wiesner, "The Christian Faith and the Common Life," p. 4, September 1936, LW, 10; Wiesner, "The Law of Nature and Social Institutions," p. 8; and Karrenberg, "Church, State and Economic Life," p. 19.

107. Barth, "The Christian Apprehension of Revelation," pp. 11-12.

108. Wiesner, "The Christian Faith and the Common Life," p. 2; and "Kirche, Volk und Staat: Bericht des Oekumenischen Ausschuss," p. 6.

109. Wiesner, "The Law of Nature and the Orders," p. 11; and "The Christian Faith and the Common Life," pp. 9-10.

110. Winterhager remembers writing this article in 1935 based on his handwritten notes from Bonhoeffer's lectures in Berlin two years earlier (Jürgen Winterhager to the author, 16 January 1987).

111. See Eberhard Bethge, *Dietrich Bonhoeffer: Man of Vision, Man of Courage,* trans. Eric Mosbacher et al. (New York: Harper and Row, 1977), p. 394.

112. Jürgen Winterhager, "Kirche und Volkstum in oekumenischer Sicht," pp. 1, 4, LW 14, folder 1.

113. Ibid., p. 3.

114. Ibid., p. 6.

115. See Bethge, *Dietrich Bonhoeffer,* pp. 59-60.

116. Winterhager, "Kirche und Volkstum," p. 6.

117. Bonhoeffer, "The Confessing Church and the Ecumenical Movement," in Edwin H. Robinson, ed., *No Rusty Swords: Letters, Lectures and Notes 1928-1936 from the Collected Works of Dietrich Bonhoeffer,* trans. Edwin H. Robinson and John Bowden (New York: Harper and Row, 1965), p. 338.

118. Bonhoeffer did not see the word "Antichrist" as too strong in reference to the DEK; the church government in Berlin, he said, threatened the death of the Christian church in Germany (ibid., p. 338).

119. Ibid., p. 344.

120. Paul Tillich, "The Kingdom of God and History," LW, 19/I, folder 7.

121. Tiefel, "The German Lutheran Church and the Rise of National Socialism," p. 333.

122. Wiesner, "The Law of Nature and the Orders," p. 22.

123. Wiesner, "The Law of Nature and Social Institutions," p. 22.

124. Winterhager, "Kirche und Volkstum," p. 6.

125. Maurice Cowling generalizes that a similar shift occurred in English politics in the 1930s. From the 1920s through 1934, he argues, the political situation was dominated by the class struggle. From 1934 to 1940 political attention concentrated on the challenge of Hitler. See his *Impact of Hitler: British Politics and British Policy 1933-1940* (London: Cambridge University Press, 1975), p. 6.

126. V.A. Demant, "The Problem of Church and State as Seen in the Anglican Church," p. 1, presented to the Paris conference, April 1934, LW, 24/I.

127. "The Kingdom of God and History," Minutes of the Conference at Schloss Hemmen, 2-4 May 1935, p. 7, LW, D242 Box 14.

128. William Temple, "Christian Faith and the Common Life," p. 1, April 1937, LW, 10; and Joseph Oldham, "The Function of the Church in the Social and Political Sphere," pp. 8, 18, October 1936, LW, 7.

129. Joseph Oldham, "The Function of the Church in Society," p. 26, January 1937, LW, 7.

130. Oldham, "The Function of the Church in the Social and Political Sphere," p. 27.

131. Oldham read widely in the German literature and was particularly influenced by the work of Barth, Emil Brunner, and Karl Heim. Few English translations were yet available. Barth's commentary on Romans, for example, did not appear in translation until 1934.

132. See Clement Webb, "Nature and Grace," p. 3, April 1937, LW, 11;

J.S. Boys-Smith, "Nature and Grace," p. 2, May 1935, LW, D242 Box 8, folder 1; and Baillie to Oldham, 20 June 1935, LW, 0.5, folder: Correspondence with Scotland. Actually the anti-Barthian outlook in Britain created problems politically. The British churches were hesitant to support the Confessing Church in the German church struggle because they did not wish to identify themselves with the Confessing Christians' preoccupation with Barthian theology. See Boyens, *Kirchenkampf und Ökumene*, p. 209; and Gordon Rupp, *I Seek my Brethren*, p. 9.

133. Webb, "Nature and Grace," pp. 2, 7.

134. H.H. Farmer, "Christian Faith and the Common Life," p. 12, May 1937, LW, 9/II; and R.H. Tawney, "Memorandum," pp. 10-11, May 1937, LW, 15/II.

135. H.G. Wood, "The Kingdom of God and the Meaning of History," p. 2, August 1936, LW 19/II. In 1937 Wood was the Director of Studies at Woodbrooke Settlement, Birmingham. He had formerly been a professor at Jesus College, Cambridge.

136. Temple, "Christian Faith and the Common Life," pp. 4-5; and Wood, "The Kingdom of God and the Meaning of History," p. 2.

137. Minutes of Schloss Hemmen, 2-4 May 1935, p. 1.

138. Demant, "The Problem of Church and State as Seen in the Anglican Church," p. 3; and Farmer, "Christian Faith and the Common Life," p. 6.

139. Demant, "The Problem of Church and State as Seen in the Anglican Church," pp. 3-4; A.E. Garvie, "Church and State," p. 1, March 1934, LW, Ehrenström Papers, Box 4; Austin Farrer, "The Christian Doctrine of Man," in Conference on Church, Community, and State, *The Christian Understanding of Man* (Chicago: Willett and Clark, 1938), p. 212. For a discussion of this theme in William Temple's social thought see Robert Craig, *Social Concern in the Thought of William Temple* (London: Gollancz, 1963), pp. 45-47; and Jack F. Padgett, *The Christian Philosophy of William Temple* (The Hague: Martinus Nijhoff, 1974), pp. 174-184.

140. Minutes of Schloss Hemmen, 2-4 May, p. 9. Oldham was speaking here specifically of Wendland's explanation of the orders. More privately he said, "Wendland's paper is pretty hopeless from the British point of view." See Oldham to Alfred Zimmern, 29 April 1935, LW, 0.5, folder: Oldham Correspondents, 1934-1935.

141. John Baillie, "Comments on Wendland's Paper," p. 8, April 1935, LW, 18/I, folder: 1.

142. Garvie, "Church and State," p. 1. For an elaboration of these ideas see Garvie's book written in 1935 to respond to the Paris conference, *The Fatherly Rule of God: A Study of Society, State, and Church* (New York: Abingdon Press, 1935).

143. Minutes of Schloss Hemmen, 2-4 May 1935, pp. 2, 7.

144. Baillie, "Comments on Prof. Brunner's Paper," p. 3, March 1936, LW, D242 Box 16, folder 2; and Farrer, "The Christian Doctrine of Man," p. 204.

145. Minutes of Schloss Hemmen, 2-4 May 1935, p. 2; and Demant, "Notes on Grace and Natural Law in Relation to the Orders," pp. 2-3, September 1935, LW, 9/II.

146. Temple, "Revelation," pp. 3-4, n.d., LW 23/II; see also Craig, *Social Concern in the Thought of William Temple*, p. 124.

147. Baillie, "Comments on Prof. Brunner's Paper," p. 4; and J.S. Boys-Smith, "Comments on Prof. Brunner's Paper," p. 2, April 1936, LW, D242 Box 16, folder 2.

148. Minutes of Schloss Hemmen, 2-4 May 1935, pp. 3, 13; see also Oldham, "The Function of the Church in Society," p. 26; Temple, "Christian Faith and the Common Life," p. 9; and Farrer, "The Christian Doctrine of Man," pp. 204, 211.

149. Edwyn Bevan, "The Kingdom of God and History," p. 2, August 1936, LW, LW/I, folder 2. From 1922 to 1933 Bevan was a lecturer on Hellenism at the University of London.

150. Minutes of Schloss Hemmen, 2-4 May 1935, pp. 2, 12.

151. Wood, "The Kingdom of God and the Meaning of History," p. 2; Webb, "Nature and Grace," p. 3; and A.E Garvie, "Comment on Brunner's Memorandum," p. 1, May 1936, LW, D242 Box 16, folder 2.

152. Boys-Smith, "Nature and Grace," p. 1; and Maurice Reckitt, "Grace and the World Order," p. 17, August 1946, LW, 11.

153. Demant, "The Christian Doctrine of Freedom in Relation to Secular Totalitarianism," p. 4, April 1935, LW, Ehrenström Papers, Box 6, folder: Papers Presented at Schloss Hemmen.

154. Garvie, "Church and State," p. 3; Temple, "Christian Faith and the Common Life," p. 1; and Minutes of Schloss Hemmen, 2-4 May, 1935, p. 11.

155. Bevan, "The Kingdom of God and History," p. 10; and Farmer, "Christian Faith and the Common Life," pp. 1-2, 11-12.

156. Reckitt, "Grace and the World Order," p. 18; and Oldham, "The Function of the Church in the Social and Political Spheres," p. 10.

157. Demant, "The Christian Doctrine of Freedom in Relation to Secular Totalitarianism," p. 6.

158. Demant, "The Problem of Church and State as Seen in the Anglican Church," p. 4.

159. Reckitt, "Grace and the World Order," p. 6, 17; and Demant, "The Christian Doctrine of Freedom in Relation to Secular Totalitarianism," p. 4.

160. Oldham, "Theses on Church and State," p. 1, presented at Paris, April 1934, LW, Box 012, folder 3; "Protokoll," Minutes of Schloss Hemmen, 4-8 May 1935, p. 6; and Minutes of Schloss Hemmen, 2-4 May 1935, p. 32.

161. Garvie, "Church and State," p. 3; and Demant, "The Problem of Church and State as Seen in the Anglican Church," p. 3.

162. Temple, "Christian Faith and the Common Life," p. 5; and Minutes of Schloss Hemmen, 4-8 May 1935, p. 12.

163. Garvie, "Church and State," p. 2.

164. Temple, "Christian Faith and the Common Life," pp. 5-7.

165. J.P.R. Maud, "Church, Community and State in Relation to the Economic Order," p. 37, April 37, LW, Ehrenström Papers, Box 9, folder:

Section III; and Oldham, "The Function of the Church in the Social and Political Sphere," p. 19.

166. Temple, "Christian Faith and the Common Life," p. 9; Bevan, "The Kingdom of God and History," pp. 11-12; and Reckitt, "Grace and the World Order," p. 18.

167. Bevan, "The Kingdom of God and History," p. 613; and Temple, "Christian Faith and the Common Life," p. 4.

168. Minutes of Schloss Hemmen, 2-4 May, 1935, p. 31; and Oldham, "The Function of the Church in the Social and Political Spheres," p. 11.

169. Boys-Smith, "Nature and Grace," p. 3; and Tawney, "Memorandum," p. 1.

170. Thomas Edmund Jessop, "The Scientific Understanding of Man," in Conference on Church, Community, and State, *The Christian Understanding of Man*, pp. 33-34.

171. Henry Clay to Oldham, 19 February 1937, LW, 0.5, folder: Miscellaneous. Clay had been secretary of a London charity organization, warden of a settlement house in Sheffield, and professor of economics at Manchester University before joining the Bank of England in 1930. Like his superiors in Whitehall, Clay was skeptical of Keynes's ideas in the 1930s.

172. Reckitt, "Grace and the World Order," p. 19; Tawney, "Memorandum," p. 6; and Minutes of Schloss Hemmen, 2-4 May 1935, p. 12.

173. Wood, "The Kingdom of God and the Meaning of History," p. 3; and Minutes of Schloss Hemmen, 4-8 May 1935, p. 12.

174. Maud, "Church, Community and State in Relation to the Economic Order," p. 37; see also Tawney, "Memorandum," pp. 6-7.

175. Maud, "Church, Community and State in Relation to the Economic Order," pp. 9, 14; and Ernest Barker, "Church, Community and State in Relation to the Social Order," p. 4, March 1937, LW, D242 box 1.

176. Tawney, "Memorandum," p. 3; and Malcolm Spencer, "Comments on Dr. Polanyi's Draft Memorandum," pp. 4-10, November 1936, LW, 14/II, folder 5.

177. Tawney, "Memorandum," pp. 10-11; Maud, "Church, Community, and State in Relation to the Economic Order," p. 13; and Barker, "Church, Community and State in Relation to the Social Order," p. 4.

178. Barker, "Church, Community and State in Relation to the Social Order," pp. 12-13; and Tawney, "Memorandum," p. 12.

179. Spencer, "Comments on Dr. Polanyi's Draft Memorandum," pp. 9-10.

180. Oldham to E.M. Hemingway, 9 December 1934, LW, 0.5, folder: Oxford Correspondents.

181. Tawney, "Memorandum," p. 17; and Craig, *Social Concern in the Thought of William Temple*, pp. 129-136. Temple's social thought came to fruition later in his *Christianity and the Social Order* (Harmondsworth: Penguin Books, 1942).

182. Oldham, "The Function of the Church in the Social and Political Sphere," p. 10.

6. Conclusion

1. "A Brief Report," p. 8 (Bell Papers).

2. See *The Social Function of the Church*, pp. 4-5.

3. Anthropoligists and rhetoricians have shown how effective such symbols and myths can be. See Claude Lévi-Strauss, "The Structural Study of Myth," *Journal of American Folklore* 68 (1955), 428-44; Kenneth Burke, *A Rhetoric of Motives* (1950; Berkeley: University of California Press, 1969); Mircea Eliade, *Images and Symbols: Studies in Religious Symbolism*, trans. Philip Mairet (New York: Sheed and Ward, 1961); and Eliade, "Methodological Remarks on the Study of Religious Symbolism," in Eliade and Joseph M. Kitagawa, eds., *The History of Religions: Essays in Methodology* (Chicago: University of Chicago Press, 1959).

4. Adolf Keller, "The International Activities of the Churches," *Review of the Churches* 7 (1930): 393-394; see also *Stockholm* 1 (1928): 181-187; and *Life and Work* 4-5 (July 1928): 206.

5. Malcolm Muggeridge, *The Thirties, 1930-1940, in Great Britain* (London: Hamish Hamilton, 1940), p. 35.

6. See the remarkable agreement between the Scottish Presbyterian John Baillie in *What Is Christian Civilisation?* (London: Oxford University Press, 1945) and the Anglo-Catholic T.S. Eliot in *The Idea of a Christian Society* (London: Faber and Faber, 1939).

7. Actually, by the end of 1937 only one Protestant pastor had lost his life at the hands of the Nazis. Rev. Paul Schneider died in Buchenwald after refusing to leave his parish on Gestapo orders. See Conway, *The Nazi Persecution of the Churches*, p. 209.

8. Eberhard Bethge's biography of Bonhoeffer, for example, lays bare the division of the movement and the reticence and conservatism of certain groups within the Confessing Church. See also Gutteridge, *Open Thy Mouth for the Dumb*, for criticism of the Confessing Church's lack of action on the Jewish question. Shelley Baranowski and Fred Bonkovsky both have argued that the Confessing Church was not born out of political or humanitarian motives but primarily organized by conservative German elites who resisted Nazi intrusion onto their traditional ecclesiastical control. Both assert this, however, more than they actually examine the question. See Shelley Baranowski, *The Confessing Church, Conservative Elites, and the Nazi State* (Lewiston, N.Y.: Edwin Mellen Press, 1986); and Frederick O. Bonkovsky, "The German State and Protestant Elites," in Franklin H. Littell and Hubert G. Locke, eds., *The German Church Struggle and the Holocaust* (Detroit: Wayne State University Press, 1974), pp. 124-147.

9. Gutteridge, *Open Thy Mouth for the Dumb*, p. 72.

10. Walter Künneth, "Das Judenproblem und die Kirche," in Walter Künneth and Helmut Schreiner, eds., *Die Nation vor Gott: Zur Botschaft der Kirche im Dritten Reich* (Berlin: Wichern Verlag, 1933), p. 91.

11. See Boyens, *Kirchenkampf und Ökumene*, p. 45; and Friedrich Wilhelm Kantzenbach, *Widerstand und Solidarität der Christen in Deutschland 1933-1945: Eine Dokumentation zum Kirchenkampf aus den Papieren*

des D. Wilhelm Freiherrn von Pechmann (Neustadt/Aisch: Degener, 1971), p. 8.

12. See for example Helmreich, *The German Churches under Hitler*, p. 142; and Peter Neumann, *Die Jungreformatorische Bewegung* (Göttingen: Vandenhoeck und Ruprecht, 1971).

13. See Wendland, *Weg und Umwege*, p. 154.

14. Shelley Baranowski, "The Limits of Discontent: The Confessing Church in Germany 1933-1939" (Ph.D. diss. Princeton University, 1980), p. 146; and Gerstenmaier, *Streit und Friede hat seine Zeit*, pp. 194-214. For Schönfeld's involvement see Bethge, *Dietrich Bonhoeffer*, pp. 660-668.

15. Boys-Smith, "Comments on Prof. Brunner's Paper," p. 2.

SELECTED
BIBLIOGRAPHY

Archival materials

Geneva, Switzerland. World Council of Churches Library.
  Eugène Choisy Papers.
  General Secretariat Correspondence.
  Germany, Church Struggle.
  Elie Gounelle Papers.
  Life and Work Papers.
  Pamphlet File
London, England. Lambeth Palace Library.
  George Kennedy Allen Bell Papers.
  Randall Davidson Papers, Box 1925:W26, Subject: Life and Work.
  Cosmo Lang Papers, vol. 76.
Uppsala, Sweden. University of Uppsala Library.
  Söderblom Archives.
West Berlin, Germany. Evangelisches Zentralarchiv.
  Kirchliches Außenamt Papers, Bestand 5.
  Personal Files: Gerhard May and Hans Schönfeld.

Published Sources

Albertin, Lothar. *Liberalismus und Demokratie am Anfang der Weimarer Republik: Eine vergleichende Analyse der Deutschen Demokratischen Partei und der Deutschen Volkspartei.* Düsseldorf: Droste Verlag, 1972.
Allgemeine Evangelisch-Lutherische Kirchenzeitung 58-70 (1925-37).
Althaus, Paul. *Die deutsche Stunde der Kirche.* 3d ed. Göttingen: Vandenhoeck und Ruprecht, 1934.
_____. *The Ethics of Martin Luther.* Translated by Robert C. Schultz. Philadelphia: Fortress Press, 1972.
_____. *Kirche und Staat nach Lutherischer Lehre.* Leipzig: U. Deichertsche, 1935.
_____. *Theologie der Ordnungen.* Gütersloh: C. Bertelsmann, 1935.

Anderson, Gerald D. *Fascists, Communists and the National Government: Civil Liberties in Great Britain 1931-1937.* Columbia: University of Missouri Press, 1983.

Bailey, Charles Edward. "Gott Mit Uns: Germany's Protestant Theologians in the First World War." Ph.D. diss., University of Virginia, 1978.

Baillie, John. *What Is Christian Civilisation?* London: Oxford University Press, 1945.

Baranowski, Shelley Osmun. *The Confessing Church, Conservative Elites, and the Nazi State.* Lewiston, N.Y.: Edwin Mellen Press, 1986.

————. "The Limits of Discontent: The Confessing Church in Germany 1933-1939." Ph.D. diss., Princeton University, 1980.

Barth, Karl. *This Christian Cause: A Letter to Great Britain from Switzerland.* New York: Macmillan, 1941.

Bebbington, David W. *The Nonconformist Conscience: Chapel and Politics, 1870-1914.* London: George Allen and Unwin, 1982.

Beckmann, Joachim, and Gerhard Weissler, eds. *Gemeinde und Gesellschaftswandel.* Stuttgart: Kreuz Verlag, 1964.

Bell, G.K.A. *Randall Davidson, Archbishop of Canterbury.* 2 vols. New York: Oxford University Press, 1935.

————. ed. *The Stockholm Conference 1925: The Official Report of the Universal Christian Conference on Life and Work Held in Stockholm, 19-30 August 1925.* London: Oxford University Press, 1926.

Bell, G.K.A., and Adolf Deissmann, eds. *Mysterium Christi: Christological Studies by British and German Theologians.* London: Longmans, Green, 1930.

Bentley, Michael. *The Liberal Mind 1914-1929.* Cambridge: Cambridge University Press, 1977.

Berger, Peter L. *The Sacred Canopy: Elements of a Sociological Theory of Religion.* New York: Doubleday, 1969.

Besier, Gerhard. *Krieg, Frieden, Abrüstung: Die Haltung der europäischen und amerikanischen Kirchen zur Frage der deutschen Kriegsschuld 1914-1933.* Göttingen: Vandenhoeck und Ruprecht, 1982.

Bethge, Eberhard. *Dietrich Bonhoeffer: Man of Vision, Man of Courage.* Translated by Eric Mosbacher et al. New York: Harper and Row, 1977.

Blackbourn, David, and Geoff Eley. *The Peculiarities of German History.* New York: Oxford University Press, 1984.

Bonkovsky, Frederick O. "The German State and Protestant Elites." In *The German Church Struggle and the Holocaust,* edited by Franklin H. Littell and Hubert G. Locke. Detroit: Wayne State University Press, 1974.

Borg, Daniel R. *The Old-Prussian Church and the Weimar Republic: A Study in Political Adjustment.* Hanover, N.H.: University Press of New England, 1984.

Boyens, Armin. *Kirchenkampf und Ökumene 1933-1939: Darstellung und Dokumentation.* Munich: Chr. Kaiser, 1969.

Bradfield, Margaret. *City of Mercy: The Story of Bethel.* Bethel bei Bielefeld: Verlagshandlung der Anstalt Bethel, 1964.

Brady, Robert A. *The Rationalization Movement in German Industry: A*

Study in the Evolution of Economic Planning. Berkeley: University of California Press, 1933.

Brakelmann, Günter, ed. *Kirche, soziale Frage und Sozialismus: Kirchenleitungen und Synoden über soziale Frage und Sozialismus 1871-1914*. Gütersloh: Gerd Mohn, 1977.

―――. *Kirche und Sozialismus im 19. Jahrhundert: Die Analyse des Sozialismus und Kommunismus bei Johann Hinrich Wichern und bei Rudolf Todt*. Witten: Luther-Verlag, 1966.

Bramsted, E. "The Position of the Protestant Church in Germany 1871-1933, Part II: The Church during the Weimar Republic." *Journal of Religious History* 3 (1964): 61-79.

Breipohl, Renate. *Religioser Sozialismus und bürgerliches Geschichtsbusstsein zur Zeit der Weimarer Republik*. Zurich: Theologischer Verlag, 1971.

Breitsohl, Theo M. "Die Kirchen- und Schulpolitik der Weimarer Parteien 1918-1919." Ph.D. diss., Tübingen University, 1978.

Brown, Ford K. *Fathers of the Victorians*. Cambridge: Cambridge University Press, 1961.

Brunstäd, Friedrich. *Gesammelte Aufsätze und kleinere Schriften*. Edited by Eugen Gerstenmaier and Carl G. Schweitzer. Berlin: Lutherisches Verlagshaus, 1957.

Burke, Kenneth. *A Rhetoric of Motives*. Berkeley: University of California Press, 1969.

Carter, Paul H. *The Decline and Revival of the Social Gospel: Social and Political Liberalism in American Protestant Churches*. Ithaca, N.Y.: Cornell University Press, 1954.

Cell, John W., ed. *By Kenya Possessed: The Correspondence of Norman Leys and J.H. Oldham 1918-1926*. Chicago: University of Chicago Press, 1976.

Chadwick, Owen. *Hensley Henson: A Study in the Friction between Church and State*. Oxford: Oxford University Press, 1983.

―――. *The Secularization of the European Mind in the Nineteenth Century*. Cambridge: Cambridge University Press, 1975.

Childers, Thomas. *The Nazi Voter: The Social Foundations of Fascism in Germany, 1919-1933*. Chapel Hill: University of North Carolina Press, 1983.

The Churches and Present-Day Economic Problems: Conference of Christian Social Workers, London July 12th to 17th, 1930. Geneva: UCCLW, 1930.

Churches in Action 1-18 (March 1933-October 1938).

Clark, George Kitson. *Churchmen and the Condition of England 1832-1885: A Study in the Development of Social Ideas and Practice from the Old Regime to the Modern State*. London: Methuen, 1973.

Clarke, Peter. *Liberals and Social Democrats*. Cambridge: Cambridge University Press, 1978.

Cochrane, Arthur C. *The Church's Confession under Hitler*. Pittsburgh, Pa.: Pickwick Press, 1976.

Cole, G.D.H. *Guild Socialism: A Plan for Economic Democracy*. New York: Frederick A. Stokes, 1920.

Conference on Christian Politics, Economics, and Citizenship. *Industry and Property*. London: Longmans, Green, 1924.

————. *The Nature of God and His Purpose for the World*. London: Longmans, Green, 1924.

Conference on Church, Community, and State. *Christian Faith and the Common Life*. Chicago: Willett and Clark, 1938.

————. *The Christian Understanding of Man*. Chicago: Willett and Clark, 1938.

————. *Church and Community*. Chicago: Willett and Clark, 1938.

Conway, John S. *The Nazi Persecution of the Churches 1933-1945*. New York: Basic Books, 1968.

Cowling, Maurice. *The Impact of Hitler: British Politics and British Policy 1933-1940*. London: Cambridge University Press, 1975.

Cox, Jeffrey. *The English Churches in a Secular Society: Lambeth 1870-1930*. New York: Oxford University Press, 1982.

Craemer, Rudolf. *Evangelische Reformation als politische Macht*. Göttingen: Vandenhoeck und Ruprecht, 1933.

————. *Der Kampf um die Volksordnung von der preußischen Sozialpolitik zum deutschen Sozialismus*. Hamburg: Hanseatische Verlagsanstalt, 1933.

Craig, Gordon. *Germany 1866-1945*. New York: Oxford University Press, 1978.

Craig, Robert. *Social Concern in the Thought of William Temple*. London: Gollancz, 1963.

Cross, Colin. *The Fascists in Britain*. London: Barrie and Rockliff, 1961.

Dahm, Karl Wilhelm. "German Protestantism and Politics." *Journal of Contemporary History* 3 (January 1968): 29-49.

————. *Pfarrer und Politik: Soziale Position und politische Mentalität des deutschen evangelischen Pfarrerstandes zwischen 1918 und 1933*. Cologne: Westdeutschen Verlag, 1965.

Davidson, Randall T., ed. *The Five Lambeth Conferences 1867, 1878, 1888, 1897, and 1908*. London: S.P.C.K., 1920.

Dearmer, Percy, ed. *Christianity and the Crisis*. London: Victor Gollancz, 1933.

Deissmann, Adolf. "The Present Position of Ecumenical Christianity." *Review of the Churches* 3 (1926): 393-397.

————. *Stockholmer Bewegung: Die Weltkirchenkonferenz zu Stockholm 1925 und Bern 1926 von innen betrachtet*. Berlin: Furche Verlag, 1927.

Dibelius, Martin. *Evangelium und Welt*. Göttingen: Vandenhoeck und Ruprecht, 1929.

Dougall, J.W.C. "J.H. Oldham." *International Review of Missions* 59 (January 1970): 8-22.

Drummond, Henry. *German Protestantism since Luther*. London: Epworth Press, 1951.

Ecumenical Review 21 (July 1969).

Die Eiche 1-20 (1913-33).

Elert, Werner. *Morphologie des Luthertums.* 2 vols. Munich: C.H. Becksche, 1931-32.

Eley, Geoff. *Reshaping the German Right: Radical Nationalism and Political Change after Bismarck.* New Haven, Conn.: Yale University Press, 1980.

Eliade, Mircea. *Images and Symbols: Studies in Religious Symbolism.* Translated by Philip Mairet. New York: Sheed and Ward, 1961.

_____. "Methodological Remarks on the Study of Religious Symbolism." In *The History of Religions: Essays in Methodology,* edited by Eliade and Joseph H. Kitagawa. Chicago: University of Chicago Press, 1959.

Eliot, T.S. *The Idea of a Christian Society.* London: Faber and Faber, 1939.

Une enquête sur l'éthique sociale des églises. Geneva: UCCLW, 1935.

Ericksen, Robert P. *Theologians under Hitler: Gerhard Kittel, Paul Althaus, and Emanuel Hirsch.* New Haven, Conn.: Yale University Press, 1985.

Faber, Johannes. *Jamaa: A Charismatic Movement in Katanga.* Evanston, Ill.: Northwestern University Press, 1971.

Frank, Walter. *Hofprediger Adolf Stoecker und die christlichsoziale Bewegung.* 2d ed. Hamburg: Hanseatische Verlagsanstalt, 1935.

Frick, Heinrich. *Das Reich Gottes in americanischer und in deutscher Theologie der Gegenwart.* Giessen: Alfred Töpelmann, 1926.

Füllkrug, Gerhard. *Die Weltkonferenz für praktisches Christentum von 19. bis 30 August 1925.* Berlin: Wichern Verlag, 1925.

Gaede, Reinhard. "Kirche, Christen, Krieg und Frieden: Diskussion im deutschen Protestantismus während der Weimarer Zeit." Doctoral diss., University of Münster, 1972.

Gaines, David. *The World Council of Churches.* Peterborough, N.H.: Richard R. Smith, 1966.

Garvie, Alfred. "The Challenge of the Social Gospel." *Review of the Churches* 3 (1926): 516-523.

_____. *The Fatherly Rule of God: A Study of Society, State, and Church.* New York: Abingdon Press, 1935.

_____. *Memories and Meanings of My Life.* London: George Allen and Unwin, 1938.

_____. *The Ritschlian Theology: Critical and Constructive.* Edinburgh: T. and T. Clark, 1899.

Gay, Peter. *Weimar Culture: Outsider as Insider.* New York: Harper and Row, 1968.

Geertz, Clifford. *The Interpretation of Cultures.* New York: Basic Books, 1973.

Gerhardt, Martin. *Ein Jahrhundert Innere Mission: Die Geschichte des Central-Ausschusses für die Innere Mission der Deutschen Evangelischen Kirche.* 2 vols. Gütersloh: C. Bertelsmann, 1948.

Gerstenmaier, Eugen, ed. *Kirche, Volk, und Staat: Stimmen aus der Deutschen Evangelischen Kirche.* Berlin: Furche Verlag, 1937.

_____. *Streit und Friede hat seine Zeit: Ein Lebensbericht.* Frankfurt/M: Propyläen, 1981.

Gilbert, Alan. *Religion and Society in Industrial England: Church, Chapel, and Social Change 1740-1914.* London: Longman, 1976.

Gloede, Günter, ed. *Ökumenische Profile: Brückenbauer der Einer Kirche.* 2 vols. Stuttgart: Evang. Missionsverlag, 1963.

Gore, Charles. *The Doctrine of the Infallible Book.* New York: George H. Doran, 1925.

Groh, John. *Nineteenth-Century German Protestantism: The Church as Social Model.* Washington, D.C.: University Press of America, 1982.

Gründer, Horst. *Walter Simons, die Ökumene und der Evangelisch-Soziale Kongress: Ein Beitrag zur Geschichte des politischen Protestantismus im 20. Jahrhundert.* Soest: Mocker und Jahn, 1974.

Grunow, Richard. *Wichern-Ruf und Antwort.* Gütersloh: Rufer-Verlag, 1958.

Gutteridge, Richard. *Open Thy Mouth for the Dumb! The German Evangelical Church and the Jews 1874-1950.* Oxford: Basil Blackwell, 1976.

Halperin, William. *Germany Tried Democracy: A Political History of the Reich from 1918 to 1933.* Hamden, Conn.: Archon Books, 1946.

Hamilton, Richard F. *Who Voted for Hitler?* Princeton, N.J.: Princeton University Press, 1982.

Hammer, Karl. *Deutsche Kriegstheologie 1870-1918.* Munich: Koesel-Verlag, 1971.

Harvey, John, William Temple, et al. *Competition: A Study in Human Motive.* London: Macmillan, 1917.

Heiler, Friedrich. *Evangelische Katholizität Gesammelte Aufsätze und Vorträge.* Munich: Ernst Reinhardt, 1926.

Helmreich, Ernst Christian. *The German Churches under Hitler: Background, Struggle, and Epilogue.* Detroit: Wayne State University Press, 1979.

————. *Religious Education in German Schools: An Historical Approach.* Cambridge, Mass.: Harvard University Press, 1959.

Herntrich, Hans-Volker. *Im Feuer der Kritik: Johann Hinrich Wichern und der Sozialismus.* Hamburg: Agentur des Rauhen Hauses, 1969.

Hertzman, Lewis. *DNVP: Right-Wing Opposition in the Weimar Republic 1918-1924.* Lincoln: University of Nebraska Press, 1963.

Heuss, Theodor. *Friedrich Naumann: Der Mann, das Werk, die Zeit.* 3d ed. Munich: Siebenstern, 1968.

Hoffmann, Peter. *The History of the German Resistance 1933-1945.* Translated by Richard Barry. Cambridge, Mass.: MIT Press, 1977.

Hudson, Darril. *The Ecumenical Movement and World Affairs: The Church as an International Pressure Group.* Washington, D.C.: National Press, 1969.

Inglis, K.S. *Churches and the Working Classes in Victorian England.* London: Routledge and Kegan Paul, 1963.

Iremonger, F.A. *William Temple, Archbishop of Canterbury: His Life and Letters.* London: Oxford University Press, 1948.

Jasper, Ronald C.D. *George Bell, Bishop of Chichester.* London: Oxford University Press, 1967.

Jones, Gareth Stedman. *Outcast London: A Study in the Relationship between the Classes in Victorian Society.* Harmondsworth: Penguin Books, 1971.

Jones, Peter d'A. *The Christian Socialist Revival 1877-1914: Religion, Class and Social Conscience in Late-Victorian England.* Princeton, N.J.: Princeton University Press, 1968.

Journet, Charles. *L'union des églises et le christianisme pratique.* Paris: Bernard Grasset, 1927.

Kantzenbach, Friedrich Wilhelm. *Widerstand und Solidarität der Christen in Deutschland 1933-1945: Eine Dokumentation zum Kirchenkampf aus den Papieren des D. Wilhelm Freiherrn von Pechmann.* Neustadt/Aisch: Degener, 1971.

Karrenberg, Friedrich. *Christentum, Kapitalismus und Sozialismus.* Berlin: Junker und Dünnhaupt, 1932.

Kater, Michael H. *The Nazi Party: A Social Profile of Members and Leaders 1919-1945.* Cambridge, Mass.: Harvard University Press, 1983.

Keller, Adolf. "The International Activities of the Churches." *Review of the Churches* 7 (1930): 390-397.

———. *The International Christian Social Institute, Geneva 1927-1928.* Geneva: International Christian Social Institute, 1928.

Keynes, John Maynard. *Collected Works.* Vol. 20, *Activities.* London: Macmillan, 1981.

———. *The End of Laissez-Faire.* London: L. and V. Woolf, 1926.

Kingsford, Peter. *The Hunger Marchers in Britain 1920-1939.* London: Lawrence and Wishart, 1982.

Kirchliches Jahrbuch 50-59 (1923-32).

Klingemann, Karl Viktor. *Glaube und Vaterlandsliebe.* Essen: G.D. Baedeker, 1915.

———. *Wo für kämpfen wir?* Witten: Evangelischen Preßbüro, 1915.

Kosmahl, Hans-Joachim. *Ethik in Ökumene und Mission: Das Problem der "Mittleren Axiome" bei J.H. Oldham und in der christlichen Sozialethik.* Göttingen: Vandenhoeck und Ruprecht, 1970.

Koss, Stephen. *Nonconformity in Modern British Politics.* Hamden, Conn.: Archon Books, 1975.

Kouri, E.I. *Der deutsche Protestantismus und die soziale Frage 1870-1919: Zur Sozialpolitik im Bildungsbürgertum.* New York: Walter de Gruyter, 1984.

Krczmar, Karl. *Einheit der Kirche in Leben und Wirken: Die Stockholmer Weltkirchenkonferenz für Praktisches Christentum vom Jahre 1925.* Vienna: Reinhold Verlag, 1930.

Kressel, Hans. *Simon Schöffel: Magnalia und Miniaturen aus dem Leben eines Lutherischen Bischofs.* Schweinfurt: Historischen Verein und Stadtarchiv, 1964.

Kretschmar, Gottfried. *Der Evangelisch-Soziale Kongress: Der deutsche Protestantismus und die soziale Frage.* Stuttgart: Evangelisches Verlagswerke, 1972.

Künneth, Walter. "Das Judenproblem und die Kirche," in Walter Künneth and Helmut Schreiner, eds., *Die Nation vor Gott: Zur Botschaft der Kirche im Dritten Reich.* Berlin: Wichern Verlag, 1933.

————. *Lebensführungen: Der Wahrheit verpflichtet.* Wuppertal: Brockhaus, 1979.

Kupisch, Karl. *Adolf Stöcker: Hofprediger und Volkstribun.* Berlin: Haude und Spenersche, 1970.

————. "Friedrich Naumann und die evangelisch-soziale Bewegung." Ph.D. diss., Friedrich Wilhelms University, Berlin, 1937.

————. *Das Jahrhundert des Sozialismus und die Kirche.* Berlin: Kathe Vogt Verlag, 1958.

————, ed. *Quellen zur Geschichtidees deutschen Protestantismus 1871-1945.* Göttingen: Musterschmidt, 1960.

————. "Stromungen der Evangelischen Kirche in der Weimarer Republic." *Archiv für Sozialgeschichte* 11 (1971): 373-415.

The Lambeth Conferences 1867-1948: The Reports of the 1920, 1930, and 1948 Conferences with Selected Resolutions from the Conferences of 1867, 1878, 1888, 1897 and 1908. London: S.P.C.K., 1948.

Langford, Thomas A. *In Search of Foundations: English Theology 1900-1920.* Nashville, Tenn.: Abingdon Press, 1969.

Laun, Ferdinand. *Soziales Christentum in England: Geschichte und Gedankenwelt der Copecbewegung.* Berlin: Furche Verlag, 1926.

Lévi-Strauss, Claude. "The Structural Study of Myth." *Journal of American Folklore* 68 (1955): 428-44.

Lewis, W.A. *Economic Survey 1919-1937.* London: George Allen and Unwin, 1949.

Lieb, Fritz. *Sophia und Historie: Aufsätze zur östlichen und westlichen Geistes- und Theologiegeschichte.* Edited by Martin Robkrümer. Zurich: EVZ, 1962.

Life and Work: Bulletin of the International Christian Social Institute 1-10 (1927-30).

Lilje, Hanns. *Luthers Geschichtsanschauung.* Berlin: Furche Verlag, 1932.

Lindt, Andreas, ed. *George Bell, Alphons Koechlin: Briefwechsel 1933-1954.* Zurich: EVZ, 1962.

Lloyd, Roger. *The Church of England in the Twentieth Century.* 2 vols. London: Longmans, Green, 1946, 1950.

Luther's Works. American ed. Vol. 26. St. Louis, Mo.: Concordia, 1963.

Maas, Hermann. "Friedrich Siegmund-Schultze und der Weltbund für Freundschaftsarbeit der Kirchen." In *Lebendige Ökumene: Festschrift für Friedrich Siegmund-Schultze zum 80. Geburtstag.* Witten: Luther-Verlag, 1965.

McCleod, Hugh. "The De-Christianization of the Working Class in Western Europe 1850-1900." *Social Compass* 27 (1980): 191-214.

MacFarland, Charles. *Steps toward the World Council: Origins of the Ecumenical Movement as Expressed in the Universal Christian Council for Life and Work.* New York: Fleming H. Revell, 1938.

Mahling, Friedrich. *Die Weltkonferenz für praktisches Christentum in Stockholm 19-30 August 1925: Bericht über ihren Verlauf und ihre Ergebnisse.* Gütersloh: C. Bertelsmann, n.d.

Maier, Charles S. *Recasting Bourgeois Europe: Stabilization in France, Germany and Italy in the Decade after World War I.* Princeton, N.J.: Princeton University Press, 1975.

May, Gerhard. *Die volksdeutsche Sendung der Kirche.* Göttingen: Vandenhoeck und Ruprecht, 1934.

Mehnert, Gottfried. *Evangelische Kirche und Politik 1917-1919: Die politischen Stromungen in deutschen Protestantism von der Julikrise 1917 bis zum Herbst 1919.* Düsseldorf: Droste Verlag, 1959.

Miller, Robert Moats. *American Protestantism and Social Issues 1919-1934.* Chapel Hill: University of North Carolina Press, 1958.

Monnier, Henri. *Vers l'union des églises: La conférence universelle de Stockholm.* Paris: Librarie Fischbacher, 1926.

Monod, Wilfred, ed. *À la croisée des chemins (organisations de la paix): Discours prononcés durant la session du conseil oecuménique du christianisme pratique.* Geneva: UCCLW, 1932.

Moore, Barrington. *Injustice: The Social Bases of Obedience and Revolt.* White Plains, N.Y.: M.E. Sharpe, 1978.

————. *Social Origins of Dictatorship and Democracy: Lord and Peasant in the Making of the Modern World.* Boston: Beacon Press, 1966.

Motschmann, Claus. *Evangelische Kirche und preussischer Staat in den Anfängen der Weimarer Republik: Möglichkeit und Grenzen ihrer Zusammenarbeit.* Lübeck: Matthiesen Verlag, 1969.

Mowat, Charles Loch. *Britain between the Wars 1918-1940.* Chicago: University of Chicago Press, 1955.

Muggeridge, Malcolm. *The Thirties, 1930-1940, in Great Britain.* London: Hamish Hamilton, 1940.

Mumm, Reinhold. *Was jeder Christ von den heutigen Parteien wissen muß.* Hamburg: Agentur des Rauhen Hauses, 1924.

Neumann, Peter. *Die Jungreformatorische Bewegung.* Göttingen: Vandenhoeck und Ruprecht, 1971.

Niebuhr, H. Richard. *Christ and Culture.* New York: Harper and Row, 1951.

Norman, Edward R. *Church and Society in England 1770-1970: A Historical Study.* Oxford: Clarendon Press, 1976.

Nowak, Kurt. *Evangelische Kirche und Weimarer Republik: Zum politischen Weg des deutschen Protestantismus zwischen 1918 und 1932.* Göttingen: Vandenhoeck und Ruprecht, 1981.

Oliver, John. *Social Thought in the Church of England, 1918-1939.* London: A.R. Mobray, 1969.

Opitz, Günter. *Der Christlich-Soziale Volksdienst: Versuch einer protestantischen Partei in der Weimarer Republik.* Düsseldorf: Droste, 1969.

Padgett, Jack F. *The Christian Philosophy of William Temple.* The Hague: Martinus Nijhoff, 1974.

Pribilla, Max. *Um Kirchliche Einheit, Stockholm Conference, Lausanne,*

*Rome: Geschichtlich- Theologische Darstellung der Neueren Einig-
ungsbestrebungen.* Freiburg: Herder, 1929.

Ramsay, Arthur Michael. *An Era in Anglican Theology from Gore to Temple:
The Development of Anglican Theology between "Lux Mundi" and the
Second World War 1889-1939.* New York: Scribner, 1960.

Rathje, Johannes. *Die Welt des freien Protestantismus: Ein Beitrag zur
deutsch-evangelischen Geistesgeschichte Dargestellt an Leben und Werk
von Martin Rade.* Stuttgart: Ehrenfried Klotz Verlag, 1952.

Reckitt, Maurice. *From Maurice to Temple: A Century of the Social Movement in the Church of England.* London: Faber and Faber, 1947.

Renatus, Kuno. *The Twelfth Hour of Capitalism.* Translated by E.W. Dickes.
New York: Knopf, 1932.

*Revolutionary Theology in the Making: Barth-Thurneysen Correspondence
1919-1925.* Translated by James D. Smart. Richmond, Va.: John Knox
Press, 1964.

Robinson, Edwin H., ed. *No Rusty Swords: Letters, Lectures and Notes
1928-1936 from the Collected Works of Dietrich Bonhoeffer.* Translated
by Edwin H. Robinson and John Bowden. New York: Harper and Row,
1965.

Rouse, Ruth, and Stephen Neill, eds. *A History of the Ecumenical Movement
1517-1948.* Vol 1. 2d ed. Philadelphia: Westminster Press, 1967.

Rupp, Gordon. *"I Seek My Brethren": Bishop George Bell and the German
Churches.* London: Epworth Press, 1975.

Schöffel, Simon, and Adolf Köberle. *Luthertum und die soziale Frage.*
Leipzig: Dörffling und Franke, 1931.

Scholder, Klaus. *Die Kirchen und das Dritte Reich.* 2 vols. Frankfurt/M:
Propyläen, 1977. Translated by John Bowden as *The Churches and the
Third Reich.* 2 vols. Minneapolis: Augsburg-Fortress, 1987-88.

Schönfeld, Hans. *Kritische Studien zum wirtschaftlichen Problem des Zwei
und Dreischictensystems in Hochofenbetrieben.* Jena: Gustav Fischer,
1926.

Shanahan, William O. *German Protestants Face the Social Question: The
Conservative Phase 1815-1871.* South Bend, Ind.: Notre Dame University
Press, 1954.

Shillito, Edward. *Life and Work.* London: Longmans, Green, 1926.

Siegmund-Schultze, Friedrich, ed. *Nathan Söderblom: Briefe und
Botschaften an einen deutschen Mitarbeiter.* Marburg: Oekumenischer
Verlag Edel, 1966.

Skidelsky, Robert. *Oswald Mosley.* New York: Holt, Rinehart and Winston,
1975.

Söderblom, Nathan, and Adolf Keller. "Echoes of Stockholm." *Review of the
Churches* 3 (1926): 351-362.

Soloway, Richard Allen. *Prelates and People: Ecclesiastical Social Thought in
England 1783-1852.* London: Routledge and Kegan Paul, 1969.

Stählin, Wilhelm. *Via Vitae: Lebenserinnerungen von Wilhelm Stählin.*
Kassel: Stauda, 1968.

Stange, Erich, ed. *Die Religionswissenschaft der Gegenwart in Selbstdarstellungen*. Leipzig: Meiner, 1928.

————. *Vom Weltprotestantismus der Gegenwart*. Hamburg: Agentur des Rauhen Hauses, 1925.

Steinweg, Johannes. *Inneres Mission und Gemeindienst in meinem Leben*. Berlin: Wichern Verlag, 1959.

Stockholm: International Review for the Social Activities of the Churches 1-4 (1928-31).

Strohm, Theodor. *Kirche und demokratischen Sozialismus: Studien zur Theorie und Praxis politischer Kommunikation*. Munich: CHR Kaiser Verlag, 1968.

Studdert-Kennedy, Gerald. *Dog-Collar Democracy: The Industrial Christian Fellowship 1919-1929*. London: Macmillan, 1982.

Sundkler, Bengt. *Nathan Söderblom: His Life and Work*. London: Lutterworth Press, 1968.

Sykes, S.W. "Theology." In *The Twentieth Century Mind: History, Ideas, and Literature in Britain*, edited by C.B. Cox and A.E. Dyson. 3 vols. London: Oxford University Press, 1972.

Tawney, R.H. *The Acquisitive Society*. New York: Harcourt, Brace, 1920.

————. *Religion and the Rise of Capitalism*. 1926; Harmondsworth: Penguin Books, 1975.

Taylor, A.J.P. *English History 1914-1945*. Oxford: Oxford University Press, 1965.

Temple, William. *Christianity and the Social Order*. Harmondsworth: Penguin Books, 1942.

Terrill, Ross. *R.H. Tawney and His Times: Socialism as Fellowship*. Cambridge, Mass.: Harvard University Press, 1973.

Theology 14 (1927).

Thomis, Malcolm. *The Town Labourer and the Industrial Revolution*. London: B.T. Batsford, 1974.

Tiefel, Hans. "The German Lutheran Church and the Rise of National Socialism." *Church History* 41 (1972): 326-336.

Tilgner, Wolfgang. *Volksnomostheologie und Schöpfungsglaube*. Göttingen: Vandenhoeck und Ruprecht, 1966.

The *Times* (London), 7-14 April 1924.

Todt, Rudolf. *Der radicale deutsche socialismus und die christliche Gesellschaft*. Wittenberg: E. Rust, 1877.

Totaler Staat und Christliche Freiheit. Geneva: UCCLW, 1937.

Troeltsch, Ernst. *The Social Teachings of the Christian Churches*. 2 vols. Translated by Olive Wyon. London: George Allen and Unwin, 1931.

UCCLW *Newsletter* no. 7 (8 July 1932).

United Kingdom. *Parliamentary Debates* (Lords). 5th ser., vol. 64 (1926).

Verhandlung des zweiten Deutschen Evangelischen Kirchentages in Königsberg, 1927. Berlin: Evangelischen Preßverband, 1927.

Vidler, Alec. *The Church in an Age of Revolution: 1789 to the Present Day*. Harmondsworth: Penguin Books, 1961.

Visser't Hooft, Willem. "Karl Barth and the Ecumenical Movement." *Ecumenical Review* 32 (April 1980): 129-151.

———. *Memoirs*. Philadelphia: Westminster Press, 1973.

Wagner, Donald O. *The Church of England and Social Reform since 1854*. New York: Columbia University Press, 1930.

Ward, W.R. *Theology, Sociology and Politics: The German Protestant Social Conscience 1890-1933*. Bern: Peter Lang, 1979.

Wearmouth, Robert F. *Methodism and the Struggle of the Working Classes 1850-1900*. Leicester: Edgar Backus, 1954.

Weber, Max. *The Sociology of Religion*. Boston: Beacon Press, 1963.

Wendland, Heinz-Dietrich. *Weg und Umwege: 50 Jahre erlebter Theologie 1919-1970*. Gütersloh: Gerd Mohn, 1977.

Weyer, Adam. *Kirche im Arbeiterviertel*. Gütersloh: Gerd Mohn, 1971.

Wichern, Johann, ed. *Die Mission der deutschen evangelischen Kirche: Eine Denkschrift an die deutsche Nation des Central-Ausschuss für die Innere Mission*. 3d ed. Hamburg: Agentur des Rauhen Hauses, 1889.

Wobberin, Georg. *Arthur Titius: Ökumenische Theologie zur Befriedung der Kirche*. Berlin: Arthur Collignon, 1937.

Wolff, Walther. *Alles, alles für unser Vaterland*. Berlin: Verlag des Evangelischen Bund, 1917.

Woods, Edward S., and Frederick B. MacNutt. *Theodore, Bishop of Winchester, Pastor, Prophet, Pilgrim: A Memoir of Frank Theodore Woods 1874-1932*. London: S.P.C.K., 1933.

Wright, J.R.C. *"Above Parties": The Political Attitudes of the German Protestant Church Leadership, 1918-1933*. London: Oxford University Press, 1974.

Zabel, James. *Nazism and the Pastors: A Study of the Ideas of Three "Deutsche Christen" Groups*. Missoula, Mont.: Scholars Press, 1976.

Zahn-Harnack, Agnes von. *Adolf von Harnack*. Berlin: Hans Bott Verlag, 1936.

INDEX